HEAR

Charlie Stuart Gay

HEAR

HEAR

is dedicated to my beloved children

Arabella and James Stuart

and Sahana

All born as Children of God

Who's Your Daddy?

"This is an extraordinary book. It is a brilliantly written, deeply engaging, emotionally compelling, and spiritually awakening call to action by one of the most profoundly wise, deeply interesting and amazingly effective visionaries of our time. I kept turning page after page as Charlie masterfully took me on a journey from his and our deeply painful individual personal pasts to our incredibly bright and hopeful collective future. I highly recommend this book to anyone who cares about their own personal evolution and the conscious evolution of humanity and our planet."

Jack Canfield, Co-creator of the New York Times
#1 bestselling Chicken Soup for the Soul series;

"Charlie Gay is one of the great enlightened, enlivened, enriching, enhancing, exciting minds of our time."

Mark Victor Hansen - Co-creator of the New York Times
#1 bestselling Chicken Soup for the Soul series;

"When I started to read this book, I wondered why Charlie had decided to write a very long essay, just for me. That's the way I read it because that's the way he wrote it. This isn't a book at all. It's a personal letter to me. And to you, and to him, and to her. As Charlie himself says in one of the early sections, I can make my own mind up whether I read it at all or when I decide to stop, or continue, or abandon it. It's the gift of choice we all have. What happens next is always up to us.

I issue a health warning to all those who decide to read HEAR. Your neck muscles will soon start to hurt from repeated nodding because much of what you will hear is already inside your head, somewhere. For all of us, we bury what we know whilst we're busy doing what we do. To have our own thoughts articulated with such clarity is a massive bonus we may never have expected, and a little scary. To refer to HEAR as a tome of magnificent advice about living our lives is to underplay its importance. Every reader will become a single beneficiary but collectively the world will be a better place every time

4

someone reaches the last words of page 294.   They are the last words and not the final word, as Charlie would remind us, which is always ours to create.

If Charlie was meant to live his extraordinary life with only the single objective of writing HEAR it's already been a sublime success. Thanks Charlie."

Ray Hanks has been a senior executive in the advertising world and Managing Director of the biggest Direct Marketing Agency in Europe. He met Charlie one day, read HEAR the next, and then wrote a review.

Far too often, when we at last open ourselves to the truth of self, we are blinded by the new light, and follow a new distorted path.   Charlie, by baring his soul to us, blemishes and all, reflects a brilliance of self, personal and for us, that provides a new path of clarity, purpose, and passion, that pertains to all.

This is a must read, for anyone who believes in humanity's infinite potential, or not ..... as we walk away at completion, knowing the truth of our unlimited capacity, if we only slow down enough to Hear, what he has written and what has always been ...

Our time is Now, and Charlie
Shows us how !

Christopher Pair
Former CEO – Herbalife

Thank you Charlie, for helping us understand how important what we HEAR is in informing the experience of our daily lives. It is always a breath of fresh air to remember that we choose either to HEAR from a place of judgment or from a place of compassion. And depending upon our choice, our whole world spins accordingly.

H. Ronald Hulnick, Ph.D., President,
University of Santa Monica

Sanara Publishing
London - Los Angeles - Tulum

HEAR
Published 2014

Printed in the United States and Europe

ISBN-13: 978-1484111352
ISBN-10: 1484111354

CONTENTS

Prologue   The Beginning

Introduction

Section 1   **CHAOTIC EMERGENCE TO**
                  AUTHENTIC EXPRESSION

1   How are You?
2   Response-Ability
3   Response-Inability
4   Navigating with Hope
5   Choosing Direction
6   How Great can you Be?
7   Belief Fans
8   Why this road and not that one?
9   How to Hear
10   Hard of Hearing?
11   History & Her-story
12   In-Sight to Hear

Section 2   **TRAVELING THE 13Cs OF LIFE**

13   Creation
14   Childhood
15   Confusion
16   Compromise
17   Conflict
18   Crisis/Chaos

19	Choice
20	Confession
21	Compassion
22	Clarity
23	Consciousness
24	Co-operation
25	Circulation

Section 3   **HEARING YOUR QUESTIONS TO CHOOSE YOUR OWN ANSWERS**

26	Re Create to Re Emerge
27	Your Shift – Here and Now
28	HEAR Out of your Box
29	Taking Inventory
30	Emerging into living
31	Implementing your life
32	Evolving with your life
33	Integrating who you are

Epilogue   **A FUTURE**

Acknowledgments

HEAR

At origin our world was good.

At birth we were given ears to hear
Yet we became deaf.
We had eyes to see
Yet we blinded our Selves.
The world cried and yet we did not hear it.

Today
Because of these very cries
We are more capable of hearing.
And despite of ourselves
We are each being re-gifted an opportunity
To shift from our own history
to our collective destiny.

It is a time of Chaotic Emergence.
And at this time, Authentic Expression is fertile.

The choice for this expression is yours.
Your old story is struggling to die,
as your new story struggles to be birthed.

What story do you choose to hear
within the mine-field of your mind?

hear   (hîr)

v. heard (hûrd), hear·ing, hears
v.tr.
To perceive (sound) by the ear:

Can you hear the signal?

PROLOGUE: THE BEGINNING

Northern Mozambique - March 2006

I cried a lot when I first went to Africa. A lot of people have.

The path was overgrown and lush. The head of the Mozambique de-mining agency turned to me and urged, "Don't stray off my footsteps, we only just cleared this and all to the right of us are mines. Someone blew up on this path just last week."

I stopped. Looked ahead, behind, to the right and then down at the grass ahead trodden down by my African friend. My next stride landed in the very same beaten down grass spot as his.

Behind me on the trail was our camera team followed by a contingency of government officials, humanitarian workers and soldiers. At the end of trail was the next target. News had come in of two incidents and I had requested that our team make the small plane trip into this lost Eden that had endured thirty-six years of wars and brutal killings. We had touched down on a de-mined runway.

The farmer's smile was infectious. It made every one happy to see him. Gemille, like all the other villagers, knew that the countryside around the village was laden with mines. His village was a few miles from the border of Mozambique and Rhodesia, now named Zimbabwe. These were fields of historic massacres.

These villages were the battlefield for security forces and rebels, and as a consequence their land was also populated by soviet antitank mines as well as every other form of land mine, which could knock out vehicles and take off the feet of troops. Now generations old wars were over after thirty six years and the green overgrown fields were so enticing with lush soil that for so long had not been ploughed or cropped. Gemille was determined to venture out from the safety of the village to a new field about half a mile away. To farm he kneeled and put a stick in front of him and then he would lean down and dig with his hands the meter around him.

Soon after he started he felt a solid object and his hand and whole body froze in an instant. He knew what could happen next, yet as a farmer he knew he needed to plough his land. He had to grow food to live or his family would have nothing to trade and be in danger of starving, so he gently dug the mine up with his hands. It was one of the small green plastic ones that were dropped down like confetti out of superpower helicopters. Their deadly reason: to rip off limbs and disable soldiers.

He was successful in not blowing his hand and face off so he carefully moved his stick forward and dug another meter and another. At the end of the day Gemille had dug up eighty-seven tiny land-mines, piled them on top of each other and blew them up, putting on a giant fireworks display for his village. His smile covered his face and we laughed with him at his good fortune.

An hour later however, we all glimpsed our own wells of grief as we faced silent tears of women who had lost their children.

We met three mothers, Amelia, Angelica and Stella and two of their children. Three of their other children had instantly blown themselves up the week before, ten feet from their mud hut in the middle of the village. We drove their relatives the half a day's walk to the cemetery and tended to their fresh graves.

Before we left we had fallen in love with the two remaining children, Josefa and Ennesto, and gave instruction to cover their education expenses.

When I did this, I also had a feeling that I knew I was limited with what I, a single man, could ever do. Once, twice but how often. It was this that made me cry in a sea of happy children's faces.

A week before I had left my own children, last seeing them peer out of living room window of our white picket fence house in Studio City, next to Universal Studios Hollywood. Arabella who was then five years young, was crying her eyes out as we both poked our bye-bye signature, with our index and middle fingers tapping against our hearts. Now in Africa I cried knowing these little Mozambique war children were so like my own offspring.

The next day in Maputo, the capital, we met at our patron's house. Nelson Mandela, the ultimate peacemaker, and Graca Machel, shaped by being the only woman alive married to two Presidents in her lifetime. We chose their beloved land with its deadly legacy to implement our massive alliance of action.

A group of caring citizens of the world, who were not held back by limiting beliefs in their own lives, had already put their names behind it.

A group that in the first stage of their lives may have been labeled rebels themselves.

These included an actor who had entered the talent casting merry go round of "No" in Hollywood before hearing "Yes" and being cast in Thelma and Louise; a personal care marketing agent who remembers living in the back of his car before he struck the mother load of hair care salon distribution with black and white Paul Mitchell shampoo bottles; a black lawyer who had spent twenty seven years imprisoned because of prejudice, and his wife who had seen her first Presidential husband die perhaps for the same reason; an Englishman who was told by England and Wales's Companies House that he couldn't name his company Virgin; and an American woman, with a Syrian grandfather, who had married and lived as a Queen amongst the hotbed of North African intrigue.

A group that had, in the journeys of individual lives, realized that a rebel is someone much more interested in the question than settling on the answers forced upon them. You know them for their labels of success and notoriety. They knew the land mine victims and each farmer beyond their suffering for the common heart shared. We therefore all shared common purpose.

Nelson Mandela and Graça Machel, Queen Noor of Jordan, Sir Richard Branson, John Paul de Joria and the actor Brad Pitt had already answered a call to be Patrons of an impassioned visionary, Mike Kendrick, who would not let the legacy of Princess Diana's humanitarian work die with her.

Seventy-million to one hundred million little plastic bombs, lying amongst fertile grounds, paralyzing villages as women and children are blown up every twenty minutes. Little plastic venom instantly disabling limbs. Governments put them there, so it is not governments that are getting them out...just impassioned heroic citizens of the world.

What should we do? What would you do? I got to work.

Then another un-expected crisis blew in. One year later the Zambezi River flooded through floods and cyclones into Northern

Mozambique, after the dam basin had overflowed in December. Now between February 14 and 22 2007, one hundred and twenty-thousand refugees streamed into camps that literally did not exist the day before.

The situation was dire. The United Nations had announced, two months before, that they had run out of money for a famine relief fund, which put another two hundred and fifty-thousand into famine. Then there was an earthquake, cyclones and floods becoming the next in a spate of worldwide natural disasters, which forces massive famine crisis in far off lands.

Entire crops being prepared for spring harvests were saturated and wiped out. Refugees were forced onto higher ground.

The leading caregiver of that country, Heidi, reached out to me one early morning, helpless, having had no sleep through the night. Clearly with this tidal wave of starving children and women, this day looked insurmountable even to her and her resolute belief. For twenty years this little lady had loved one, and then another one, and over the years tens of thousands of "ones" had been picked up on the shores of her compassionate faith walk. A walk committed to making poverty history. Today though it was a tsunami of misplaced souls that she saw and there was nothing for them as they came towards her. She looked at me and asked, fatigued, "How do I cope?" She cared so deeply, and yet now she questioned what to do.

Reactions to my own life would never be the same again. In that moment I began to hear a question, just as I questioned the answers, that until that moment, in the utter chaos of a day, I thought were right. A new question asked at the end of one journey in the wilderness and a question that births an answer. A question that in its instant of asking opens the kingdom door to a new birth, a new creation, a new hope, a new life.

I had looked into too many faces to ignore what I saw. I had felt my heart well up and expand into a place of utter compassion one too many times for me to ever believe I could sleep again.

I had heard the mantra of "Making Poverty History" as a young man in 1984 impacted by the brilliance of Live Aid and dozens of artists urging us all to be the change we wanted to see.

Now my awareness was deafening. I had been working for a

year since sitting down in Mandela's garden with Graça Machel and Mike Kendrick, Richard Branson's long time collaborator and the founder of the Mineseeker Foundation. We had come up with a plan to fuse together an umbrella of non profits working in the sectors of food, water, health and education, creating a sustainability campaign for Mrs Machel's beloved homeland. She herself is referred to as the mother of Mozambique having been married to its former President who was killed in 1986 before she married the legend that will always be Nelson Mandela in 1996.

The passion we had as we birthed this unifying idea was overwhelming and throughout the year I had left behind my other Hollywood business endeavors to commit myself to helping shift a country, regarded as one of the poorest in the world.

Yet despite our efforts, I was witness to Heidi's tired and broken resolve after nineteen years of herself working towards making poverty history around her; of taking children off dumps just before some of them literarily became dog meat, eaten by equally ravenous animals; of taking stray children into her schools which had become the highest graded in the country, as she had received provisions and donations from the West, having tirelessly travelled through Europe and the USA to promote the most needed of work. To compound the issue, the United Nations food program was not available because they too cried poor. Heidi and all the non-profits did not have money or food. The patrons of Mineseeker, great people in every right, were not there when the refugees poured into the camps. However great a philanthropist is, nothing prepares us for the next unexpected disaster wherever it may hit.

In addition Mandela had shown us all that aid alone is inefficient to making poverty history as an estimated two trillion dollars has been "given" in relief work to Africa over the last thirty years.

Questions started pouring into my consciousness and in the silence of this moment, amidst the chaos, came a space for healing.

Questions relating to the effectiveness of an age-old charity model that is reliant on you, the donor, giving. What happens when you are not there? What happens when you get fatigued of giving and your own bank account is dry? How can the recipient plan a strategy around the work they are doing if they do not know next months donation is coming?

They had food but now they did not. Their suffering was real.

I was witnessing it in front of me and it was undeniable to me. I had come to this place knowing my own doubts, my own lacks and my own desire to lift myself and those close, from interior sufferings. As I questioned the answers that were around me, I became overwhelmed with peace and then excitement. What if we have all got it the wrong way round?

What if we can make our own suffering history, not as you and I give, but when we learn how to receive and then share our collective resources and skills.

What happens also if Africa, the cradle of the world, shifts itself from knowing how to receive charity, to learning how to give first to itself and then its surplus to others?

What if food could be cropped in wonderfully fertile countries like Malawi, Mozambique and Liberia and exported to Ethiopia and Sudan? What if small solar panels could be manufactured in Kenya? What if banana weaving could circulate the bananas from the street traders of Sri Lanka, Nepal and India to women co-operatives working in eco factories to be made into clothes for export? What if woman and young people everywhere could be put through vocational training on portable devices and stimulated into small micro enterprise co-operative ventures?

What if we cared deeply enough for our planet and its people and even ourselves yet did not yet know how to hear it's cries and respond beyond how we were told to respond?

Today in 2014, many of these "What ifs" are no longer dreams and these questions are receiving millions of purpose-driven "How can we do this?." Yet our world still suffers more every day.

"What ails thee, oh majestic planet?" A most simple of questions and yet, for all of mankind, the hardest to come. The question of caring. A question that has been systematically and artfully hidden from generation to generation until the day it is revealed as we individually and collectively are once again able to start hearing it.

A question that, in my quest, would bring me to caring portals of trust and of faith all over our suffering, divided, fragile world.

A question that in my asking of it over the years would allow me to encounter those that are guided by it and give me a chance to ultimately heal and know better the answers to "How am I?"

There was, and is nothing more expensive to me than ignorance, and in Mozambique at that time, having journeyed into a far off field in perhaps the cradle of our world, when I asked my question, access to my own chaotic emergence was granted.

It has taken me a while to emerge through the door, with new questions for today flooding over the answers of even yesterday.

What happens to you in your home, in your schools, in your bank, in your community and ultimately because of your world?

What happens after Africa inevitably feeds itself as a continent and the USA does not - do charity advertisements of American's dealing with malnutrition and obesity run on African televisions?

What happens after most other economies becomes stronger than the USA? What happens to you when your country wakes to its own poverty? Surely the austerity cuts, which have happened in Greece, in Spain, in Cyprus and in Portugal, can not happen to your country? "Please God don't let my money disappear. We just have to keep our country's currency strong. Don't we?" What happens when inflation hits and all your hard earned money looses value?

What happens if Russia, China and the United States have discord over how to deal with the chemical wars in the Middle East? What happens then when by 2025 over forty countries will have critical water shortage, and wars will be started over water rather than oil? What happens then if China pulls the economic plug on the USA and also you cannot afford to pay for your own water at home?

Or what happens when we learn how to catch water to drink and wash with, rather than catch all the fish we can? Until then dirty water will kill more than Malaria, TB and AIDS put together, with us being able to only have available use of 0.1% of our planet's water.

What happens after our children kill their teachers? And most importantly when we do not care to do anything about it?

What happens when we all ask 'What if we?" and if we don't ask these questions, how expensive will it be for us to ignore our cries and for how long can we before the world says "Enough" to what happens when and decides to cry from its fatal wounds?

Today is that day when "What if" has become "What now?"

INTRODUCTION - 2013

What happens next?

Can we lift ourselves out of our collective suffering?

Today you are asking yourself for these answers and many more.

However like the life changing story when I first visited Mozambique, what happens when you too do not settle on the answers you have settled on for ever..... until now.

What happens now in the midst of the greatest questions of our life? How are you?

Nearly everyone I meet is in transition, and it doesn't matter what country, what business sector, what gender, and what perceived economic status. Only one generation ago we would not have confessed to this. We all knew the answer or held trust in our leaders who did. Today I can hardly find someone who isn't in transition and either panic or apathy exists. Every one, whether we admit it or not, is asking ourselves "What's the answer to all of this?"

Why? Because we see our economic, political and environmental paradigms changing tumultuously in front of our eyes. Chaos seemingly has been verging closer to our doorsteps and is today discussed at water stations in offices and in homes across the world. The gateways you thought were stable entry points to prosperity, careers, pensions, relationships, and the very ways you were meant to live your life and run your businesses no longer beckon you. Your world has never been so uncertain.

Around our planet, the legacies of our past generations have become increasingly meaningless. Hope for our children and their future is now unclear. In many paces they are still being massacred.

In our lives we have constantly strived so earnestly, even vehemently, to give and receive answers, which we hope will help us change the way our lives are to be. We did trust. We did hear opinions first from parents, then friends, business partners, staff and loved ones; we were led by politicians, by bankers and we got swayed by what we heard through media opinion. Long ago an answer would be given and multiple generations would follow it. Today multiple answers are given by everyone all the time and the source of clarity is totally confusing.

In our confusion we have lost confidence in people's decisions and even in ourselves. Many, seized by self pain, keep asking for another result. Some of us go to hear in churches, more turn our backs accusing God and every one we know of desertion.

We are acting out our own will or we desperately will the actions of others to finally fix us, as if we are broken. Heck, if we can't find answers within ourselves or through our partners and our businesses, we can always look to hear answers through our children. Our children, the torch bearers of our legacy. How important it is to be right for them? But what is the ultimate "right" answer to leave them with as our legacy?

My own life, like yours and like everything around you, started with creation and childhood. Next I moved inexorably into confusion, compromise and conflict. It was then in the epicenter of chaos and crisis that the only choice left to me, confession for my own responsibility, become clear. Renewed with a compassionate heart, consciousness for what is true returned to me. Later, becoming better with myself, I was gifted a chance to collaborate with others, circulating, as best we can, collective talents and resources.

I found that all my life I have been navigating this maze of Cs, thinking I was coming to a dead end, only for a new path to reveal itself. Sometimes I would feel sore and tired with no exit in sight, and then a light at the end of a tunnel would flicker ahead in the gloom.

I am today amazed by this journey of life. HEAR is here to help you at this moment of your life and whenever you need it.

So how have your answers been treating you? Does it seem that all you can do in your life is to keep seeking to know more answers? Answers that victoriously may allow you to find peace and trust, to be loving and loved with the perfect partner; free as a citizen of your homeland with a legacy that is meaningful to the future you leave your history to.

Today, you may be like so many others in our world who, despite delivering the best creative answers they knew, are at best confused and conflicted and at worse heading into crisis and chaos.

This is happening to countries, their presidents and people, to multinational bosses, to heads of churches, to marriages, and in so many families. It happens now to our global environment because of the answers we have thrown at it, and it may be happening to you or you are sensing it is ebbing towards you, as you watch bad news flood around you. Despite the collective yearning wills of seven billion people the answers have not come. What is also clear is that we have become lost in other people's answers.

For thousands of years the world has offered us every answer. Every single person born throughout time, each with their own clear opinion. Politicians, religious and business leaders, financial controllers, military generals, even politicians that used religious interpretations to reach their own business goals, using military force to create financial controls. How much danger has been created on delivering what they wanted people to hear?

Every one of us has absolutely always delivered the best answers each of us can conceive, from what we know.

This single statement is hard to agree to. A personal experience of murder, genocide, abuse of children, human trafficking, financial corruption and any other human tragedy would have us cry out in anger, judgment and recrimination.

However if someone, however limited and isolated they are in the true way, is delivering an answer that results in diabolical consequences, it is because that is the choice they have made in that moment. They cannot help themselves to know any better.

That's the single reason why they were delivered as earnestly as they have been and are still being. However if answers were all that was needed then the world would BE, AND you would BE, and it clearly is not, and probably so you are not.

Yet there is an opportunity like no other for you and for all of us to accept right now. At the epicenter of ultimate chaos is the very point of your ultimate emergence and because of it, our worlds own prosperity. A place that you do not know that you know until you can hear yourself living your question which, whilst you are, will in its midst deliver your ultimate answer.

There is chaotic emergence unfolding today.

However much we tried for it not to happen, however much we remained deaf to it through our own answers and actions, it is happening and it may just be your saving grace and mine.

It has had its struggles to surface.

En masse we have looked for the opposite of what is emerging. We fought and persecuted over color, over geography, over creed and even over gender. Gosh how we fought and we still are. Today nearly every nation has unrest. We staunchly stood for political values, and every few years rivalries ebb and flow them in and out of their own period of power. We have perpetually enticed and baited ourselves in how we valued money and yet we face the world's worst financial crisis with nearly half of us living on less than two dollars a day, and the other half victims of debt.

Today we are stumbling, with many falling as we hurtle towards the truth. It may pain us as we have been so separated from it, but it is only through the clarity of a Grace-bestowed authentic expression for a time such as this, that we are being forced to at last wake up. We are connecting with truth and, vitally now, when we are not willing to listen, the truth which remained alive in us throughout time, is painfully connecting with us.

The world is saying, "You didn't hear me. Well, hear me now."

Despite of us, the world is changing. There seems to be an answer forming from the question posed by Shakespeare.

"To be or not to be? That is the question"

Today countries are changing from within. "Old" paradigms are desperately and painfully trying to hold on, yet the collective voice of the "New" emerges in a way never judged and critically never felt before. What happens in the Middle East is in natural order through cause and effect of changes in the environment, money, gender, color and creed - all compounded by social connectivity and flow of information through modern media. No one is anonymous!

Money is changing. Today a dollar is worthy of what? Yes, it is just one dollar. A pound sterling is only that. The trouble was who actually knew that until now? Maybe the only people who knew this fact lived in the slums of our world and we called them underdeveloped! There is no mortgage crisis today in those slums.

We called ourselves in Europe and North America developed. Who or what allowed us to believe our money was worth eighty times multiple earnings or one hundred percent no money down mortgages? We pointed fingers at bankers in Iceland as its financial markets crumbled. Who taught them how to build their house of cards? Surely we would be ignorant if we did not say it was Wall Street and Europe's financial centers, which expertly created peripheral ways of stretching the value of currencies. The US Federal Government shutting down, how on earth have we let that happen?

Color is changing. An African-American was able to sit in the most powerful seat in the world at The White House. A black man in a White House got re-elected. How much suffering throughout history took place for this chaotic emergence to take place? What answers then prepared him and others to deal with what may have been his country's worst ecological disaster in the Gulf of Mexico, which in itself became a saving grace for the coast of California as former State governor, Arnold, reversed his decision the next week, preventing further off shore drilling. For years activists with answers campaigned to keep safe the whales and dolphins and precious marine life off the coasts of Ventura and Santa Barbara, and to no avail as the governor approved drilling. Then in one day the Gulf of Mexico disaster changed everything forever. Chaotic Emergence.

Its tough to accept change. Obama is examined by an opposition across his nation viewing his administration with vehement hate. Television shows, newspapers, Republicans, and many citizens in the world. All knowing their own answers are right. How can brilliant and committed people be so contrary in their judgment of each other? Yet most of the time fifty percent are because their hearing and communication is limited to what they know in opposition. Multiply this error of judgment through the history of time.

We had to stumble to finally fall on the sword of our own answers. Money, color, creed, sex - all weapons of mass destruction.

Who let us allow gender chauvinism, or religious chasms to prevail, both of which rely on judging as their core foundation? How did we let color divide us? Why did we let ourselves disregard the health of our planet? Who taught us to accept credit card debt and student loans to set up our lives for scarcity rather than abundance and joy? Who said in the USA that it is okay to give over seven thousand dollars per person per year on health care and yet nine million children have no coverage and unpaid medical bills cause half the nation's bankruptcies, whilst some of the poorest women in the world today in the slum of Kibera in Nairobi both receive health care and thrive through micro loan trading with ninety seven percent success? What western banker would not crave that pay back ratio through hard honest work? There is poverty of sorts in slums but how long can the word 'poor' in the slums be maligned and misunderstood?

How do we indeed navigate through the chaos of our world?

What has brought forward this need for countries, businesses and our very lives to be in the midst of change in order to discover long-lost truths? It's undeniable and denying it may mean that our children will not be given the opportunity to question our answers.

Our world is at a crossroads and, as we stand in front of the signpost, dripping the blood of ancient wounds, most of us are desperately confused as we try to trust our choice of which direction will lead us back to safety.

The massive barrier to being how we want to be has been that we are ultimately limited in our answers. All of us, and that means you. We are limited to what we know we know, rather than by what we don't know we know. Each answer we have given since Adam and Eve, in each generation, in each sex, in each color, in each nation and in each religion has inexorably taken us away from a truth of who we are as individuals and as a collective world, and what we now must be to ourselves and for our world.

Generations have known to have fought wars over religious views; religions have held generations in the vice of their dogma; men chauvinistically victimized women; women fell victim to hiding their light; white threw judgment at black; black judged white for judging black, both armed themselves with heavy rocks that they carried on their own backs; political, social, geographic and economic separation occurred as governments sought to control with a survival of the fittest winning the day. The West used to fear both the old Soviet Union, hiding behind its own iron curtain and also the red menace hidden in the vastness of China. Today Africa is embracing Chinese money for construction, and western bankers will take anything a Russian businessman will put their way. You will buy Chinese everything, and even our beloved sports teams are being swept away in the gravy train of promised glories. Banks and accountants have taken our basic pound, dollar or local currency and multiplied it a thousand times over through ingenuity motivated by greed and need. We have been baited and motivated to live outside what is real.

All our answers, my history, your "her-story" and all the stories of our ancestors have therefore resulted in what?

Surely the sum of all our brilliant parts throughout time adds up to more than just endangering ourselves and the future of our planet? We have stretched ourselves and who knows our breaking point as our past struggles to die and our future struggles to be birthed? Yes our history has created so much good, yet at what catastrophic expense? Polarity; chauvinism; murder; and a blind love of power that conditioned a collective minefield of our planetary mind.

Over time we became blind, deaf and sadly mute.

What if all these answers by all people throughout all time, when heard and responded to, have now taken us on a course navigating our collective planetary ship towards the most hazardous yet essential waters, swelled by a fundamental struggle that has, at its core, shaped all our history? A love of power's struggle to usurp the power of love.

We all know this titanic story. Edward John Smith was a very skilled, responsible and a conscientious person. I hope just like you. He wore a bowler hat to go to work and he was considered the finest at his chosen skill in the land! On the morning of April 10, 1912 he boarded RMS Titanic as its esteemed Captain. The course he initially chartered with his maps was the course of a skilled professional in the knowledge that the safety of his cargo, the world's finest society members, was his paramount focus. The owner of the White Star Line, the ship builders and owners were thinking differently. They wanted the jewel of their fleet to break all records on its maiden voyage across the Atlantic. Once at sea Joseph Bruce Ismay, demanded to take the engines to maximum drive and Smith was forced to revisit his maps and charter a different course, a path that would lead north closer to known icebergs. A path that would not have safety but speed and public acclaim as its chief motivator. On the night of April 14, Edward John Smith went into his cabin, closed the door and went to sleep. A few hours later 1,517 of the 2,223 on board perished and Smith's body was never recovered. Conscious and confident in his own abilities Edward Smith captained his ship to its legendary watery grave because of one massive fact:

He was, at his end, powerless over the love of man-made flawed power.

Have we done the same as a world? Have we, satisfied with our answers as the captain, had the compulsion to go down stairs, into our cabin, close the door and go to sleep as our world suffers?

What about you? What have you ignored?

What can you possibly hear through your world's cries that can have you emerge from chaos to clarity? A hinge moment that has you emerge from a life path that in the past had you judging what happens around you, and instead brings you to recognize that YOU are what is happening to you.

The heart of HEAR brings us to these central questions, "Who Am I?" "How am I to be?" and "What effective roll can I play within a generation faced with the challenge of choosing the destiny of this planet?"

The pulse of HEAR can lead you to your answers, which will better equip you to face the challenges brought finally to the surface by the accurate questions!

Embarking on your journey through this book of discovery, please remember this. The answer is not to be found in the past or current answers of man or even me!

However before we go further please believe nothing you read here! Nothing. Unless it absolutely resonates with what you sense, and trust, with who you are and how you can feel. Travel into your heart to hear. Then and only then what is to show itself instantly ahead will open the door to your own essential questions.

Questions that only you can and will ask, connecting to what is inherent within you, nurtured by your trust, faith and hope.

Heart centered questions, which will connect you to the Spirit that has always been alive and so very well inside of you. Despite it being ignored, disregarded and not seen or heard, it has brought you here.

There is no more important time in history than here and now for you and our world. Yesterday is past. We are still here. What's next?

HEAR questions your answers
to answer your questions.

What was central has become peripheral, and
What was peripheral has become central;
With our world, our relationships, our businesses,
Our religions, our colors, our money
And our own precious lives.

You, this generation, are starting to recognize this.
We do have ability to respond as we learn

History does not determine your Destiny
Her-story does not determine your Destiny.

We are emerging to live our lives as Ourselves
And not as Another.

And if you think you need saving,
that's not what *HEAR* is setting out to be.

Our world never ever needed you to save it.
Not the money, not the environment,
Not the color and not the creed.
And not you.

All it needs is each of us to serve it and ourselves.
When we do, then our world, and all in it, flourishes.

SECTION 1

Chaotic Emergence
To
Authentic Expression

Chapter 1:   HOW ARE YOU?

Hello. How are you?

There comes a time in everyone's lives when this question becomes the most meaningful question to ask. Not in my asking it of you. That's easy, and you are being asked it by complete strangers every day. No. It suddenly becomes the toughest question in your life when you turn it on yourself and ask "How am I?"

So "Hello, how are you?" Now are you really going to respond with your customary yet ultimately evasive "I am just fine, How are you?" Gosh you are so good at this rapid automatic response, making sure no will ever know how you really feel.

Or will you say " I would be fine, if only I had more (blank)" Usually the word is money that we want to fill any blank with. The judgment that is caused by the missing "because" can propel many of us for a life-time, without ultimate change.

Or would you be vulnerable and present enough to say "Well Charlie, thanks for asking and the reality is life is not all good for me right now and I think I need a lot of help."

Who am I today to ask such a personal question to you?

Life for me has been a big chaotic mess many times. For the first part of my life I would have given you the first two answers above. For the last twenty years I may have been able to give you my truth. Regardless though life could have been, and still can be, a chaotic mess. What I do in these moments is I look to get rid of stuff.

If things are a mess for you, consider unpacking as well. You don't need to get new things. You are probably traveling heavy today. Most of us our as we have spent a life time packing the back-pack of our lives. Our emotions, our judgments, our physical stuff that we must have to keep us who we think we need to be. All this messy stuff is being carried by you and its heavy!

About twenty years ago I started to unload and now years later I find I am still unpacking nearly every day. Chaotic emergence happens and I have to unpack! When I empty the back-pack of my life, I find my own authentic expression and, as every one who knows me, it's been hard ever since to keep me quiet, even though I love silence! So I express.

There was the first stage of my life, when my message and voice were not often in tandem and I had packed heavier and heavier to cover up who I was. I was shrunk and not much good to myself let alone you. Yet now I unpack. I let myself vision organizations and experiences to help others do the same. The compounding result is, because I have been in the freeing action of what I do now, I have been forced to look at what else I can unpack.

I have accomplished quite a few goals and learned from more misses along the way. Recently using my developing skills, we have been able to circulate multi millions through creating branded business communities and actioning social enterprises that sustain lives. We have also been delivering creative messages through live music, films and appeal broadcasts within the ecosphere of social networks, reaching billions of fans. Now we are building Sanará spaces to support healing and wellness. All these enterprises happened simply because I had confidence to say to myself "Just Start." Importantly I went ahead and actioned what I was visioning.

Today I remain guided by amazing people like you, and from the slums of the world to the grand halls of Western capitals; and by real queens and divas to not so real ones; and even by a combination of religious and Spiritual leaders, each one in love with their brand of faith, as well as others who question whether there was or is a God.

My life is guided by a series of "Ands" rather than "either, or"

You all collectively help me unpack "and" this diversity happens because the light and potential I see in all has no hierarchy. I trust in potential and this gives belief and hope for what is possible in fellowship with others. Importantly as I remained on the learning line of my life, buffeted by the tempestuous changes of my world, I had become better at one thing - desiring to hear myself and then knowing a little better in the next second of my life. As this happened I became deafeningly attuned to a variety of sounds from around the earth, to the awareness of how our forefathers responded and how all our answers have been little more than band aids, as we and our world cried out with greater veracity. This now keeps me awake.

It's vital that we pack with compassion our every case, our every action, our every breath. All those answers delivered by all our peoples, including all good intentions and the well-meaning activists have brought us to this. Every government goal to eradicate poverty, end wars and gender prejudice, prevent slavery; bring a fair and just platform to our nations economies have brought us to this place. Every thing has brought us to this.

To enable our collective consciousness to be willing to reach a dormant question that, once reached, will become the active answer to the way we are to live, we must each choose to lead every action towards ourselves and others with compassion for everything.

I encounter this when I open my eyes like at Heavens Hill, which can be found by passing through the gates following the most bumpy of drives in a four-wheeler through continuous potholes. Officially it is fifteen and a half acres on the outskirts of Monrovia, the capital of the West African country of Liberia. For over twenty years utter terror had held Liberia in a disabling vice as political despots zealously stirred rural tribes into unconceivable violence on themselves, their families and their opponents.

Daily village raids by guerrilla warlords plucked a terror fruit from families. Children were seized to be fashioned into the formation of sickening child soldier forces and to become the main weapon of individual aspirants to go down in the history of genocidal dictators. Knives were nonchalantly without seeming care wielded across necks and tens of thousands of arms were cut off from those that disobeyed.

Across Liberia no family was safe from the aggression of teenage generals like General Benjamin. He was so brutal that even as a teenager he had forged two child soldier forces together to make one massive army in his puppet-like support of Charles Taylor, his insidious President.

The only living souls left in Benjamin-raided villages after all would flee or be seized would be the most seemingly tragic little life bodies, that even the soldiers would not feel worthy of death, a bullet or even a machete swing. The physically handicapped babies and children. Deemed useless to the armies and not capable of running away with their fleeing parents.

In African history a baby born with physical or mental deformity caused men of a village to discard both baby and mother, viewed possessed by evil spirits that they should deliver such a pathetic creature into the midst of the village. Even to the soldiers, evil in their killing actions yet afraid of these so-called evil spirits, leaving these helpless children far alone was better than interfering and inflicting their miserable lives with death. They let them be. However today, only a few years later, change has occurred and there exists a situation that is the action of God on Heaven's Hill.

What you will find on the Hill when you visit is two hundred and fifty of those abandoned souls each with his own history or her story on how an abandoned baby from the raided villages could have found their way to such a place.

Often these stories had angelic appearances of nuns or heroic village members. Exceptional divine interventions that rekindled the fragility of life flames at their very point of being extinguished. In the case of these souls they were collected up by an impoverished Catholic nun from the United States as some of the final actions of her own very long life.

Today when you visit you will see a sign that reads "The Enabled Project".

Today you will hear the songs of celebrations as tiny six year olds push wheelchairs with elder limbless children and youths into a circle of celebration. You will know that the fifteen acres of Heavens Hill is owned in its deed by the very community of souls left in all those villages.

Also you will meet young Benjamin, no longer a General of destruction, who now knows that he knows that his history does not determine his destiny. Today he is committed to his role in the global shift with Morris and other child combatants. Their leadership of a growing community of former child soldiers committed to bring basic utilities and irrigation to lead their country back to self-sustainment. Now they partner with other forces for good in the fields of compassion led by one courageous legendary child, now African youth activist, Kimmie Weeks, who himself passed through the bounds of all bravery by walking into war lord camps to say, "Enough. Put your guns down." Then, after hiding from assassination by Charles Taylor's inner crack hit men of twenty-seven guards, Kimmie was smuggled out of the country until it was safe to return.

There was a day when Kimmie was eight, supposedly dead

wrapped in a blanket on a pile of dead bodies in a hellish refugee camp with war all around his corpse, but that day was not to be destined to be his last. His mother released after two hours by the men that had dragged her son away saying that he had died from multiple diseases, had rushed from pile to pile of bodies. She found her son and his pulse was still active and she nursed him back to health. There was a day when he stood in front of those genocidal generals and instructed them to put their guns down. There was a day when he hid in his childhood friend's attic as President Charles Taylor's assassins searched to destroy his light.

Ultimately there was a day when the brilliant first female premier of an African nation, President Ellen Johnson Sirleaf, invited a young twenty four year old folklore hero to be the national orator on Independence Day of their beloved nation, Liberia. There was a day when Kimmie came to speak about Africa at a conference we were staging in Los Angeles, and since then there have been many days when humanity has united with his brilliance, and because of this we all converge today for a nation's people to impact themselves with goodness.

Kimmie Weeks and his colleagues in Youth Action International, represent caring, hope, courage, conviction, responsibility, action, co-creativity and co-operation, youthful integrity, family, unity, leadership and joy-filled commitment and love. Isaac was Kimmie's friend whose attic hiding place allowed Kimmie to escape Benjamin's murderous intent. They are both twenty-eight years old now, seasoned after twenty years of commitment to their cause, and all Isaac wants from me this day is the shirt off my back. Its not hard to get me to hear him, as he smiles and banters. A young man that was at the center of horror and chaos within his country for years. His authentic expression of passion for what I was wearing was not lost on me and so I stripped off and gave him my blue shirt, Chelsea's new home football shirt. We all laughed, joked and danced to the "Blue" chant of Drogba and Isaac.

Today Benjamin's weapon is not conflict, crisis and chaos. He carries manuals not on how to assemble rocket launchers manufactured and given him under the full knowledge of super powers. Today Benjamin's books are "how can I be better" books as he reprograms himself back to the fruits of his spirit, and as Benjamin does reach back into his heart he meets again those that were deemed to be given the least but in fact inherit the most in the kingdom of hearts.

As I stand in the middle of Heavens Hill and am honored with my fellows, for the sustainment of our social enterprise by these wonderful people, I feel the hope carried by Kimmie and his team and I feel the trust that all on Heavens Hill have for their young savior. I also feel the warmth of Benjamin's embrace and I see the signpost through the pupils of his eyes to the soul of his heart, I am a witness to a celebration that only God knew until now and I see and feel unconditional love. I know what love is today.

I am home on Heavens Hill, utterly at home beyond any boundaries of this life time, and in this field of Compassion, I am able to feel more and because I can, I rekindle original senses.

I recounted a prediction on another hill voiced thousands of years before. *"Blessed are the meek, for they shall inherit the earth."*

I hear "Heaven is right here in the midst of you." It really is.

Chapter 2:   RESPONSE-ABILITY

How is your ability to hear and then respond?

What are you hearing right now inside of you with what you have read in the first few pages of HEAR.

Did you have a response that was triggered by a word or sentence? Did you feel an emotion of sympathy, or anger, or contempt, or despair, of did you just nor care? If you are caught in automatic judgment of the characters, the drama or even me, you remain in fact a great distance away from hearing what you need to know to navigate through chaos. How is your ability in response?

There are true stories laid out throughout the book - as the journey through life is - randomly. It is likely that you have judged banks and governments recently, such as people finding ways to let one bank lend over two trillion dollars with limited cash assets in its reserve, and then allow it to borrow over twenty five billion dollars of US government bail out money as well as over sixty billion of UK tax payers money and still be audacious enough to want to pay its CEO a four million dollar bonus in 2012. How are we all at dealing with the issue of money? With chronic ailments not very well it seems.

How are events to occur that will change us so we can once again rediscover peace within the depth of our soul? Today it is clear that the issue is never, ever, the issue, it is how we respond to the issue, which IS the issue. The lingering issue most of us have most of the time is that we are not effective in how to respond, as we have Habitual Emotional Automatic Responses, especially as we resist facing pending chaos. When we sense challenges or see danger ahead or look to force our own way, we nearly always try to do this with responses and actions that we have used in the past – from our old story. We do this even though we often are aware what we are doing has not worked in the past, although we might not be hearing ourselves admit it as we impulsively use the same tactics again. Often at this pivotal point we are deaf to the world around us, and disconnected to the truth within.

So right away let us stop. Stop here. Your drama and the drama of your business, your life, your world. Let the next silence heal you.

Before we start to journey on, there is a poem that I ask you to experience that may additionally prepare you for receiving what this book is offering you. You may have heard these words said before. This time though please put into a different context, even if you have encountered the poem before. As you read it maybe for the first time, stop the drama of your past, of all your past. Release your mind of all future events or thoughts of data.

Just Be.

These words are pure, yet their representation in such a short time in a world, of television, CNN and internet, highlight how much we can trust history and how much credence we can give to the facts of how history and drama is taught to every one of us.

Did the great Nelson Mandela choose after twenty-seven years, not to point his fingers at his incarcerators when he finally became free? Did he utter these words the day the world's media had their cameras on him as a free man? Mis-labeled a "Black Gangster" he had twenty-seven long years to consider what he would say and these words would have been worthy indeed of this great peacemaker.

With all my heart it would be so apt to attribute them to this mighty humanitarian leader of our times. Most people do because Google says so too! Every year the Nelson Mandela Foundation receives thousands of request to provide clearance and permission for others to use them. Each requester believes they know that Nelson Mandela said these words. They can justify and mirror the words to the man. It is written in countless books that he said these words. Millions of people today understand in their own minds that by looking at himself and not others, Mandela gave an entire African nation, gripped for decades in apartheid and atrocious supremacy wars, the permission in that second to choose freedom. He changed the world by his own act of looking inward, rather than out. They are right and they are wrong. The Nelson Mandela Foundation website even know as well and they post in "Frequently Asked Questions." He didn't and has never used the words attributed to him, or in any speech. They were written by a wonderful American woman, Marianne Williamson.

However Mandela walked this talk throughout his life and walked out of prison into history in a way of "don't judge lest ye be judged." It was the same way that Gandhi and Martin Luther King had catalyzed national and cultural transformations. It is a way you too can choose to be, if you choose to. Marianne Williamson's words were voiced through her and written in A Return To Love: Reflections on the Principles of A Course in Miracles, 1992.

Our deepest fear is not that we are inadequate. Our deepest fear is that we are powerful beyond measure.
It is our light, not our darkness that most frightens us. We ask ourselves, who am I to be brilliant, gorgeous, talented and fabulous?
Actually, who are you not to be?
You are a child of God.
Your playing small doesn't serve the world. There's nothing

enlightened about shrinking so that other people won't feel insecure
around you. We were born to make manifest the glory of God that is
within us.
It's not just in some of us, it's in everyone.
And, as we let our own light shine,
we unconsciously give other people permission to do the same.
As we are liberated from our own fear,
our presence automatically liberates others.

Chapter 3:   RESPONSE-INABILITY

Chaotic mind-fields laid by my mind-power

Once upon a time, in the beginning, when our precious world, the only one we have, was created what was central to our creation and to this planet was indeed central. All was good and plentiful across the lands and in the oceans.

Yet in the years since, we as humans have slipped, and then slipped again. Each time we did we systematically navigated away from the vision of our Creator and moved what was central to become peripheral in the ways of our lives. Worse still was what was once peripheral had become central within much of our society. The lands got ravaged and wasted and the oceans became polluted. Over the centuries anger raged, self-will governed and dogmas were applied. Countries went to war first with others and then with themselves. Politicians became powerless to effectively govern as select individuals became too powerful, and the policing forces powerless to hold them accountable. The people of our world, isolated from their own Selves, and under the pressured labels of achievement, gave scant regard to the beauty of what had been first created. What needed to be "mine", "mine", "mine" caused the world most dangerous mine field to be laid.

A mine field that we did not have the ability to defuse or disable.

As we got angry and hurt more as people, the world received daggers to its core. Crisis after crisis rained and reigned in the power kingdoms of chaos. Prejudice, greed and a need for greater convincing tactics manipulated and, in the case of money, valued nothing into something for the sake of someone.

The Power of Love once had a clear pulse, connected from the beginning when there was the Word, and the Word was God. We were all connected, through God's creations through Mother Earth. We were even left directions by Jesus as written in the "Red Letters" of the Gospels. Yet after time we became less connected. The Power of Love was being suffocated.

The Love of Power became the pulse that we the people, in our trance, sought for our very comfort. The near tragedy was, because our hearts had been effectively veneered by the mind-field, of one mind after the next, we didn't sense, feel, see or hear the fundamental difference between central and peripheral.

Our will enabled us to create missiles that could denote on a pin head at the end of their flight half a world away, yet our will was not able to innovate ways to eradicate poverty.

In our desperation for power, we had indeed become powerless, power less and that is when it happens.

At that very point of recognizing our disability, when we finally were forced to comprehend we did not have the ability to deliver an answer, we were faced with no other alternative.

Thank God that when you become powerless, you actually have moved yourself into ideal conditions to heal yourself!

As we buckled to our knees, a change occurred. In listening to the throes of our planet's fatal cries, in the utter crisis and chaos that was descending, we were gifted the opportunity of how to hear. This is a gift that comes through vulnerability found only in a tumultuous eye of chaos. As we were given grace to hear, we gave ourselves new vision and could glimpse the glittering coins gleaming at the bottom of each of our own personal well of grief. In this moment of individual awareness a collective consciousness started to emerge and hope re-birthed itself, followed by new revelations that we knew was not previously of our own mind.

Today, beyond all that we have been taught or we thought we

knew, we do have a choice if we have the ability to examine our every motive, our every step, our every problem, our every solution?

Can we choose to look at our creations that stimulated the childhood of our ideas, and their subsequent compromises, that brought forward conflict, crisis and chaos?

In our choices today can we confess with compassion in our hearts, so that we can consciously reconnect with our Selves, which inevitably will lead to co-operating with others as we freely circulate our resources, serving each other and our planet?

I hope you possess courage enough to hear in the eye of chaos and navigate a path through your uniquely designed amazing maze.

Chapter 4:   NAVIGATING WITH HOPE

Hope only needs just one second.

Thankfully despite all the veneer and pollution of our own selves, as we slipped from generation to generation, this one kernel of brilliant essence remained within each of us. Hope.

Hope can be held onto kindling life itself as it was amidst atrocious suffering in the diabolical Nazi concentration camps, or it can be rediscovered at any moment.

At first the glimpses were isolated in the light surrounded by the darkness. Often in their physical forms they were stifled, crucified, shot or shot down. Then as a new millennium dawned these unique treasures, each carrying often unconsciously the DNA cell of what was and is central, started to hear each other in the dim light of distance. Today now millions of us, "We the people" are hearing these cries, asking the question "What ails thee?" not only to the world but through its vulnerable yet penetrating question to ourselves, an all powerful reflection that currently pierces into the very hearts of ourselves. In this courageous action we rediscover the very brilliance birthed in each of our origins. We become better again, conscious within our own persona, and in this receiving we contribute to our local community and we can converge and impact all our world issues.

The Power of Love conquers for all time the Love of Power. It is a time like no other before it. It is your embrace of the Power of Loving for yourself that has you recognize the awakened "cells" in other and compels you to join together, making change inevitable for all time.

In the past governments, organizations and businesses success was based on how successful were they at convincing. Today you ask them to connect with you.

The fact is we are actioning "Chaotic Emergence." The signs are clearly here, and despite our best efforts to keep our world out of alignment, we have unintentionally set up our own route to safety.

An African American in the White House; fresh and hopeful thought in North Africa and the Middle East; a coalition between Liberals and Conservatives; female presidents of African nations; one hundred and twenty million micro social entrepreneurs triggered into prosperity through micro loans today in a strategy that directly contradicts any banking loan you have ever received; your own bank accounts that are based on the true value of money however painful the statements are; energy manifestos to curb our fossil fuel consumption and offshore drilling at a time of potentially the world's most disastrous environmental crisis; free range labels that are affecting how we purchase chicken, pork and beef, as we are conscious to the consequences of factory farming or sugar in our children's school milk; cars that can drive one thousand miles on a tank of petrol; water purification innovations stimulated by extreme weather bringing rain and drought

Companies today recognize that they can increase their value, whilst engaging stakeholders and consumers by being corporately responsible and employing cause marketing branding and advertising campaigns. Vitally in this decade because "We the people" are converging, these companies also know if they do not live up to your expectations of them they will be punished by you, a very savvy consumer. Today we see social enterprise business strategies that drive social and environmental change. Companies are shifting from the survival of the fittest and winner takes all mentalities to connection and collaboration, creating a more sustainable business demo-culture ecosystem. This is all now underpinned by transparency and an authentic admittance when a business tactic fails.

The world, at its brink, is showing us the signs and we are demonstrating we possess not only the capacity to hear its cries and requests but an aptitude to co-create the action that will soothe the tears.

Emergence from your own Karmic Placenta

Now it is your turn but what can you do if you are at your brink, your bank accounts have diminished, your business cannot make profit, staff are being laid off and you are stressed at home? Now more than ever, you judge that your cries are not being heard, your position is becoming hopeless and you are beginning to not know how to believe it can be different in the future.

However don't despair. You are now clearly being forced to breakthrough what I term as Karmic Placenta, residue from past generational answers, inherited by you as gunky mess to clean up within your life time. As you do and pass through this transformational threshold, you will both change forever and will be joining others as the only generation that faced the challenge of choosing the fate and ultimate destiny of this planet.

What had been introduced within the lifetimes of our parents and ancestors cannot continue in the lifetimes of our children and grandchildren. Insignificance is becoming Significant.

People who may have been judged as the most insignificant people are becoming the most significant support for our planet. Humanity today indeed unites us, regardless of our past, our color, creed, religion and socioeconomic condition. Together the celebration of our diversity, the very diversity that past generations delivered every answer to keep us apart, is now the co-operative pulse that drives our current actions of co-creation, summoned through convergence. Together, and only together, we change the world forever. This is real and I know it as I am a witness to it. It is happening inevitably already. There is hope in humanity.

Thirty cents health insurance on micro loans in the slum of Nairobi provides the most power filled nation in the world to be liberated from its scarcity. The most insignificant clearly show our political and business power leaders what is possible. We have millions of people receiving social enterprise micro loans and most significantly ninety-seven percent of them are successful in repaying them in full. That is one hundred and twenty million people out of the so-called bottom two billion that yesterday were living on less than two dollars a day. Fabulous products being produced by innovative artisans and small co-operative groups all over the world, are now finding their way into your high street stores. Micro trading is becoming integral to our macro economy.

How can we hope to trust each other again?

Women all over the world, coming out of the carnage of their nation's collapse, are immense today and great examples of people asking each other with deep caring the simple question "How do we trust each other, how do we trust ourselves?"

In Liberia, under President Ellen Johnson Sirleaf, the women finally marched in Monrovia to stop the war that had taken so many of their own child soldiers and said, "No Sex, Enough death!" The war ceased that day. Funny what the threat of no sex does to most men!

When Dr. Mohammad Yunus starting running up to women in the streets of Bangladesh brandishing money to give as loans to them, they ran away from him. He wanted no collateral. No paperwork and they were women who never received let alone should receive loans in their history. At best they were being pursued by a crazy man, and at worst he was after what little they did have. Today simply because they learned to trust this man and each other as they engaged in their own micro social entrepreneur circles, their world and ours has changed for ever. These and many others are at the forefront of a new, emerging deep trust that is shedding from our generic skins the old paradigm skin of an archaic world wide banking structure. Those that work on the Exchanges of the world will face greater discernment and accountability for a world demanding trust. Dr. Yunus asked the question in the late nineteen seventies that was critical to him one day in a village in a rural countryside of his beloved country and his question has changed our world.

Back in March 2007 when I was confronted with the crisis that the caregivers of Mozambique were faced with, I trusted myself.

All it took was awareness to what I could do and then action. I trusted myself to call my friend, Larry Jones, who had founded Feed The Children, and was moving food and resources all over the world to help the needy. I had worked with Larry often, using his trucks and food boxes to feed homeless across the United States. Now I needed food fast in a remote African country. A year before I had invited Larry to Mozambique and I had given him firsthand experience of the issues of land-mines, floods and wars of Mozambique. I had taken him to meet Graca Machel at Mandela's house. Larry responded to my call for help.

I was trusted by the caregivers. I trusted Larry. Larry was trusted by a global company called Nuskin, whose millions of product users and home based distributors trusted as their global company to help give them a good product and a livelihood. Nuskin also made a Nourish The Children meal with factories in China and Malawi for Feed The Children to distribute. Larry called me back and a few days later through a chain of trust and then action, our caregiver Heidi received containers from China to support the need. Later Nuskin trusted us as they continued supplies to us.

Trust is often exclusive. We must move to make it inclusive.

How can many of us trust a network marketing company in Utah? Network Marketing. Absolutely no trust in that. Yet when a network marketing company looks to eradicate malnutrition and has the food supplies I needed, I immediately trusted and so did everyone in Mozambique who was a caregiver or starving. The United Nations was not there that day.

We must today hope for trust to return to ourselves and around the world. Trust must be inclusive, starting with us trusting ourselves.

We can kick start economies, countries, and ourselves with hope, trust and belief.

Let us choose to trust "We the People." and let us trust the "And" that connects each of us.

A trust that must now be inclusive of color and creed and gender and geography, and otherwise how can we be we?

Our global world is shifting
as you read *HEAR*

"We, The People" are returning and, like it or not,
You are a play maker.

I hope you will value your immense role
in your own life.
As you do the world will be served
and we will all be better because of you.

What is your opportunity today?
&
How can you grasp it?

Chapter 5:   CHOOSING DIRECTION

History authentically written.

In 1300 the poet Dante started The "Divina Commedia," an allegory of human life, in the form of a vision of the world beyond the grave, written avowedly with the object of converting a corrupt society to righteousness: "to remove those living in this life from the state of misery, and lead them to the state of felicity."

Dante was thirty-five, the day before Good Friday, when he started The Inferno which is the first part of Commedia with these words

"In the middle of the road of my life,
I awoke within a dark wood
Where the true way was wholly lost"

Does it get more appropriate to today, our world and our lives? Are we as people not waking today in our millions within a dark wood where the true way of our world has become wholly lost?

Dante's first of nine rings in his journey to the center of hell is "Limbo." How many of us live in limbo, in a trance, in a dream state even when we think we are awake and even we tell ourselves we are functioning driving to work, bringing up our children. How many of us are awake living someone else's dream or life?

Did the people of Iceland not awake within a dark wood where the true way was wholly lost? Now people are being woken to being forced to be awake to what is economically real across Europe? The worst crisis is hitting a bankrupt USA since the 1920s and everyone is blaming and judging each other.

Was it not in the middle of family lives that one day one hundred and thirty-two million mortgage owners and families woke in the USA to a realization that had been lost to them a short time before?

When have you been in your business and realized the true way was wholly lost as your staff were caught in confusion, compromise, conflict and crisis?

Where are you now and what surrounds you as you wake?

Seven hundred years after Dante, I was a young man who left school, lost my friends and then lost myself in crowds of people, amongst hundreds of thousands in stadiums and arenas and in bars, clubs and parties. I was also thirty-five when I awoke in the most abrupt fashion in the middle of the road of a life being lost.

It was September 2, 1994, the Friday evening of a long Labor Day weekend. A weekend that Americans see as the end of the summer, and the start of the new business and school year. I was celebrating another business success. A sip of the good wine at dinner turned to a series of malt whiskeys. The tipping point was passed as all the suppressed memories and demons took over, pained by compromise, and once again I hurtled into the abyss, goaded now by the rock and movie stars around me.

I knew where I was going and I didn't seem to care. The fleeting sight of the signpost to oblivion, flashed by me. It was carelessly passed. I had been to oblivion before and knew very well those signposts pointing towards compromise and at worst complete chaos. I had been lost many times before I was officially released into the world after school and then once I found myself in the world, I had found myself lost amongst the divides of differing societies.

Now I was powerless. Maybe this would be the last time and a life that had started with the promise of creation and childhood, that confusion had triggered into compromise and conflict would lead this night to the ultimate crisis and I would find the grave that I had seen for many of my friends. If I was to die, it would be with little known feeling and probably not much loss.

Love would have let slip this Being by in this lifetime. Yet the power of love, often derided and heckled at by the love of power, was not ready to let go. Redeemable by being powerless!

When the moment arrived, when insight and outlook collided, fused together in an instant indelible choice, which changed my actions for ever I was not in a grand Cathedral or within the gaze of an Eastern mystic. I was in the dirty bathroom of a hotel on the Sunset Boulevard strip. A hotel that had seen many Hollywood acting lights abruptly extinguished as youth flaunted life and death took over.

For me the three course meal for the night was running its predictable and dangerous path. Drink, drugs and, if at all possible, sex, which if it did not come, would soon be overcome by oblivion until waking up sometime the next evening. The problem was that from eighteen to thirty-four the hours of oblivion would lead sometimes to crisis and to the edge of life itself without any apparent human hand to guide me back to safety.

I appreciated the art of excessive behavior in every conceivable area. Business success around the world had opened many doors. In London my chairman of our new arena had got shot in the chest one night and I was lost with nothing but fear all around me. Then less than a year later having been gifted an incredible renewing of life by the top rock promoter in Australia, I was in Sydney at the end of a month concert tour with a super group. I had my watch, wallet and all my belongings taken from me, whilst I was tripping through a hallucinating nightmare, and the next day when I woke my car was smashed in a hotel foyer. By me! Two years later in New York I found myself crashing again, this time through a Harlem second floor glass window, a few hours after finishing a massively successful five nights as I managed my superstar Diva at Madison Square.

I had scared myself, but I was only afraid for myself after I had woken. I was lucky sometimes that I could wake up. This night, in the City of Angels, His-story lead me to a different result.

In that Hollywood bathroom mirror, I saw myself for an instant and what flickered back was not the circumstance of the room and my immediate surroundings of girls and drugs. What I found myself looking at in the mirror was not clouded in the compromise and conflict of my intent or acts.

What I witnessed, accessed through seeing into my own eyes, was the child I was born as. That was enough. I remembered.

Suddenly floods of thoughts came to me. I saw my mother and father, my lost loves, my brilliant moments and as I did I felt a concoction of past self-loathing, regret and yet of warmth in my heart. I was no longer cold to myself. The demons that held my mind in a straight line to oblivion vice one second before, fled. What was so inexorably to be happening in one second, suddenly became the most foreign of actions in the next?

In the same instant, the light led me within myself. I heard my cries inside and I was given a gift of choice. "How I am."

It was enough for a life, my life, to be reclaimed.

It was the most exciting moment I had ever experienced. From living a life in the third person, looking at my life from outside my skin, suddenly I was within myself, at peace and connected to myself.

The feeling was not foreign. I remember it once on the moors of Dorset, when I was first lost as an eight year old. Now it would live with me for ever.

As abrupt as Dante's experience seven hundred years before. As sudden as "In the middle of the road of MY life."

Where darkness and fear had gripped me just a fleeting moment before, now waves of excitement and enthusiasm flooded through me. My friends, who were anticipating a weekend party at my Hollywood hills home, once the home of Greta Garbo, were left behind apparently by a shining smile on my face. I was gone. I didn't look back as I stayed in "How am I?"

"In the middle of my life, I awoke within a dark wood where the true way was wholly lost" For the rest of my life I would be content, knowing that the "woods" of self-judgments could be felled, whatever the circumstance.

Suddenly misery became a journey in this world of ministry and in Dante's immortal words "to remove those living in this life from the state of misery, and lead them to the state of felicity."

So what is your choice now?

Over seven hundred years later it is a new generation, YOURS, that is awakening within your own dark wood. The moment is abrupt, not only at the point of age you are in your own life, but also to this moment in the history of our world.

Palestine, Israel, Egypt, Syria, the Middle East. You are suddenly attuned to the cries of your historic lands and to what is central in your quest for your own power of love, your own caring both of yourself and for your brothers and sisters.

China, India, Mexico and Nigeria you are now awaking to the question of your great power and responsibility.

Now you. Is it now your turn? What awakes you in the middle of the road of your life? Can you use these current powerful incidents to bring you to an abrupt moment of choice: Iceland; Ukraine; Span; Your business; Debt and economic meltdown. Social Entrepreneurs and Fair Trade; A black man in the White House; The Gulf Coast and earthquakes as in Haiti and Japan; Indigenous lands being seized; Animal extinctions; Polar caps melting; Plastics in your oceans; Your divorce; Your marriage; Always your children; Death; Life; God, Christ and the Holy Spirit coming alive inside of you. What ever it is, the choice may be abruptly upon you right now.

The choice to which path you take is yours to make today.

Chapter 6:   HOW GREAT CAN YOU BE?

Bill Clinton was once being interviewed on CNN by the great questioner, Larry King, who asked, "Do you think the Clinton Global Initiative will be your greatest legacy?" Clinton replied, "I did a lot of things I am proud of as President, but yes I believe it will be, if I live long enough."

I was in a room with this former president in Toronto in 2008 when he was asked another direct question, "Do you think Rwanda will be your greatest regret of your Presidency?"

Clinton replied "Yes one of two greatest regrets that we did not do something. The reality is that 800,000 people died in only ten weeks and we did not believe it was important enough to convene one single meeting at the White House on the subject of Rwanda. If we had maybe we would have saved a few hundred thousands of lives. I was distracted trying to convince tenuous allies to get behind our similar interventions in Eastern Europe and it just didn't happen. It is a great personal regret."

Today Bill Clinton, often maligned by so many for the things he was not proud of, works across party lines to eradicate malaria and poverty in poor countries and helping serve his country when natural disasters hit its shores. You may like Bill Clinton, you may dislike him. Yet what is unquestionable is that any one, man or woman, who rises to a position of such prominence has done many, many things greatly. From being a child to a young person educating to the highest standards, to a career in business and in state and in federal service, greatness has to be evidenced. Every high bar set and met has to be because of a great capacity of something and yes you can indeed put your word in there, even if it is "the gift of speech" which is a polite way of gifting the former President one of his greatest virtues! Throughout a life a person that takes on great things also assumes great responsibility. Therefore you can believe and hope that such people may apply greatness to a legacy of their life. In the case of Bill Clinton, he has used his position wisely in society since 2004, gathering thousands of pledges made by leading businessmen, contributing by 2013 over seventy three billion dollars in humanitarian efforts, effecting 400 million people. He recognizes his Belief and cannot be ignorant to it.

As for the people of Rwanda? Rwanda does not wish to forgive him as there is nothing for them to forgive him for. He has caused the building of hospitals schools and infrastructure and in a few short years the countries income per capita has risen from four hundred dollars per year to over one thousand two hundred dollars.

How great may Obama be as an Ex-President with nearly half his life still to live when he leaves the White House after two terms as the first black man in a White House. He was destined to have a tough time in the White House, being dealt cards called global recession, international relations from wars, competition with the regrowth of Russia and the impact of China. We all also demanded he responded to our growing environment and health care crisis?

Would Hillary as a woman or another right wing media friendly force have made a better President for you? The fact is Obama was elected and then re-elected President and like Bill Clinton, beyond the rights and wrongs of how he and his collective supporters deal with the issues during their White House days, he may be constructing one of the strongest platforms to deal with global priorities when he joins the hard-to-get into Ex-President club. He is living a significant life.

The legacy of life, which nearly always appears in the second stage of life is often fashioned by the first stage of life. I, like you, Clinton and Obama and the leader of your country right now, was born to be brilliant, beyond measure.

Past Presidents who, lifted from the compromise of office, can remind how great we can be. We can all release ourselves from fear and give permission to others through our own actions.

It is likely that there have been incidents throughout your life to give you signs as to the talents that you possess. You may be a great innovator, visioning the future and creating things out of nothing. You may be a performer or salesperson, brilliant in the moment, being able to deliver on a stage, and perform in front of people. You may be a producer, making things happen and completing tasks. You may have an accountability brilliance, like an accountant or home carer who see what hasn't been done. Every great team usually has innovators, performers, producers and accountants.

Some people like to put people into label boxes. I caution this as I think I started out as a performer, with a great gift of the gab! Yet as I came to know myself I gave myself permission to be an innovator and as I appreciated others, I supported them as a producer. I am not much good though as an accountant or making my bed!

You, like every one of them, are powerful beyond measure.

Believe?

The first stage of your life
Whether you judge it great or not,
Does not have to govern the rest of your life.
Not if you have Belief in your Self.

Are you able to Believe
In your own Belief in your Self?

Do not ignore what you learnt in the first stage,
Consciously or Unconsciously.
The passion that crafted these talents
Will never be diminished and can be used.

Chapter 7:   BELIEF FANS.

Belief changes everything.

Can you believe you are powerful beyond measure? Can you believe that everything will be OK and that you can be healed? Can you believe that our planet will heal itself?

Belief in knowing that we as a world spend one trillion dollars on arms and weapons every year and yet if we spent only an extra ten billion dollars towards education, every one of the children of our world would today be receiving primary education. Belief that education is indeed the world's most powerful weapon. Yet today one out of five children don't go to school and then only one of out of four that do have primary education go on to further education. We can build better secondary schools and more vocational training centers.

Belief in knowing that even though we love ice cream and consume over forty seven billion dollars worth eating its different flavors, if we spent nineteen billion dollars on food cultivation and preventing malnutrition, every starving person would no longer be going hungry. Belief is believing the President of Malawi that turned his country from famine-ridden to exporting surplus food to neighboring countries within a four year Green Belt agricultural subsidy plan. As Chairperson of the African Council he declared the continent of Africa can be free of famine in only five years. Belief is that we can catch and purify water so that everyone has the healthy basic for all basic health. Clean water that can turn desert dwellers from a life of thirst to a thirst for life.

What is the hope at the heart of our world's belief? Can it be that Muslim and Hindu and Buddhist and Christian hearts are to be connected beyond the judgment of the generational minefields of separating religions? How uncertain has the certainty of one religion, as opposed to another, made us all as we walk the streets of our world confronted by the conflicting certainty of the minds of another? Surely we can hope for a day when we can all be united as we honor and celebrate each others belief.

Belief rekindled by what connects us rather than what separates us can change ourselves and our world. Do we have a choice in a world of unimaginable suffering; in a world of perverted priorities, and a world of mindless massacres and devastation?

Do we have to continue to choose our own lives to be in enormous uncertainty? What will it take for us to awake into a world of hopefulness? Belief is knowing that hope needs but one second! Just one. As you now cast your eyes on your 13Cs of life how is your level of belief? As you know your world has taken itself, our collective masses and no doubt you, from creation to crisis and chaos, where are you, in your most authentic expression of yourself, on your self chartered journey?

Insignificance is about to become significance if you believe.

Increasingly, people all over the world are becoming fans and participants of "We the People." Interested people are doing extraordinary things everywhere. People who work in their regular professions making a living and being responsible for their own families and yet finding time to now do more. Through the connectivity of modern technologies we are connecting each other to each other and there is no barrier to entry to choosing to be significant and believing each of us can make a difference.

I became a trustee of the Barefoot Foundation in Cheshire, England, started by a woman, Dawn Gibbins, who ran her own commercial concrete flooring company. The television show *Secret Millionaire* invited her to spend time undercover on the streets of Bristol. By the end of her show she gave away a staggering £250,000 and more since. Yet equally important to her was what she received from the street charities themselves. This lovely lady with an exuberance for life has turned her life to service and she has rallied interesting people that are doing extraordinary things to help stimulate training, trade and jobs around Britain.

Everywhere there are interesting people doing extraordinary work, like doctors and dentists who take themselves off in the jungles and deserts to conduct thousands of surgery procedures. I admire people like Sophia Swire of Future Brilliance, Martina Fuchs of the Real Medicine Foundation and Jennifer Trubenbach of Operation

Hope. I also admire the night club owner who goes out in his yellow Hummer at two in the morning and gives supplies to the homeless who are in the corners, alleyways and gutters of the Toronto street where temperatures are sometime dropping to below minus twenty wind chill. He does this from two to six every night of the week. I did it with him one night and I was freezing. Yet this man, who could be partying or doing anything else he wanted, went out every night of the week, every week of the year. You know your own heroes too.

Choice and Belief - Two vital ingredients for life and living.

Chapter 8: WHY THIS ROAD & NOT THAT?

Stay Simple Stupid

The world was created, went instantly into its childhood, and then Adam ate an apple and what had been simple and easy suddenly became sinful and difficult, and has been ever since.

Adam covered himself up, as he thought he should. The next generation made it worse, when Cain killed his brother Abel and tried to cover that up with a lie. "Am I my brother's keeper?" has become a phrase that many since have uttered. Every generation since has taken what was central and made it peripheral and what was peripheral and made it central, allowing our minds to prevent us hearing our hearts and this ignorance has been expensive. Our mighty brains led the world to confusion, and it has lingered in compromise ever since. Our frustrations raised, hurt and angered, we pushed and baited ourselves to conflict with what was central and beautiful at our planets creation and as a result we have been forced to witness its outer reaction of crisis and chaos.

Everything about the world, everything in it, everyone in it, every business in it. You, me, our relationships with our selves, with each other follow this self-navigated path. We laid a path to danger.

The mantra of "Stay Simple Stupid" was simply stupidly ignored. The path led the world to thousands of years slowly becoming deaf.

Nations became deaf. Our leaders became deaf - Utterly deaf and totally handicapped.

Then today came. This hour. This second. The very moment, the very second after we had heard nothing, when our cries in ultimate crisis of "God get me out of this" may not have allowed us as people to continue. Our people died in shopping malls, cinemas and offices.

The crisis was too great. The hurt too deep and the judgment too lost. Inevitably we would have continued in the isolated choice of being lesser than, slipping away and losing the beauty and spirit of the world for ever.

However this was not to BE. Confession as authentic as the world's origin, and then self-compassion is flooding the world and into us as a people.

As we moved past distracting signposts of the Millennium bug of 2000, the 2012 end of the world doom-sayers and into our "share" "like" and "post" social network community, the ranks of those that could hear have swelled exponentially, with the knowledge that humanity, not the awareness of it but the very the action of humanity, could save us. Now interestingly, as we all become fans of authenticity, it emerges that the confusion in the word "saved" becomes its truest meaning for our world and ourselves. We are learning that the way to save is to serve, as the world knows how to heal itself.

Our world just needs serving.

Humanity's dimension of grace given to us two thousand years ago with *"don't judge lest ye be judged"* and *"help those that don't have what I have"* has become a pulse that is felt by a rapidly growing portion of our world today. What can never be erased is a faith-fuelled judgment centered around man's ability or inability to be his brother's keeper, which itself may have been foretold in ancient Jewish and Hebrew text although not included in the compilation of the Bible.

The reopening of our heart through compassion now leads the world back through clarity, a consciousness that endorses not the survival of the fittest, but a new paradigm, a new law of co-operation. This leads you and I to be connected. We are being connected within a new revelation. A power of love uniting us in our

Spirits beyond the man-made walls of righteousness and judgment systematically built over thousands of years.

Now we are joining, united with each others brilliance, free of judgment of color, creed, religion and politics.

We circulate our resources and talents and we re-create with what is central and true to all.

Chapter 9:   HOW TO HEAR

Can you remember so you can get better?

Or are you happy to stay the same and not change anything?

Have you ever had a feeling that you wanted someone else's life? Are you resigned to the way your life has played out its cards and you now find your body and mind are stuck in a world far less than your own childhood dreams had for you? If you have a desire in this moment to enhance your life, you can and it will help you and everyone else in your world.

Change will be forever, the very second you know how to choose to hear.

It's most likely you have perfectly healthy ears and you are saying right now "I've been listening all my life and look where its got me!" My question to you is "Do you know how to hear?" and not "Do you listen just to the constant rant that is happening around you?' Indeed can you hear yourself now?"

Think about it. Are we able to hear ourselves at our Creation, or as we go through our Childhood? When we were pulled into the Confusion of our youth, where we were led to Compromise, doing something we knew wasn't right, we did it nonetheless, didn't we.

Then did we ignore the inside voices that allowed Conflict to separate our mind against our heart. Those singular moments when even the ugly head of Crisis showed up so that we could not hide our problems from those close around us.

All of these Cs: Creation, Childhood, Confusion, Compromise, Conflict and Crisis happened to me and to various degrees continue today, because I do not have clear ears to hear. Clearer maybe, but not crystal clear. My navigation charts were off without the awareness of the Cs.

The Cs arise in my life nearly every day, in my business, in my personal choices, in my walk with my faith. In fact from the very second any passionate idea is birthed within me.

However I know your life can change as you hear yourself clearly inside recognizing that your life examined will become a life worth living. Mine has. I have witnessed tens of thousands of others change the course of their lives for ever and now I am seeing nations getting ready to change for ever. They cry out in authentic expression. A wonderful country like Iceland, a nation of givers to the world. Yet in a moment caught in the manipulation of a few bankers, and trance to the true value of a dollar. Their penalty. The first country to declare itself bankrupt with its entire cabinet government resigning. It was a potent of things to come.

What opportunity Iceland has to release itself from its own fears and allow their presence to support others to be released from theirs before they too fail, or as they fail like Spain and Detroit.

Now in collaboration and connectivity with a growing number of the world's business and humanitarian leaders and millions of people purposeful in their common reawakening states, there is a new sound we move to. Today, we serve an emerging world through humanitarian campaigns to change the history of nations for ever. What has been sensed and held dear for years by some as their highest intention, has now found its time within the conviction and belief of the masses. Actions are clear and throughout our world we now experience this change. It is a time when we know we cannot choose to hold back, or be held back by any limiting belief.

We know it is possible, because we know the power of: personal Choice. Not need or a want, yet with hope that takes but one second to rekindle us, and with trust and belief, we do know that we can hear once again. We hear as Faiths connect. We hear in the silence of our hearts. We hear as we release past judgments from our mind.

We hear as we cease fearing the future of our souls. We hear only in the now, honoring the past fir its shaping of today, and its hope and belief for tomorrow.

The Purpose of Now joins forces with a Power of Love.

What is this "now" second and why is vital for us to be conscious of it? The purpose of now, the "I AM THAT I AM." It is woven as the backbone of every teaching found in the Bible, the Koran, the Vedas. The Now is taught to athletes today, in business schools and every counseling session. It is not holding the past or fearing the future. It is present. The ancient Hebrew translation, Ehyeh asher ehyeh, "I am what I am" can also be translated as "I shall be what I shall be." Even this future "shall be" is phrased as a present moment of clarity, being at an another time in the future.

The reading of this last paragraph, or any moment when you seek or take counsel, may not be producing the desired results for you. The reason. As you move through the experience, you are not fully present to it. Your mind is either holding on desperately to other past moments of your life or you are fearing a moment yet to come. The purpose of Now needs but one factor - A personal choice by you to be living for and in the now.

It is a choice that once you make, you will discover that you will always have the ability to do. Like riding a bicycle for the first time without safety wheels, you may be petrified to be exposed but once you are up and pedaling you will never ever again concern yourself to not being able.

A choice in Childhood between identity and inferiority; a choice in Confusion between the light and truth of the heart and the darkness and minefield of the mine; a choice in Compromise when we act out the mind and ignore the fruits of the spirit birthed and dwelling in our hearts.

Indeed there are now acute Conflicts and Crisis in the world, in governments, in church and religion, clearly as severe as they have been since World War II. Yet for the hope to exist in the world, we must first confess to the conflict and crisis in ourselves.

If we choose Choice, we Confess and in the Confession the deafness around our heart falls away, dropping us in to our personal wells of grief and we start to feel Compassion for that which had always been inside. Choice, Confession and Compassion open the door wide for us to come to that one second when all else changes for us. We see the veneered mold that we alone have placed ourselves around our hearts to protect ourselves suddenly crack and fragment, never to return.

The miracle results of confession and compassion usher forth Clarity and Consciousness to what lies within and a Co-operation with our self and towards others. The Spirit placed within us at birth is rekindled and comes alive. Mercy has shown itself and now, Grace-filled and gracefully, we cannot help but passionately become an active response-able participant in Circulating freely our individual resources.

The one second when the past can be understood but no longer be held on to and when a future cannot be feared yet we can look responsibly towards. A passion, an enthusiasm, an entheos to ourselves, the clear definition of having God within, a God-ing, a pure actioning love that we give to another without an iota of expectation of a return.

If you can flow through the Cs of your life, and recognize you pass through one to another, then you will be attuned better to hearing, and your life will flow without self-obstruction.

In my life most Cs most days are showing up. They have to be as I create business opportunities or look to stretch outside a conforming box, or within my relationships and with my children.

I am split. Being there for the children in my life - bringing up my love, Daniella's Luca and Kai and supporting Sahana and her mum. Yet because of the choices that I took around life and love and the disappointment I cause their mum, I am prevented from being with my beloved Arabella and Jamie. All five children are now between thirteen and four and all 13Cs show up every day for me, for their three mothers and for them.

The Cs show up for you as you live today. You do have a choice. My hope is that you do want to HEAR in every way possible and you will possess the courage to come and knock on the door of your life, that can both bring change to you and also serve change for ever.

There are open invisible, mysterious arms for you on the other side of the door you may now see before you.

Your old is to merge with your new, and for the rest of your journey just being able to acknowledge the Cs is to give you a smoother transition from what was to what will be.

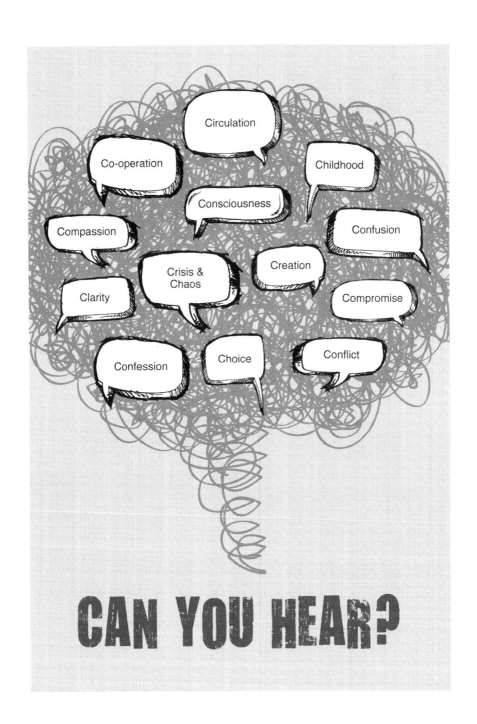

Chapter 10:   HARD OF HEARING?

This is not easy. If it was, the world would be well. Are you realizing yet how hard it has been for you to hear beyond what you know and how much this has prevented you from being you.

"Though seeing they do not see:
Though hearing, they do not hear or understand"
Matthew 13:14

What are we therefore really able to hear now?

RECEIVING

How hard is it to receive?
How skilled I was at deflecting
Can you hear me? Do I hear myself?
I ask then again, how hard is it to receive?
Receive the wisdom of a sage and the tutorage of a teacher
To receive the words of a friend and the love of another.
How skilled we are of giving to others,
yet how hard it was to receive.
Like pointing a finger out from a hand
It's so simple to blame another
Or blame oneself for not being another.
Do you see how easy it is to give and how hard it is to receive.
Yet in the pointing of the finger is the very signpost to receive.
Please look at your hand when you next point a finger.
When anger or aspiration takes you to give to another.
For in that moment you have three other fingers pointing back.
Personal signposts guiding what feelings lie dormant within.
Seek faithfully within and you can be healed.
Let your fingers point you to your own shadowy soul.
Cast a Light through your armor and open your wound,
Let Christ's piercing truth restore life to your heart.
A Hope of compassion and forgiveness, the remedy for all.

Within all of us lies that secret to receive,
As an open hand leads us to an opening heart
And an open heart is worthy and loveable
And as we realize our worth and our love
We realize how easy it is to receive.

Chapter 11:   HIS- STORY & HER- STORY

Now if we cannot hear, what do we really know about history?

History, first written in Godliness as His own Story, but then gradually erroneously and self-servingly rewritten, revised and misconstrued by man. Written by the winners, and those that held control through the centuries of time. Then influenced by the views of many. Until now.

What was real and what was not? What really happened and what was manipulated by love of power to make us believe it was fact? History was meant to set the records straight and settle any debate with its factually answers. Yet now more than ever we find ourselves questioning these historic answers to answer the questions of today.

What is fact? A fact that through history, and stories being told, we know to be true? Which ones stuck with us to become integral cornerstones of what we know we know and which ones were obliterated through generations past?

We are taught history's heroes. Hercules, Odysseus, Caesar, Cleopatra and Mark Anthony, of Nelson, Wellington, and Washington, or Roosevelt and Churchill, of Gandhi, Mandela and King. We know every date through time. When the art of Da Vinci and the music of Mozart was given to us. Beyond the fact of dates, we have become increasingly drawn to historical back-drops. A visit to Moses's Sinai desert or the great Pyramids, or Jerusalem lets us touch questions held throughout time. Why were the stones at Stonehenge arranged as they were and why there, on the hill above

Amesbury on Salisbury Plain? When will the other circles be discovered? Why, when King Arthur died, did Guinevere be banished and die at Amesbury Abbey? What is the real history of the Knights Templars, the originators of commercial business networks? Who wrote their rules, and were they the real historical purveyors of the knowledge to the life and death of Jesus?

Where, when and how was divine female grace obliterated from records? Her-Story's grace filled and compassionate truth, erased by man's singular love of power.

Throughout HEAR I reference to writings that have stood as our central source for what is good. History that shows us how to act. We are brought up with the Bible, and the Koran, and their understanding of history, the good, the bad and the ugly. God made the world. His story is centrally scribed through the Good Book. We know the journeys of Joseph, of Moses and of David, and the family of Abraham, yet how well do we know the journey of Mary of Magdalene? Why has her story remained largely a mystery.

Central to the Book which has both divided so many through time who did not have eyes to see or ears to hear, and yet has brought untold healing and comfort to the masses of our world, is a story. His story. A story of one man's travels, his miracles, his brokenness yet ultimately eternal encouragement for us all through the historical event of birth, life, death, resurrection, ascension and return of Christ. Good news that has been handed down through time so whenever we slip, all can be repaired.

A Book connecting Old and New, interweaving father and son, laying out a path for us. A historical story of one who lives the perfection of his own life, who pays the penalty for our broken lives and whereby opens up an access for us to find a restful place for us to reside in a spiritual higher power. The Good News. Yet a New Testament and Gospels written decades after the death of a Messiah and maybe a thousand years after the Torah texts. What would have been the effect of the Old Testament and the Jewish tribes if the New had not been written causing the birthing of Christianity? The actions of a "turn us to salt" God in the Old may not have been interpreted as an enduring hit, unless His central compassionate character had not been brought to us through the life of his son, weaved through the stories of the Gospels. One of my own life mentors is perhaps the most simple and brilliant communicator of the Word today, Alistair Begg. He is a Scotsman, living in Cleveland and he is able to extend his teachings every day on the radio across the United States through "Truth for Life." Alistair is a very humble man even though he is considered perhaps the greatest preacher of the Word since Dr. Billy Graham. In his humbleness he asks many questions of himself as he looks to understand the historical line of Paul who wrote about Christ.

"God made Him, who had no sin to be sin for us so that in him we might become the righteousness of God"

People have tried to answer by interpreting this as they have every other line in the Bible. Luther and teachers like Dr. Begg point to this as "The Great Exchange." In this great exchange God took our sin and charged it to Christ and took all of His righteousness and credited it to us. "God treated Christ as we deserved to be treated, so that He might treat us as Christ deserved to be treated."

God had already warned Paul with "You do not have in mind the things of God, but the things of man." How much has religion sinned because of religious minds?

What did Constantine change in the history of the Bible? Were there other gospels that didn't make the final compilation as we know it? A compilation that Christians know as the hand of God, and, as so, what editorial ego of man could have determined such a change in the way we would view the eternal history of God?

The Bible has been the context to so many generational questions of history, all of which led to being mixed into the "cause and effect" of our own Karmic Placenta at birth. A Papal decree was defiantly ignored by an ego-driven King who wanted to bed and marry a Lady Anne. The King said let us change the course of religion and create a Church of England, and then his daughter, Elizabeth, after living longer than any King or Queen in history, (until surprisingly another woman, Elizabeth II), in order to prevent Catholics coming to the throne, allowed for England to accept what it had fought four hundred years of wars not to have, a northern King from Scotland.

The USA celebrates the Pilgrims and the birthing of the New World. Yet how many of us know that the separatists were thrown out of England thirteen years before, after the Hampton Court

Conference? Queen Elizabeth's heir, James 1, who was formulating the King James Bible and actually correcting verses from poorly translated European bibles, said in 1609, "Harry those separatists out of my lands, they neither acknowledge Rome or Me as heads of their church." The Separatists had congregated their church in Scrooby and saw history as acknowledging Jesus and God first. Not the Pope and not their lands sovereign, James. They were hunted and harried out of the land by James's soldiers, with many of their women raped, and spent thirteen years in Amsterdam without prosperity. They were looking for a better solution and started to hear the history of travellers to a New World. Putting up all their money they acquired two boats and some resources. History states in William Bradford's journals that one of the boats leaked, they had left most of their children behind and when the Mayflower finally did leave there were only twenty seven pilgrims on a ship of one hundred and twelve. The rest were made up of criminals, deserters and pioneers wanting to buy their way on to the ship.

Not much history was written about the journey. One person died on the trip, and they nearly had a mutiny half way across but the twenty seven pilgrims were a group and they convinced the remainder to continue on. One baby was born at sea.

Landing in November and ill prepared for a severe winter with no supplies, two-thirds of the Mayflower's passengers were dead and buried four months later in February. Young William Bradford lost his wife in the harbor drowned as they came ashore, and by the next year he had become the Plymouth Governor.

Cause and Effect

The point of this factual story, or as our history books chronicle as fact, is really the cause and effect of the King James's Bible, a Bible that became the cornerstone publication of the church as we know it. Our book of knowledge. If James had not been determined to stamp his sovereign authority on the Word, having already piously tackled the prayer book before he came south from Scotland, then a small group of universal God lovers would not have traveled for thirteen years before bumping into their destiny. The destiny of the Unites States of America.

So how was our history written and how do we know it to be true? Even more vital, what has taken us in referencing facts from historical books or circumstance, whether it be gender, geographical, creed or commerce and has turned our current circumstance and actions from central to peripheral.

More recently the arrival of CNN and Fox News with access to open sourcing your social media, means we can have your own video edit from your camera of a breaking news item broadcasted within minutes to the world. Yet for thousands of years we did not possess a worldwide internet and history was written by the.........winners.

What about our own history and our relationship with our own history? Nor where the BBC, CNN and Fox are pointing cameras at our families. Big Brother or MTV Real Life cameras probably have not being pointing at your every moment since you were born, so that you could study your every movement, analyze how you responded to the facts of your life.

A simple test is to ring a friend from your school days and ask them what they thought of you, and what talents and strengths you showed then. I made a call and the answers were completely different to what I thought I knew of myself, and liberating!

How does cause and effect show up today?

In recent years the world has become enamored by the lives of celebrities. Every hairstyle, every phrase, every detail on how they live their lives or how we think they live their lives is adopted immediately by a vast group of impressionable people. We have greater perceived access into their private lives as today we have literally thousands of television shows, weekly magazines and internet portals dedicated to making money by finding the stories that you want to know. "What happened to Paris Hilton's dog?" became more important than the world economic meetings or famine in Africa.

One simple celebrity story gave me insight into cause and effect through media reporting. It relates to something I witnessed whilst I worked with CHER, who had welcomed me into her personal management inner circle in Los Angeles, after we had met when I worked promoting her Love Hurts concert tour of Australia in November 1990.

I should also say at this stage of my writing that even though there are a number of stories of people, famous or not, that have been known to me, I respect their lives and what my interaction has been with them during my own journey of discovery. Therefore any reference to anyone that is known in HEAR is as a reference simply to bring forward a point in context to the book.

Back to the cause and effect of celebrity reporting.

What starts as a personal tale often became a reporting inaccuracy in USA's first and most popular scandal weekly, The National Enquirer, which itself was an approved reference to People Magazine which was an approved reference for Vanity Fair which was an approved reference for The Washington Post, which of course was the lead newspaper that broke Watergate and therefore has earned the right to be an approved reference for anything and any one.

As was the case when the respected French magazine Paris Match reported CHER had had rib removals. I had met her just after this report, but I know two things. First in 1992 we did a television show with the television day time host Maury Povich, who was the first to expose the story in his "Current Edition." CHER's rib removals had become for ever historical celebrity folklore by the time we did another "Maury" show around a real issue of cranio facial disease and the children that suffered from it. CHER, as the champion of the cause following her acclaimed movie role in Mask, wanting real first hand publicity and Maury agreed to give this to us along with a healthy donation to these incredibly brave little souls.

Nothing CHER could do would ever erase the inaccuracy of the initial report about her ribs. Not even a visit to an ultra conservative and respected British doctor with his results directly published by the most respected newspapers would ever change what the gutter brought up. Not even the bare bones fact that CHER has been an artist that pushed the boundaries of scantily clad dressing, way before bare bodies were allowed on prime time. Did ever any one see or point to scars? No. Did the doctor confirm that all her ribs were intact? Yes! The very sad truth is that this inaccuracy in reporting probably promoted painful and costly procedures with many others wanting a "Forever Fit" body like CHER's. Cause and effect at its modern day worst.

Regarding my own history with CHER, when someone asks "What was CHER like?" The answer is simply. "Amazing, and a living demonstration of both an energy and a human being, never ever held back by limiting beliefs. She's touring in 2014, nine years after her "Farewell Tour!" Outstanding! "

Chapter 12: IN-SIGHT TO HEAR

Intuition or Ignorance?

Ignorance in your case means not what you know, but what you are choosing to ignore in this second. For you, if you continue this deafness in any area of your life and for our world, it will be the most expensive mis-action of your life.

"He came to that which was his own, but his own did not receive him" John 1: 11

WHAT DO I KNOW?

When I was born I was what He knew
When I was ten I wanted to be known as you
When I was twenty I needed you to know me
And When I was thirty I really didn't want to know.
Then at forty I was renewed.
Now I travel onwards from fifty and I Am,
I am hearing what I know I know,
Becoming aware of what I don't know I know.

HEAR

And as I reclaim the innocence of my child
I know what willful cost is man's Ignorance of Belief.
I see now there is nothing more expensive than Ignorance.

You have known your intuition all your life. You have heard it speak to you probably more than any other live voice. You hear it at night when you put your head on the pillow, when you lie in your bath or take a long shower. The voice is clear even as you walk into a meeting and meet someone for the first time. The voice of Intuition is never dumb. We are just dumb when we ignore that voice.

"The light shines in the darkness but the darkness has not understood it" John 1:5.

As I look at the future my intuition says this. The world will continue to evolve, despite of the pain and conflict, until such a time as the very least are given the most. In a period of years there will be mountains of trash all over our world and the slum pickers whose children today are in danger of being eaten alive by dogs, will be making profit from bundling and recycling trash. The commodities that we value and trade will be water, education and garbage, not gold, silver and shares.

The world will be in a state of healing itself and we will finally be learning to live in the light of a just and holy society. The pain we live in now will have been eased and we will all feel home with each other. There are many Cs to travel before we are home. Unavoidable hurdles including the ultimate breakdown of the way we rule ourselves and earn our ways through our lives to keep us safe will need to be faced as "We the people" will have collective insight to how to overcome these seemingly impregnable barriers.

Do you see how good we have been hearing our answers and knowing our questions through the darkness of color, creed and gender, and our desire for our own love of power over another?

As we now embark on the journey through the 13Cs of HEAR and we have been packing the ingredients of this first section into our travel bag, my hope is that you are traveling so lightly that you have courage to examine your current life thoroughly, as you continue to seek to HEAR yourself most accurately.

SECTION 2

Traveling the 13Cs of Life

INTRODUCTION TO SECTION 2

So what do you HEAR?

For you to hear what you hear, now is the time for us to set out on a journey that can reveal the truth to your history and what you know to be true about yourself, past and present, which obviously is related to the rudder to your liberating future.

To get there I have chosen for us to examine history around cornerstones that may be the cause and effect of how your life is viewed today. These cornerstones may carry for you the most weight, most attention, most drama, most effect, and most intention in your past as well as fear for your future. If this presence exists, then the heightened awareness will also bring forward the opportunity for the most learning and therefore the most ability to transform.

Cornerstone knowing of the "World" you inhabit.

Cornerstone knowing of "Money" and your interaction with it.

Cornerstone knowing of "You, which you have intimacy with, and which you are to recognize more than anything else you ever know.

I have belief that these three cornerstones are critical to facilitating your experience of HEAR, and for you to know more accurately what to do and how to do it, wherever you are. To help identify their importance and relevance to you I have put them under the energetic microscope of the 13Cs. How are they?

Also before we jump into this quest together, let us remember what I have written intentionally earlier, that indeed I am limited in what I know, and if anything I may write here does not absolutely resonate with you, please do one thing for me after you put this book down. Discard any judgments you might have from reading the book. Do not let them go into the backpack of your life. Do not travel more heavily because of them. Let us have you travel light, and the way you do this is simply to live what you believe deeply inside to be true.

Past generations would hear and hold true to ways of living, of survival, of trade and banking for an entire generation if not for centuries. Because of the ways our world has sped up through the passing of information between us, you have changed what you have wanted to hear at a rate where now the alarm bells are constantly ringing in our ears.

Indigenous tribes in the remote corners of our world follow unchanged answers passed through time from elder to youth. In Greenland where Eskimos are able to burrow under the ice for a few days of the year to collect mussels left from a receding spring tide, they build an igloo and survive minus fifty degree Celsius nights, because the inside of an igloo can heat to plus fifteen degrees. This knowledge of hunting and survival is clearly heard and adhered to. In the extremes of our planet their alternative would be death. However tragically the elders today fear that their youth are not interested in learning the skill of carving blocks of ice and constructing a life saving home which would keep them safe.

So we all have an immense capacity to survive and when we are in the extreme conditions of our world, we adapt so we do survive. Yet today most of our western world have been conditioned and reconditioned not to hear.

How can you hear me when I say that the bottle of water you are drinking today is not making profit for its manufacturers like Nestle or Coca Cola from the water but from oil? It is oil that these companies are trading and banking on as they make the plastic bottle and distribute the water to you. It is oil that is the greatest cost of goods for you to drink the bottle you are holding. Those that are in the mass water business are in fact oil tycoons.

There are many that hear that plastic needs to be recycled, but the cost of breaking down the plastic bottle, makes it prohibitive for this to happen. So how do we survive with islands of plastic in our oceans? How do we survive when the Middle East fights over water? There will be cause and effect that will lead us to the answer.

Me, what do I know?

I used to know everything.
There certainly was a time I knew everything: Everything and

everyone around me proved that and I was very clear that I knew as much as I needed to and anything I didn't know was either irrelevant or I wasn't going to admit to not knowing it. Actually in the darkness of these shadows, what I knew was of little meaning, because somewhere along my life-line I stopped hearing, first others and then even myself. What I knew was influenced by yesterday's judgments, which provided a filter of expectations and judgments for my thoughts of the moment.

How could I know? I had expertly and systematically put up roadblocks to the only thing I needed to know: My Belief. Belief that reveals the Faith in Truth, without the lingering, strangling influences of the past, or the shrinking-through-fear of the future. The knowing of the perfection of this moment, this very second when I live "Thy Will be done." I have now found that with the absence of Belief there is nothing.

Once upon a time in a far away land I was a very little boy when I opened a present and found a "Batman" outfit. It was the must-have gift of the year and I quickly put on the shinny vinyl suit and glistening cape of the Crusader. There was no dark knight history that day for me, not even an Adam West, Michael Keaton, Val Kilmer, or Christian Bale, and who knew Clooney would don the cape or that Ben Afflick would make it his?

I rushed to look at myself in the mirror, with my mother's words trailing after me. "Just don't jump out of the window Charlie Brown." These were vitally important words as there were news stories circulating of little boys doing absolutely that; sailing catastrophically off balconies, across London, and why not?

At the time at night I dreamt I could fly, I loved Peter Pan. I had a "Mary Poppins" look alike as my nanny, and an umbrella had flown Julie Andrews into our hearts and minds that very year. Concerns amongst the adults of my family were well founded and our penthouse balcony with me looking to launch myself was a constant danger to them. I hurried into my room with my new uniform and looked into my mirror and asked, "Who is the fairest of them all?"

"I am, I am" I shrilled as I jumped, twirled and "powwwed!" In my childhood, frolicking in the morning dew of youth, I would only ever see my own reflection in my mirror. Then one dark, drizzly day dawned and it all changed. I glanced, but I could not see myself. I looked harder and I could still hear the loving voices of my mother and father but all I could see was my four year's old best friend, Andrew Macpherson, playing with his new toy farm, made out of shiny wood with dozens of livestock. I did not have it in my toy chest and I wanted to possess it. That's what I knew. I was not smiling as I rushed out of my room in search of my angelic Mary Poppins nanny, with the single purpose of dragging her to biggest toy department in the land to buy myself that cherished toy farm. As I ran out of the room my mirror cracked. I did not see it. I was not told that I was going to suffer any years of bad luck. Yet my mirror had taken a mortal blow and I did not have the innocent ears to hear the cry that whispered deep inside.

A cry that would travel through my world.

I did not know that I had started to dig a personal well of grief into which glittering coins would be dropped. Most critically I did not know as I looked to play with a toy farm that was now in my possession, I had taken a seemingly innocuous step away from recognizing and hearing the source of my own self, inherited from the Creator of all things.

At four years old I wanted Andrew's toy farm to be known as mine. I was loosing my way as I got my way.

When I was born I was what He knew, but by ten I wanted to be known as you.

Bon Voyage!
Time to travel 13 Cs traversing

OUR WORLD and YOU?

MONEY and You?

YOU and You?

Just ME!

Creativity - Childhood - Confusion - Compromise
Conflict - Crisis

Choice - Confession - Compassion
Clarity - Consciousness

Co-operation - Circulation

Chapter 13.

Creation

There has to be a beginning,
before a middle and an end. If you fear the beginning nothing gets
started.

Creationivity

Today more and more people are trying to do something. They know they need to create, so they are.

Wherever I travel in the world, I witness the nativity of creation everywhere. A moment when all senses feel through what I witness, I experience and I hear. Creativity is live, participatory and an utterly unforgettable experience.

No other experience is like the internal rush of a creative idea, unique to you, in the moment you think it or even blurt it out. You know it is creative genius born within you. How? Because in an instant all your senses are dancing together in heightened awareness. You know that feeling don't you?

When you birthed your last business idea, there was no toil or strife.

When your eyes first fell upon your spouse or lover, was there anything other than a flutter of a giddy heart?

When you painted and drew. When you mastered your theme and launched your first blog!

Hear now inside for yourself what voice speaks at the signpost of creation, and yes, you too have created, who ever you are. What do you creatively hear?

In this moment of time around our planet there is creativity everywhere being born, and it is amazing in its..... simplicity. Millions of creative ideas as you read this single page.

When we birthed the first micro loan women's circle in the toughest slum in Nairobi, Korogocho, it was creativity. Noraya and her daughter Amina stimulated it through their fragile HIV plight in July 2008 in an awful tiny dark hut. The next day Noraya danced up the streets of the slum with ten other friends who went on to form a trade circle. Today up to one hundred and twenty-million women of what the West erroneously and self servingly call "The Bottom Billion" are creating. Imagine such a force for good. One hundred and twenty-million people, active in innovative ways of daily enterprise that only a few years ago lived on less than one dollar per day.

Women and youths, simple in their lives, respecting their family unit and the desire for learning, now creatively comprise an army of social entrepreneurs. This army grows in size every day. There is so much love in being witness to creativity.

In December 2009 I was about to spend a Christmas break in the UK and I was honored to witness, in the same week, two pieces of creativity. Signposts to let us know we are all alive to the possibility of being creatively penetrated at any time.

Years before, during the first week in London of world record runs for Les Miserables, I sat spell bound in the audience and witnessed the experience of creation, inside of me that slumbered until they were pulled out of me by "I dreamed a dream." The song granted me access to my own well of grief and I had cried, which for a twenty something who had gone to schools that had taught a non-crying policy, was surprising, strange and memorable.

Now I had returned to England after twenty years of my own journey exploring business, personal and humanitarian creation, and I had been invited to a taping of a television show. The presenter of the show, Piers Morgan, introduced what I, together with the studio audience, was to witness and he added that today was probably the toughest thing the star of the night had ever done.

The lights at the back of the stage suddenly became a massive ball of illumination and the cameras all turned to pick up her entrance, her music stardom career catapulted by the nativity of her ability to create an instant "Hearing" inside millions of us around the world.

I stood with every other admiring audience member, in applause of Susan Boyle. As I had no idea of the production of what I was invited to be at, I was overwhelmingly surprised by the appearance on stage of the full cast of Les Miserables. I was now watching the 2009 cast of the musical that had moved me into hearing my life, that had then been a constant mirror for me to the aspects of confusion, conflict, crisis, choice, confession and compassion in the two aspects of the two central characters, Jarvert and Valjean.

The London company of this great musical stood surrounding this small forty-eight year old, who had auditioned for a talent show in the UK on April 11, 2009, an audition that was then viewed by over one hundred million on line, a world record, before releasing an album in November with highest album sales in fifteen countries including USA since records began.

How can this happen? In a world dominated by youth, by high tech video games, by multi platform brands trying to target and advertise to younger demographics.

A simple, older (for the music industry) lady from a rugged West Lothian village simply created an ability for all of us all over the world, regardless of who we are....to hear ourselves, to inspire ourselves because we heard her. Susan Boyle's emergence into our world and into our lives has given permission to each of us to create for ourselves.

Adele also gave her self permission and as result this adorably round, love-lost princess of our music collections outsold Lady Gaga and Rihanna put together in the States to win 2012 Grammy.

The other creative experience two days later was the invitation from my friend Suzy Cameron for my partner, Daniella, and I to attend the world premiere with her and her family of her husband's new movie, Avatar.

Jim Cameron had spent twelve years on taking images and words from his mind and placing them into a vivid dimensional movie. Five years previously the two of them woke one morning in Malibu with creative knowings. Suzy knew it was time for her dream of a shared curriculum in a holistic school environment, which is now called "Muse" with schools spanning the globe. James Cameron knew that same morning that 3D technology had caught up with his dream world. Both went to work on the childhood of their ideas.

We partied together late into the night in Piccadilly with cast and crew and we knew we had witnessed an experience that we had never had before and, most importantly, what no state of the world forum, rainforest petition, or United Nation Millennium Goal had ever been able to accomplish. We were given a masterful yet simple experience of how we can love our world better.

You and everyone else around the world voiced this too over the next few months as Avatar became the first picture to crash through the $2 billion box office threshold because of your Global Film audience appreciation. It approaches $3 billion box office and that is before sales from DVD's and licenses.

Why? ... .because we the people now feel good to be made conscious in creative ways of the issues of our world and a possible way to move forward so that good wins through.

Creativity. What a moment. I hope you have one this week! Do not be held back by the lack of belief. Susan Boyle gave herself permission to have a dream; James Cameron was a truck driver. Suzy was a model, born and raised in Oklahoma. In their own individual ways they epitomize the facilitation for you of this question.

What creative idea can you have that entertain so it can educate so that it can enlighten?

Creation - OUR WORLD

"Any philosophy that can be 'put in a nutshell' belongs there."
- Sydney J. Harris, American journalist (1917-1986)

The World was created. The World created itself. There is a theory about Creation. The air, the delicately balanced hemisphere, the water and tides, the mountains and lands, the polar caps.

You do agree that we can ALL agree that the world we live in somehow happened to be created?..... unless of course it was always here. Even before we move out of the simple form of "Creation" we are a little stuck to know what is the truth. What do we hear now about Creation?

Creation in the Bible's Genesis is clear. "In the beginning God created the heaven and the earth." He then went and created light and everything we see, eat and use up in it. It took Him six days. He rested on the seventh. Everything that we are connected to was therefore created by God. Christians know that the Bible's first story happened 6,000 years ago and for the first 1800 years after Christ that was what all our forefathers knew.

Then science showed up to change history and scientists then and now point out that the Bible's first book, Genesis tells a 10,000 million year old story. To them rings in a tree and radiometric dating points clearly to millions of years, so another group of religious minds claims as "Old Earth Theory" saying God did create our universe but includes the idea that Genesis is not a literal description of creation. This branch of creation theory accepts scientific dating of the Earth and the physical universe, but questions evolution theory.

Then there are other religions and their "Creation" belief. The Vedas, the oldest texts of Hinduism, assert that living beings are part of a cycle of creation and destruction that began millions of years ago. Considering this theory, the existence of humans and the rest of the physical world is eternal. Hinduism does not support the concept of evolution, as Hindus believe humans have been unchanged since the beginning of time.

So did God "do it" or is Charles Darwin's Evolution Theory going to win the day? Currently in the USA over fifty percent say God created everything, yet being opposed by science minds and what they know they know. Ninety-nine percent of their scientists have sided with their hero Darwin.

What do you believe?

My belief is that as with everything else known to man, science is limited by what we know we know - however much that may be and our scientists have indeed fashioned their lives by successfully knowing as much as they can. Science has offered most of the innovations and advancements delivered by humankind. Scientists are also gifted at debating and publishing new theories. Yet as we have created and embraced theories around creation, backed by all the data that man can conceive to be true, we have let slip the simple beauty, joy and brilliance of the act of creation and made it peripheral in its central importance to our nature. By clouding creation and not dwelling in its sheer brilliance, we let every other creative act slip.

My belief as is the case with any Big Bang in my life, is their was cause and effect. Something or someone caused a Big Bang. For me this was God's being and doing.

What is essential now is for us all to embrace the central divinity of our world's creation and our own inter connectedness because of its simple roll within each of us. The light of creation always shines within us, even though the darkness may not comprehend it.

Creation - MONEY

"Money was a symbol, a metaphor for the divine, the creator, having power to create, to do. Utilized ceremonially, it had the ability to attract the attention of spirits and god." -Joseph Kulin

Who doesn't talk about Money? We all do. The lack of it, the expense of it, the need for it, the use of it. We talk about other people's money. We talk about our own. Its a huge topic in our world today as we start to realize what money really is.

You can now make your tottering (if you are vulnerable) or arrogantly purposeful stride into the history of creation around money. If at any point during this simple segment you find yourself doubting what you read and your mind is taking you hurtling through childhood, compromise, conflict and crisis and your choices are not clear, please know its OK.

When was money created and why and with what?

The origins of money as we know can be traced back around 7000 years as far back as the inception of a barter systems, using grain, barley, beads and shells as people traded resources.

However there is deeper history that can point to the creation of what we know as money and we must look back to prehistoric Palaeolithic times of 40,000BCE when our ancestors were tribal hunters and gatherers. We know from cave art that these people were worshipers of divine gods, originating with their daily worship of the Earth itself, Mother Earth.

They had no history of barter. It was an idea whose time still had to come.

These tribes people lived in a "Gift Economy, "a pre-monetary society. Thousands of statues that have been uncovered during archeological digs confirm that Mother Earth was seen in early dwellings as the Spirit of the Earth. Mother gave birth to all things, and everything important to keep these pre historic peoples alive came from the mother earth, with basic focus on food and shelter. Ceremonies of daily worship, giving thanks for the harvest, food and shelter were given up to the Great Spirit Mother, as well as the plants they gathered and the animals they hunted - ceremonies that remain with the indigenous peoples of our world today, and brought to 3D life by the Navi in James Cameron's Avatar.

Nothing would happen in their world as they knew it unless they had prayed and worshipped its being or action first. Before hunting for the day, before foraging for food, they would gather and give thanks to the Spirit of their Earth. As they eat they would give thanks and in giving thanks they created a Gift Economy, giving up food and supplies to Mother Earth and giving each other the divine rewards gifted to them by Mother Earth.

So was everyone's understanding and connection of pre-money divine, and was there no disconnection whatsoever with no evidence of hoarding, no guilt and greed and fear? Was there no interest, no credit, no inflation, no killing?

It seems clear that in the creation of what we now know as money, that money was indeed love and it was indeed spirit itself.

When money is printed and put into circulation a dollar is a dollar, a pound is a pound sterling. Bankers and Mortgage companies may have tried to convince us differently but this pure fact is painfully now clear again. At origin money has a value, which is what is printed on the note or the coin. Whatever currency you have in your possession clearly the number on it, is the exact value of it when it is given to you.

In its creation for you it clearly is what it says on the paper or the coin.

Creation - YOU

Yes, you were born too. Your father, whether you know him or not impregnated your mother, whether you know her or not, and sometime thereafter out you popped into OUR WORLD.

You are a Creation. An utterly unique one at that....

You know this to be true. It is indisputable. You were created by the actions of two people and there is no confusion with this fact - unless of course you are the first sheep to be able to read a book and then I would just have to say, "Hello Dolly!"

If hearing was as easy and clear as knowing you were born or you were going to die one day, then your life would be simply full of clarity from which place you could be choosing to co-create in co-operation and circulation. Hearing about the creation of you is simple for all of us to understand. You were born.

That's the "what." The issue is that the "where," the "when," the "how" and the "why" immediately took you out of this simplicity, and into your life journey, to traverse the path that I now have bumped into you on.

This trend is pretty much similar for every track of your life, if we applied business or falling in love or anything that has been birthed in your life. The what is clear to define. It's what comes after the what that tends to break your smooth stride.

You probably know the where, when, how and even why of your birth, and if you have followed astronomer, astrologers and numerologists you may even have been given an insight to who you are, based purely on the exact when-moment and where-place of your birth. However you may not wish to hear anything from an astrologer or numerologist, as you may choose to stop at the shepherds who as astronomers at night, were guided by a sky to the when and where of Christ's birth in Bethlehem that starry, starry night.

You were born on this earth. You also have created everything that is around you. You created what you are doing with your life. You created the relationship you have with your partner or spouse. How you are as a parent. The brilliant business ideas or the art that you are involved with were created in instants by you.

How you are with everyone in your life is created by how you choose to be with yourself and with them. In other words, whether you know it or not, you are a creative mega person. How you live your life is creatively up to you. In a box, out of the box. Traveling or staying in one place. How you eat, what you cook. How you have your room set up. How you fold your clothes. How you drive your car. How you speak to your children. How you look to love. How you conduct your life.

Every action, every breath is a new choice point for your creative creation whether you love the idea or not and importantly whether you do anything with the idea or not.

You were created by two human beings having their own special journeys. How much can you love them for what they did to create you? They were both very special creative forces to come together in their creative origins to give birth to you.

I know that the birth of my own children also showed me the unpredictability of creation. In some ways creation is performed under perpetual vulnerable motion with no safety net.

Often we can look back and say "Ha, that how I did it."

My second child, James's birth is an example of "Who Knows what is in store in the future."

His sister, Arabella had a very fast birth three years before. The hospital in Santa Monica had told Gina, her mother and I to go home when we first arrived, as they said Gina was not yet dilating. Gina though had other intentions and we went out to the corridor and for forty-five minutes she got herself ready! The nurse let her lie down again and in a shocked state after another examination rushed out saying "A baby is being born." The answer that the intern hospital doctors that rushed into the room, and there must have been at least a dozen, was "give her an immediate C section." Very zealous young doctors were hovering to do what they wanted to do, a surgery.

Fortunately our own doctor, who had been called, arrived and all the interns vanished immediately, with calm immediately filling the room. A few minutes later Arabella was born.

We should have learned from the past about the future.

The plan was to have a neighbor to come in and look after a three year old Arabella, if we needed to get Gina to the hospital in the night. So at 2.00am when she woke me to say she was ready to have the baby, our plan went into action. First part was I was to walk the dog and summon the neighbor and she was to have her things with her. Plan accomplished and as Arabella slept in her room, the neighbor smiling at the door, we drove out of the driveway. The journey was only seven miles on a freeway.

As we drove with no cars to be seen on the daily packed highway, we were grateful for the time of night. Then Gina said "I am having our baby." I looked across assuring and said "Yes you are." "No" she said "I am having a baby right now."

The certainly of creation suddenly turned into chaos. "Stop the car" she screamed.

I question now what would have happened if I had not come to a halt, which allowed Gina to waddle out and be spread-eagled on the bonnet of the car with her legs wide apart. So there we were in the middle of the night on a turn off road from the 101 Los Angeles valley freeway.

I question too what would have happened if we both did not have mobiles. Gina was speaking to her dueler, someone who Gina trusted as a pro, who had been present at Arabella's birth. My phone was connected to the hospital and as I was imagining what Patrick Dempsey would have done in the hit program ER, I was telling the hospital I needed them. The issue was I did not know where I was as I had panicked under the screams of a birthing mother.

Fortunately I do not question the irrevocability of the dueler, who far from the scene, calming coaxed Gina back into the passenger seat. I set off again and this time Gina was kneeling on the seat, facing the back window with her bottom pointing to the windscreen. The very top of Jamie's head was already showing. The hospital guided me the few lefts and rights to their emergency entrance, and Gina was put on the hospital gurney. By the time I had got out of the drivers seat, James Stuart Gay was born.

By the time I left the hospital it was 4.00am. As I walked out of the main exit, euphoric and thanking God for taking care of the birth, my mobile rang. "Is this Mr. Gay? This is the police, we have your daughter."

Arabella had woken. Our neighbor had fallen asleep. Belle had in only her nappies opened the front door. She had opened the main entrance door to the road. She had walked across the side street that we lived on and then in the March night she had walked on to Moorpark, one of the main roads that runs along side the valley hills that we lived beside. Apparently a gentlemen on his way to his early vegetable department shift at the local large supermarket, swerved to miss my beloved daughter. Had stopped and then he, then the bagel shop keeper and then the police had congregated. My good neighbor had also woken and in shock had been out searching for our lost daughter. They were all gathered and a beaming Arabella was handed over to her father at 4.30am.

A few days later we had two wonderful children at home. It could so easily have been different. The vulnerability of fragile creation is also a reminder of how blessed we are to be alive. Your creation, like my witnessing of Arabella and Jamie's birth stories, was as every baby born through history – Miraculous.

Creation - RELATIONSHIP WITH MYSELF

The first quality that strikes us when we look into the eyes of an infant is its innocence; within the eyes of a baby we can see that everything is simply what it is.

I was born early one dawn on April 15, "on the right side of the sticks," at Hampton Court, which is the Royal palace in London that was used by the sixteenth century Tudor Kings and Queens and made famous by the lavish parties of Henry VIII and the intrigue permeating Elizabeth's court. My parents lived in a large Royal lodge by the gates of the Palace, and I vaguely remember huge flower beds, fruit cages and sweeping gardens that went down to the historic River Thames. Three weeks after the due date, I popped right out in the bedroom before the doctor could even get there. Father was downstairs having a cup of tea.

During World War II my mother was a WAAF in the English radar system and was responsible with her radar women for capturing a German bomber pilot. She was engaged to a dashing young Australian bomber pilot, but he died. After the war she became a model and journalist and met my father, then an up and coming real estate man. My father's ancestry dates directly back to Bonnie Prince Charlie, who tried to reclaim the throne of England for his Stuart clan. I was named after them, Charlie Stuart Gay.

My father's grandfather, on his mothers side, Sir Henry Lytton, was Knighted for acting by King George V in 1930, and was the most famous actor of his day having enjoyed a fifty year career as the lead actor and singer in all Gilbert and Sullivan operas. He played Broadway in the 1900s and was a great friend of Charlie

Chaplin's. He would stay with Chaplin or with Douglas Fairbanks and Mary Pickford at their legendary Hollywood home, Pickfair. His daughter, my grandmother, Ida, was born of independent character, pursuing acting in a day when women were not to be on the stage. She also became a golf champion of the Southern Counties. She called me "ducks." It was fortunate that I knew her. She and my grandfather were planning to travel on the Titanic as he had established furrier trading offices in New York. Ida had become sick before the sailing and they had to postpone the trip.

My dad's family lost everything during the great depression and dad left school, St Pauls, at sixteen, and a family friend got him an internship to work for Sir Knight of Knight Frank, whose offices were off Bond Street at 20 Hanover Square. Dad was hauled into Sir Knight's office for running down the stairs. He was asked what he wanted to do by the great property man of London and dad said, "To sit in your chair!" Dad fought the second war including being one of the last infantry troops off the beaches of Dunkirk and finished the war on the North West Frontier, in command of the district. He rejoined Knight Frank and did indeed go on to sit in that seat as he become senior partner of Europe's largest real estate agents and chartered surveyors and world president of FIABCI, the world wide federation of realtors. He helped build cities for governments. He bought land for the great post war Jewish hoteliers and developers. He was awarded the Knight of St John, and served as a governor of Benedon girls school, a trustee of Glastonbury and Vice Chairman of the General London Council.

He was a great man and he was my dad and I was certainly created by him and my mum. Birth is utterly clear, one of the only facts that is within the triage of consciousness, sub-consciousness and un-consciousness.

Throughout HEAR it is important to recognize the pure central stunningness of creativity. Much has and will come at you to cast dark shadows that take you away from the bliss of creativity. If you can stay in it, your life will be magnified and harmony will surround you, just as occurred when through chaotic emergence you arrived into the world, with your authentic first cry.

Chapter 14.

Childhood

Either

You were nurtured in your childhood
and you feel warmth.

Or

You can reclaim it today as it lives within you,
and then you can feel warmth.
It is never too late to be a child.

Childhood

Thomas Hardy wrote his epic novels with this land as his literary canvas. Tess, the Mayor of Casterbridge and Far From the Madding Crowd. Each set on the wild windswept downs and moors of a Dorset Coastline. The ancient silhouette of Corfe Castle destroyed in 1200 yet still standing tall with folktales of a headless horseman and jangling chains in the chill of night.

On the farthest tip of the foreboding coast, standing as a stone fortress, was the boys Preparatory School, Spyway. This is where I arrived with my trunk and tuck box as I turned eight years old. Like every well produced boy I had been sent off for ten years of boarding schools.

I was beaten a number of times my first term. I was too innocent to understand why, but I was told I had transgressed. I didn't like the consequences. I learnt quickly the feeling of "fright" and wrote to my parents requesting a rapid departure. The letters were given back undelivered and I was beaten again.

Twelve weeks later I had a month holiday and my parents didn't quite hear my chirpy appeal when I pleaded that I did not want to go back. There was no reason for them to hear. Prep schools were where boys like me should have been. My second term they were in London my first night so I was shipped off to the London train station, and picked up by the old rickety school bus to be deposited again into the monsters and hell of my child mind. I had made up my mind on the train what action I would take. This time I didn't unpack the trunk and acted out the first stage of the plan. I walked down the school drive, out through the huge gates. I had escaped.

My quest was the love of my mother, my nanny and my dog.

What I didn't factor was how unprepared I was for a January winter, the razor sharp gorse bushes and deep wet soggy ditches and the fact that our house was over thirty miles away across the other side of the Dorset County. I was armed with resolve and that delivered me deep into the bleakness and solitude of a windswept countryside. I fell many times, bruised I lost my shoes, my skin was quickly slashed by brambles and gorse. Then I saw and heard images and words deep inside of me that I had no comprehension of until that night.

Alarms had been urgently put out from Spyway when I wasn't in my dormitory for lights out. My parents had been called and the police and coastguards were alerted. They were not sure whether I had headed for the hills or across a ferry. I was tiny, hurt, freezing and now lost. In the middle of this ultimate turmoil, I became aware of a peace for the first time. Right in the middle of a confusion of the childhood I lived within. There was no road, no light, no one. Just howling wind and foreboding country. I connected my outward cry to my own heart and in an instant a peace came about me. This glimpse of a feeling was instantly imprinted into my cognitive being and would be carried as a treasured glittering coin throughout time.

That epic night, I distanced further than any other child that had attempted the Great Escape. All our fathers and mothers had been survivors of World War II. Many of them like my dad in my eyes were heroes of the war. I read war picture comics that gave night time visions of daring sorties behind enemy lines. Even Steve McQueen, Dickie Attenborough and their honorable friends had shown us all in 1963 what the Great Escape was. Now I was carrying out my own great escape and I wasn't going to get caught. The night was black and I was lost but I did not stop, even though I tumbled into ditches and got caught up in razor like brambles. The feeling of conviction and fearless action was to stay with me forever.

Childhood - OUR WORLD

You know what the world looked like in its unspoiled infancy, all those centuries ago. The times you look up at the stars and see nothing but clear blue nights and twinkling lights all across your hemisphere. If ever you have been in a mountain range, or deep within a rainforest, or just sailing on the sea a few miles off a coast, a timeless vista leading you back to the question of its eternal beauty; The morning sun rise off Martha's Vineyard or a sunset off the Pacific Coast Highway; The light at the end of a day along the Suez in the Middle East or on Ayers Rock in the epicenter of Australia or above a canopy of South American jungle. Close your eyes and you can see the image of innocent enchanting simple natural beauty.

If you can, travel to a beach like Tulum on the Yucatan coast in Mexico. Mayan ruins give constant reminder, similar to the Egyptian Pyramids, of past happenings by a civilization that was clearly very able to hear a lot a thousand years ago

At any time of your life, you can be helped and even healed by the planet, its energy, its waters, its plants, its civilizations - if you believe you can be. The Spanish word to heal is *sana,* and recently we started creating small wellness retreats called Sanará.

Tulum beach, which Trip Advisor has rated third highest ranked in the world, is a massive stretch of never ending sand, populated at its north end by small eco-resorts ideally for you the discerning traveler. Its south end disappears in shimmering sand and cascading gentle waves as it tails off into a nationally protected bio-sphere.

When you visit and rise before the sun, place your feet in the water's edge and wait. The creation of the day as the sun rises is swiftly followed by flickering sun-rays which will make their way as a golden highway to your childhood toes.

When you visit you can climb the steps of a giant pyramid at Coba and gaze across the jungle top and a mystery of the Yucatan. When you visit you will swim in underground rivers and pools called cenotes and, in your water immersion, you will be invigorated.

Sanará translated means "It will heal" and we all can!

Our wondrous, amazing, stunning and plentiful planet had millions and millions of life forms sprouting, fermenting, growing and each one from birth is connected through our global network. We are not only linked to the ape, we are forever connected to every creature and species.

When our world was a child and we were early generations we had a very deep understanding of the interdependencies - the Circle of Life as The Lion King so meaningfully portrayed. A Circle of Life which around our world started majestically with clean air, unpolluted rivers teaming with fish, and a population size that was able to enjoy the plentitude of food, supplied from luscious trees and creatures big and small.

The world has been orbiting the sun every day since its creation, yet only one hundred and fifty years ago this earth and all of us in it relied only on sunlight to grow the food we eat and only one billion people lived on the planet.

Go treat yourself. There's a never-ending supply to go around.

Then one day only a very few generations before you, we learnt how to use our reserves of fossil fuel and all the immense energy sources in our grounds. Since then we have found ways to farm more land more intensely and...... our population has shot up to nearly seven billion people.

The childhood of the sustaining sun and the moon governing our every step was taken away and through rapid morphing from confusion and compromise to conflict and crisis our children are to be faced with one fact.

Our orgy on consuming fossil fuels can last two hundred and fifty years. Two hundred and fifty years from the beginning of the Industrial Revolution. We have less than one hundred years until the tank is empty. Our children and their children's children are to grow and ask increasingly this burning question.

"Is todays sunlight able to support the additional five and a half billion?"

This comparative infancy of only a few generations may have been the most infantile of actions that our history may one day chronicle.

Childhood - MONEY

I remember when I was given my first ten shillings, a big brown note, by my dad. I was ten and I remember how I lost it. It was on a bet on a horse at an amateur steeple chase. I loved horses and rode them across the fields of Dorset. I had no fear of falling at every ditch and fence. Then I got to see a horserace and fell in love with one handsome slick bay in the parade ring. When I saw his eyes looking at me I knew he would win. With no reservation I peered up at the bookmakers blackboard at the Bradbury Rings race course and flowingly made the bet. The odds of thirty-three to one meant nothing to a ten year old as I confidently leant the man with the loud voice and trilby hat all my money. I would soon get it back times thirty-three. Twenty minutes later the horse cantered past the winning past, stone cold last in the field. I remember when the next time I was given ten more shillings how I felt....I remember hoarding the money so I wouldn't lose it.....then I lost it. I don't remember how I lost it but I do remember hoarding and I can still feel the guilt and shame. Later I remember also becoming the official bookmaker at school and taking a blackboard to the amateur steeplechase when I was fourteen. The bookmaker nearly always wins, even a fourteen year old, even though my youngest gamblers were thirteen.

Money quickly moved from its creation source to its first movement around the world. Shifting from 40,000BC to 9,000BC, from nomadic lifestyles of hunters to more settled areas of agrarian developed cultures and dwellings, brought the introduction of crop planting and the raising of animals.

Now the sacred ceremonies of communities dedicated to Mother Earth centered not on hunting and the kill but in the ceremonies around planting, harvesting and the celebration of the animal. In this early childhood of money positioned between human and divine, between our creatures and ourselves and our sacred Mother Earth, the male dominance was birthed.

Where there had been only Mother Earth and Goddesses, over the next four thousand years the male, the farmer, the warrior, the hunter came into the sacred circle of life. Food was sacred and therefore the way it was traded was sacred. Man started to govern the way food was traded and the deity of mother earth and goddesses began to give way to man's whims of male Gods.

Money, in the form of grain and other traded foods had existed for thousands of years and the transaction of trade remained sacred and in divine accord.

In 4500BC metals were introduced. Metals allowed for the ultimate birthing and childhood of money as we know it today....or at least we did before plastic took over. With the invention of metals came coins, the coins that would later pay the soldiers for stealing the gold metals that would let us all recognize the childhood of "hoarding."

We all have a different experience around money, when we

create it. Some of us have to spend it right away, even deciding to keep spending at a greater rate than before we had it. Governments, sports teams and large companies have fallen into this trap often. Debt becomes the conclusion.

Some of us look to build up our cash reserves. We have our rules. A third on the home, a third on all our living expenses, and a third on savings. Some of us fear making money, some fear giving it away to others. A few of us experience a Scrooge like epiphany as the control of our mind lets go and a new joy is found within us because of a new attitude around money.

It is clear that the early moments of money, as it finds its way into our pockets and accounts, fashions the way we lead our lives.

Childhood - YOU

How was your childhood? Just as you ask the questions in your world today, it is important for you to ask the question of your child.

Over the years have you purposefully or ignorantly put a hood on your inner child? Now it may now be very hard for you to answer the question. You may be able to deflect the question by saying what does it matter, I am me now and I am getting on with what is my lot. My child is long gone and it does not serve me to answer that question. It's OK. Nearly everyone has the same response.

Another question can be "How did you stop from being the very fruit of your own spirit?" *"But the fruit of the Spirit is love, joy, peace, patience, kindness, goodness, faithfulness, gentleness, self-control; against such things there is no law"*. Galatians 5:22-23

As a child perhaps self control was not the greatest of your virtues and patience with your mother. Noooooo. You were however curious, you were full of laughter and joy. You were inquisitive, you danced, you sang, you played with anyone you could find to play with, you would talk to complete strangers in shopping malls and when you would sleep your mother and father would gaze at your peace and goodness and gentleness and they would have faith. Against such things there is no law.

Hearing your child now will bring you to hear life again.

Are you hearing what you know you know? Becoming aware of what you don't know you know? Can you reclaim the innocence of your child, and know what willful cost is man's Ignorance of Belief?

Can you see now there is nothing more expensive than ignorance?

To HEAR more accurately now can you unplug some ignorance?

Throughout HEAR I ask you to participate with me. Write about your childhood and the aspects of it that bring you loving memories. As you look at your own childhood, and the experiences and thoughts about yourself, can you now turn your attention to a creative idea you have recently had. As you prepare to move from creation and childhood into your next C, confusion, can you have an early insight to how one of your brilliantly creative ideas got quickly derailed in its early days, stuck quickly in confusion, your confusion and as a result did not have the ability or chance to reach its potential?

"Though seeing they do not see:
Though hearing, they do not hear or understand"
Matthew 13:14

Childhood - MY HISTORY

I was brought up as one of the so called privileged class. After all, I was born on the grounds of an actual palace, a palace whose walls had birthed the Church of England, when Henry VIII said compromise, conflict, crisis, enough! "I am taking my church away from the Vatican so I can marry the woman I choose, Anne." – a fine example indeed of mind and judgment of one individual shifting the complexion of history and adding an ingredient to the Karmic Placenta of varied religions.

I was christened at the Chelsea Old Church on the Thames next door to the Thomas Moore statue. My pre-prep school in London where I went as a five year old was where Prince Charles had been and I occasionally went to Buckingham Palace to see the Queen.

Well, not exactly to see the Queen. I was there because my mother was in charge of the Buckingham Palace Girl Guide troop.

When Princess Anne wanted to be a Girl Guide, it wasn't practical for security reasons for her to go out to a troop. So, as they had for her mother, Queen Elizabeth, they created the 1st Buckingham Palace Company and my mother was selected as its leader. She brought my eldest sister, Vivien, who is two years older than Princess Anne, into the troop, and she would occasionally take me along when they went to meetings. On my first play date at the Palace I cried because they wanted me to go inside for tea and I wanted to stay outside and stare at the soldier's red uniforms and amazingly tall Busby hats.

Around the time my mother took on the Girl Guide troop, we moved from Hampton Court to a penthouse across from Regent's Park in Central London. Princess Anne had a guide excursion from the palace, and they selected our penthouse apartment to be the location so that she could get her cooking badge. I remember all the commotion one day when the palace staff arrived. Once they decided that I and the rest of my family weren't a national threat, the Princess was ushered in.

That night I decided I was not going to sleep until I was kissed goodnight by my Princess. The fairytale fables told to me at bedtime had already had their impression. My vocal cords moved into wailing siren mode and had their desired effect. As my mother tells it, Princess Anne kissed me on my cheek, and that wasn't good enough to quieten me. I demanded a kiss on the lips. For me, Princess Anne was the noble in my nightly fairytales, which were my top choice for being put to sleep entertainment, and I had the power to bring them to life. That was my reality as I began forming my very earliest self-image.

Mary Poppins

The life of Mary Poppins was created in the pages of the book the same year that I was born and four years later Hollywood brought Julie Andrews flying on her broomstick into my heart and mind. This was my life. I too had gone through a few nannies that had force fed me bananas which I did not like and I learned to scream like the two angelic children in Mary Poppins. After the last dismissal my mother interviewed a new bunch.

I spied her as she entered the lobby, a woman from Yorkshire, where so many nannies came from. There even may be a factory producing Yorkshire nannies. Her son and daughter were grown and had moved out of her home and her husband had died, so, as she approached sixty, she decided to take a nanny position. Lawly radiated caring and warmth. The clincher, though, was when she bought me that toy farm I had been pestering my mother about, right out of the toy store window. I was hers. What I didn't know then was that my mother had given her the money to buy it with, as a way for her to cement the relationship with me.

Lawly and I went everywhere together. Living opposite Regents Park we often went walking there. It was she who took me for my first bicycle ride and she was there when we took off the safety wheels. She was the one who waded into the lake to retrieve the green soccer ball that I had vigorously toe poked into deep water and then cried as hard as my little body would support. She became the person I played with, getting down on her knees and fighting with me as I poked her with my plastic toy sword. She was the one I cried to and the one who made sure I was in bed and kissed me good night. Whenever I needed anything, I went to Lawly. She utterly spoilt me. She became the personification of love to me. My mother and father weren't with me so much. It's not that they didn't want to do things with me, it was more that that wasn't what was done in our social class.

My father was often away working and my mother had the obligations that went along with being the dutiful wife a highly influential London businessman. Their behavior was normal and predetermined by their largely Victorian upbringing. It is said that a newborn first comprehends a mother's smell and a daddy's voice. A typical childhood memory I have of my parents is my father in a black tie and mum with her expensive fur coat and perfume leaving for a party. They are walking out and I am in bed with the lights out, knowing I am alone. The extent of my early childhood memories of social interaction is birthday celebrations, going to the London circus with a few of my friends, and other occasional outings.

I could fly!

Before I had real live friends my own age, I used to communicate a lot with myself. As a child I had many dreams that I could fly. I was convinced that I could propel myself up and down stairways without touching a step. Frustration built when I tried and it took me time to propel off the ground and then I kept having to land, rather like a plane making a bad landing. I remember too the day that I tried to take off and landed with a thump, only to rise bruised and confused. Gravity has a way of being authentic in its expression and yet I didn't know that and so I was furious with God and his angels for deserting me at this serious time of need.

Mary Poppins, Peter Pan and Chitty Chitty Bang Bang could all fly, so could Santa Claus. Why couldn't I anymore? I was confused.

My first human childhood friend was Andrew MacPherson. We lived next door to each other and we went to Hill House together. After school our nannies, the elite Mary Poppins corps of divine beings, angelic presences and mercy mercenaries, used to take us to the most famous London store, Harrods, on Friday afternoons where we could pick out whatever toy we wanted. Our favorite was a Sean Connery James Bond gadget brief case with a hidden camera and fake knife. Then we would get on the red double-decker London bus where we would take it in turns to be Bond, chasing each other, swinging around the poles on the upper deck. Andrew, his nanny, and Lawly were the primary inhabitants of my childhood world. Andrew grew up and today is one of Hollywood's most demanded celebrity photographers.

The eye of an eagle

Since we lived across from Regents Park, we often went to the famous London Zoo. The first memorable incident of my life occurred. It shows the power of the media and national attention can have on an impressionable mind.

Britain had become obsessed with a media story. Goldie the five year old giant prized golden eagle, had escaped his cage in London zoo when it was being cleaned, leaving his mate Regina behind. Each day crowds in the park were swelling as stories circulated as Goldie had been seen devouring a Muscovian duck in the American Embassy's garden, and other small animals out strolling with their owners. The House of Commons cheered whenever he appeared on television. Traffic had been brought to a stop more than once.

I lived with my family in the penthouse overlooking it all. Cumberland Terrace, a beautiful Georgian style building with a sizeable balcony ringed by large classical statues.

That March day, when I was five, I was out on the balcony playing in the sun, when all of a sudden it got very dark and windy. It was if a huge storm was about to hit. Suddenly Goldie was swooping onto one of the statues a few feet away from me. I felt the howling wind as the great wing span passed and perched itself on a Greek Statue. He landed and I gazed spellbound at this gigantic creature. I was fascinated by the mess of feathers and felt a gentle peace as I looked into those huge deep dark eyes and for a moment we were kindred five year olds, both free. Then the regal bird took flight again. As I remember Goldie I recall too I felt a great sense of being alone in this world, one moment free, the next in captivity. Goldie, in turn, was caught in a big net on the twelfth day of freedom and returned to his aviary prison.

I went to visit him from time to time and for a while he was my favorite imaginary friend. To this day I do not know whether I had a Narnia experience or whether it actually happened but its reality is imprinted into me.

Time to leave the nest

As I approached the age of seven, my parents began considering which prep school would be best for me because every proper child around that age goes off to a preparatory school before they go to public school. Public school in England is vastly different from public school in the US. In the US, public schools are free and open to everyone. In Britain, the term 'public school' denotes very exclusive institutions for the upper classes. Nothing public at all about them! The school they chose for me was Spyway, which served only about fifty-five boys. It was as I detailed in the story at the beginning of "Childhood," to be the setting for my first test that I would consciously give myself. There could be no more dramatic a location perched on the rugged rocky cliffs of Dorset where the South Downs meets the squalls of the union between the Atlantic and the English Channel. When the sun shone it is an enchanted land, when the wind invited the sea's spray to penetrate a mist fog, the land was inhospitable to anyone that would dare to walk it.

I cried for the first week and then I got to think about the next ten years of being a boy away from home.

Within a month of arriving at Spyway, I had my first experience with disciplinary beatings. I started to crave the attention of the only woman in the school, the matron. I started drilling a hole behind the mirror on the wall between my dormitory room and her bedroom, and after about two weeks I was caught out by a trail of plaster dust. I was motivated more by my longing for a female presence than by lasciviousness. After all, I was only eight. I was surrounded by boys and men, and the warmth from my mother and then Lawly, had been ripped out of my life.

I was beaten and, to my dismay, so was the captain of the dormitory. He hadn't done any of the drilling and I suddenly felt I was responsible for someone else's pain. I comprehended that my own actions could lead to direct pain for another.

I watched the scales balancing between the satisfaction and reward of taking initiative versus the guilt and punishment that resulted from (what was considered al least by the adults) immature purpose.

Shame and confusion entered my little head.

Beatings aside, I was initially troubled at Spyway. I didn't like being there and I missed my home. My parents had been the constant presence, along with my nanny, and were the foundation of my security. During the first term I wrote letter after letter to my parents on Sunday mornings before chapel, begging them to take me back home. The headmasters would intercept them and bring them back to me for rewriting. When I wouldn't change them, the headmasters would write notes of explanation on my letters or not send them at all. So, of course, nothing happened and I stayed at school. My mother sent me a box of sweets telling me to be "a brave little fellow."

At holiday time I eventually got the chance to talk with my mother and father. I did not manage to communicate what I wanted them to hear. My cases were packed and off I went for my second term.

My mother and Lawly dropped me off at Waterloo railway station with my big blue trunk like a billboard screaming C. Gay in big block letters. For the whole train ride down to Dorset I was in a fog. I was surrounded by other boys, but I was feeling very alone. I realized that writing letters was not going to get me out of there and back to my mother's love. So, if letters and personal pleas weren't going to produce results I was going to have to act myself. And I did not possess Harry Potters magic, only perhaps his will.

The Great Escape

As soon as the old school bus dropped us off and I had put my cases into my dormitory, I made my escape. I walked through the school grounds, across the vegetable patch, down to the playing field, and through the main gate. I walked through brambles and along an overgrown path to the moor, staying hidden from the road so I wouldn't be seen by parents who were driving their kids back to school.

As I have already written, when I started running away my intention had been very clear, as if I was being driven by an inner knowing that I needed to go home. It was winter and I was wearing the casual classroom clothes I had dressed in that morning in London; grey shorts, a white shirt, grey woolen jersey and sandals. As evening approached it started to get cold. Very cold and damp, much too cold for what I was wearing.

It also got dark and the fog rolled in. I soon found myself shivering, wet, lost and very alone in the wilderness. I dropped from resolve to being scared as a loose stone wall crumpled and I fell. Now every shadow was a fantasy that someone might attack me. I wandered along, miserable slipping down ditches and hitting myself against stones. Yet whenever I saw a light I ran away and hid. I had promised myself I would escape and get home and no one was going to prevent this. Goodness I was old enough to be a young war hero.

However after I had tumbled down one embankment, landing in a bramble heap and cutting my head against a rock I felt a cold sticky substance ooze out from my forehead. My fortitude buckled and I needed to be saved.

If I didn't get murdered by a headless horseman or the ancient Black Knight I would surely freeze to death, I spotted a house light. I was past running or even walking, I was now stumbling, grazing against rocks, bruising myself as I fell down more holes and slicing my flesh horribly in the bramble bushes. The light was coming from an old stone cottage in the middle of nowhere right out of a Bronte novel. With not a little trepidation, I knocked on the door and fell crying.

It was answered by a little old lady. (Although her face was warm I still surreptitiously checked in my head to make sure the house was not made of gingerbread and candy!) A wood fire was burning and she gave me blankets and some steaming hot chocolate and asked what I was doing out in the middle of nowhere. I lied. I came up with a story that I was on holiday with my parents and had gone on a walk and had become lost. In my charmingly innocent way I asked if she would be kind enough to take me to the hotel where we were staying in Studland. This was my first memorable experience practicing deceit, and it paid off. She was aghast that my parents could lose me, and I was awash in self-judgment at her reaction to my lie. I cried more. (That feeling is what I remember most of this incident with her.) She popped me into her old car and took me to the hotel whilst I lay in a deep sleep.

Of all the places in my world, which were limited to homes and shops and train stations and parks and a few friends houses, I knew the Knoll House in Studland. Studland was very popular in the 1950s and 1960s, before the English all started traveling overseas for holidays. We had gone there several times and my family were friendly with the family who ran the hotel, the Fergusons

Like a shredded rag doll I went up to the front desk of the very imposing hotel and plopped all my candy money I had, twelve shillings, onto the tall table and announced to the receptionist that I had come to stay. The receptionist glanced at my coins, looked at me covered with bloody cuts and immediately hustled me over to the hotel's owners. They apparently also called my parents who were now at the country home in Dorset, about 15 miles away, because things began to happen. They were not the things I wanted to happen.

My father had been out searching for me as soon as the school realized I was missing. There was a massive hunt underway involving the police and the local authorities. Some bad things had happened to a few children in years before in the area, and the worst was being assumed. In quick time everyone was over at the hotel. The one person who wasn't there was my mother. She wasn't allowed to come because they felt that it would be too traumatic for her. Not for me, but for her! The whole reason for my escaping was to find my mother's love. I wanted to be with my mother, and they wouldn't let her come because then maybe it would be too hard to get me back to school. Instead I got my father, who was only there to take me back to the school. I think I was very clear again when I saw my father. I told my dad, "I don't want to go back." I was not heard again. He took me straight back to the school anyway. My plan had failed, but there was a benefit I hadn't anticipated. Thanks to my adventure, I had become the school celebrity for the week. I had apparently lived out quite a few of my fellow pupils fantasies.

War Picture Boys

As I have alluded to before, at its deepest roots, the British consciousness is quite war-oriented. My generation always assumed that we were going to be in a third world war, because all our ancestors ever since 1066 have been fighting wars. War has been a generational event and, even as children, we knew quite a lot about war lore. Our comics were filled with war stories. Steve McQueen had driven his mangled body and motorbike into the barbed wire of the Swiss border, with freedom dashed at the last hurdle. What I knew was The Great Escape. What I whistled was its theme tune. I even bounced a cricket ball against the wall like my Hollywood hero. Like Americans know sports statistics, English schoolboys knew battle statistics, victories, defeats, even minutiae like who escaped from prison camps or the concentration camps, the number of tunnels that had been dug, and how far escapees had got if they were captured.

I was now something akin to Steve McQueen. It was late at night by the time I was reinstalled in my dormitory, and everyone else was asleep, or supposedly asleep. My dormitory mates sat up and began chattering. They gasped at my war wounds and asked how I was and what it was like to be out there all alone. For all practical purposes I had acted out what every one of them had considered at one time or another as they cried themselves to sleep. In whispers they told me that, in school folklore, I had traversed across foreboding lands further than anyone ever had. I was celebrated by them. But I didn't get home.

Love Hurts

For various small infractions I was beaten too much at Spyway and that eventually became simply part of the routine for me. We had two brothers as headmasters. One, Eric, beat with a wooden paddle and the other, Mr. Geoffrey, with a whipping cane, which was more severe. We would be called into their rooms, spread over their knees or knelt over a chair and handed our pain. Normally it was three, four, and six strokes. The punishment was also meant to be an experience we would not forget or want to have repeated.

One summer day I had seen a little girl down in the village when I went out to buy sweets one Sunday. She was playing in her garden listening to the radio playing the hit of the day, "Telegram Sam" by T-Rex. For the next month I often went to sit with her for a while and we would marvel at Marc Bolan, the lead singer of T-Rex. One day I gathered my courage and held her hand. That afternoon, I went back to school and, during my French class, wrote my first letter of undying love. I proposed to sneak out of school to see her in the evening after the sun had set. Unfortunately, I left the letter in my French homework where the teacher found it. I was to be beaten.

If you to ask boys who went to school why were they beaten, most would shrug and say they really cant remember. There were a few times that the incident merited my eternal memory, but usually not. There was one time when I knew that my sentence was a foregone conclusion. I decided to take matters into my own hands and so I sneaked into the headmaster's study, stole the wooden paddles he used for discipline, and threw it away. When he went to get ready for my beating, with me standing outside his door waiting, the paddle was gone. He called the school together and said the whole school was suspect. We all had to sit there until the culprit owned up. With that as the threat, I confessed because I knew the whole school would have been in trouble, and I didn't want to again be the cause of the other boys' hurt.

When I confessed to stealing the paddle, Eric meted out an unusual punishment. It had two parts. I was to receive a beating, of course, and I had to make a paddle to replace the one I had swiped. The project took me about two days, and I felt like a condemned man building his own gallows.

Signs of Success

Fortunately there was another side to my life as a school boy. Success. I had become a star at sports. I was the hurdle and one hundred yard dash champion; and our rugby and cricket teams were unbeaten in my last year, which was a huge achievement, because we had far less boys than our competitors and in previous years were always considered the minor league side. I also was the golf champion, having been playing on the school nine hole course.

Also by ten I was considered one of the top pony riders in the area and my father, who had helped donated a new science laboratory, a swimming pool and my leaving present, a cricket scoreboard, strongly persuaded the school to let me keep my pony at stables next to the grounds. I was able to now gallop across the fields and jump the ditches that a few years earlier I had fallen into as I had made my great escape.

I started fox hunting as well at the age of ten as a natural part of emulating my ancestors, for whom fox hunting was a tradition. I was already an excellent horseman after years of lunging class lessons and whipping my mum and nanny to run faster in my first foray into competition, the local pony club leading rein classes. Like many kids who take to a sport young, I was a daring rider, usually at the front of the hunt. Since I never feared falling off, I often did. It happened one icy winter's day that I lost my seat, and as I fell, my pony slipped and kicked me in the head so hard that my helmet shattered. I was lucky, one of my best friend's mothers died on that hunting field and in that moment my friend's life changed.

At twelve, I was old, a Latin scholar and it was time to get ready to move on to the venerable school of all schools in the world, Eton College. I left Spyway prep school quite prepared, instilled with qualities of bravery, will, purpose, hope and success. The bag I packed the day I left also included mistrust, shame and guilt and that the real playing field that I had created was not one on which my ability to read Chaucer or regale the exploits of Ulysses were celebrated. It was simply that the fertile seeds of judgment and fear had been sown and were inexorably growing and crowding out the childhood fruits of my God given spirit, love, curiosity and joy.

I had started to develop two personalities, distinctly different. One stimulated by love and light. The other fearfully expecting the darkness and moving alone in my thoughts.

What I knew was I was different from you and that was a worry.

Yet how could I comprehend that? I was only twelve.

Chapter 15.

Confusion

Someone that says they are not confused is confused.
They just don't know it yet.

Confusion

The innocence of birth. Its utter open vulnerability. The innocence of the birth of your idea. Uncluttered, amidst the purity of your passion-filled heart. An innocence repeating inner sense leading to outward action, often appealing to those that are met by its needs, yet as often looking foolish to the masses. Confusing.

A childhood full of inquisitive tests, a child's will testing a mother's un-conditionality - innocent enquiring from the child yet a chore at the end of a long day for the mother. Confusing.

There is an inevitability about confusion, simply becomes each of us is living separate lives and has a different outlook to the same situation.

History confuses us.

He had travelled so very far. In fact he had traversed the hottest of deserts, lands that give you nothing but foreboding heat and a constant hazy golden landscape that forces the eyes and the mind to confront confusion. He had united the desert's own people, confused themselves before he arrived amongst them, about who of their own they could trust. He turned them into an efficient guerilla force, with a clarity of vision that caught their much more equipped enemy unawares. He had strategized with their generational family leaders to attack from land. No one crossed the desert to attack the town from land so all the guns were pointing out to sea. Yet he did. He had been uniquely qualified before the Arab desk had persuaded his superiors to send him off to muster the greatest and most expensive distraction. Surely he would die in the desert from the severity of the desert itself, or the mass enemy that he was to confront or even at the hands of his own Bedouin forces.

In every way he was victorious. He was acclaimed by those that knew their land, that owned their land. They had looked him in the eye and were not confused. Now he needed a drink after the longest of journeys. He was clear he needed nothing but to quench his thirst. He knew too of his gratitude and respect for the young Bedouin, Farraj, who had been with him all along through their every hazardous travail.

He was clear as he entered into the officer's mess, unclean from the journey, with his young manservant that he wanted two glasses of water, with the first to go to Farraj. Yet as he walked to the bar, all he attracted was stares and consternation. Not because of anything that was clearly brilliant in all that he had accomplished. But simply because he simply had brought an Arab native into the mess. The best of the British army tried to figure out how to deal with this massive threat to their personal way of life, it was an affront on everything they stood for as English officers and gentlemen. Finally one came forward to confront the situation. "Now look here Lawrence, you know the score, old boy, you cant have that in here", reportedly the officer said with his perfectly polished holster and boots and pressed uniform.

Lawrence looked at the bar man and with clarity of purpose and vision asked again for his simple need. Two large glasses of water. The bar man poured them. Lawrence of Arabia gave the first to his manservant and then as he gulped his water down he uttered the simple line. "We have taken Aqaba."

Aqaba was settled in 4000BC and was the strategic gateway to the Suez. By seizing the town, Lawrence and Sharif Hussein opened the supply chain for Arab and Allied forces and swung the tide against the Turkish threat. This was accomplished not by an officers mess of well trained Sandhurst officers doing soldiering, but by someone proven to be passionate about the affairs of its people, who lived as them and was appreciated by them for who he clearly was being to them.

A few hours later, Lawrence was now in the company of General Allenby and he re-entered the mess with admiration all around. Eyes and ears that were confused only hours before divided by class, creed and geography, could now see and hear.

What is very clear to the person that is at the center of their own being and destiny is often confusing to the masses.

A year later Farraj was laying a mine on a train track and he slipped with the detonator in his pocket. Mortally wounded he looked up knowing clearly what his beloved master, the great Lawrence of Arabia, was clearly obligated to do. The Turks would capture and torture him. Lawrence looked down at his kindred spirit, the cries of his heart piercing his confused head, and then he pulled the trigger.

A few years later Lawrence himself confused by the Allies renegading on the deal of land rights to the Bedouin, had tried to confuse the English again by changing his name so he could enlist in the Royal Air Force. Confused this great hero in our history continued to find conformity too hard to bear. Finally boys playing on a winding Dorset lane forced Lawrence to swerve and crash his motorbike. The fact that he sustained head injuries and died in hospital a few days later was the clear catalyst for the campaign that brought in crash helmets for motorcyclists.

Judgment makes our adult ears confusingly unable to hear and yet what is not confusing is that clarity can be around the corner if we open ourselves to hear.

Most of us have experience of this. Confusing, even chaotic and then "aha," clarity. I knew that all along!

Confusion - OUR WORLD

When Henry Ford introduced the automobile for the mass market, commentators looked on scoffing that for this to be accomplished there would need to be a mass web of tarmac laid all over the country and even more absurd there would have to be filling stations every few miles. Less than a hundred years later roads lead to everything and everyone and pumps are primed to give you gas or petrol at prices you scoff at but still accept, just as you now do paying more for your water for yourself than gasoline for the car! We the people call this progress. Yet, as commented in Your Planet Needs You by Jon Symes and Phil Turner, when we take into account the eight hundred and twelve hours spent every year earning the money to buy and keep a car plus the time spent using it and the distance travelled each year, our average speed is LESS than that of a bicycle. Confused?

Why would a diminutive Swedish lady, Ingrid Munroe, in Nairobi, figure out how to include health care on one hundred and twenty thousand micro loans, which directly resulted in hospitals flourishing and every one of the poorest women in the world within her Jamii Bora program now receiving both health care and life insurance? Yet in the USA in 2009 sixteen percent of gross domestic spend was on health care at an average of over seven thousand dollars per person, but, staggeringly sixteen percent of the nation as well as nine million children are uninsured and an American baby is born every minute without healthcare. Those that can afford the premiums complain about what is not covered by their exorbitant payments, and that President Obama is letting them down and yet over seventy percent of Capitol Hill are lawyers and of course lawyer's number one source of income is....health care. Confusing, or are we just living in compromise?

Are we globally dim as we look up in the sky and see the consequence of global dimming?

Confusion - MONEY

So how did money shift so dramatically to the opposite meaning and life force of its creation and childhood? How did we become so confused about money and allow our financial systems to be built on sand?

The Bible is a really good place to start. We have been confusing ourselves over the Word for two thousand years. One church person said, "Jesus's shirt was red" and then another said, "No, it was certainly blue, so, I am going to start a church over there with a different name." Jesus started Christianity, yet people since confusingly have used one church name after another to misinterpret what was central and clear. What does "judge not less ye be judged" mean when I am a Catholic and you are a Muslim, when I can speak in charismatic tongues and you can't, when I am man and you are woman?

Yes, simple words have created more confusion. *"Render therefore to Caesar the things that are Caesar's and to God the things that are God's"* Matthew 22 v21. We have taken this as a statement, a fact, to separate the physical world from the spiritual world. Yet can you believe that Jesus was not talking about money, but about the consciousness surrounding money?

When we are able to alter the energy we have around money from fear to love, we are able to traverse the gap between the material and the spiritual world and make it possible for the unlimited abundance of the Divine to flow freely into our own lives and throughout our world.

When were the signs that this separation occurred? It came with humanity's obsession with symbols around 3000-2500BC. The first crack in the holy oneness of the Divine and the human. Two worlds - material and spiritual started their inexorable journey towards separation. A journey that by Nero and the Fall of the Holy Roman Empire was complete and later by the Industrial Revolution was so ingrained in our psyche that we set to act out the Love of Power with money as our casino chips, and governments so confused ready to print up whatever they wished. Because money is energy it must flow freely. If we are fearful of it, ranked with guilt and shame and acting out in anger over money, we stop the flow of energy. Hoarding it creates a wall of stopped-up energy. Because ultimately money is energy directed by people's collective thoughts, there can be enough money or there can be not enough money. We through generations of manipulations, media commentary have taken the decision that there is not enough money for everyone.

We have agreed that there are to be three groups. The very poor who do not have enough, and maybe out of charity we can give them a hand out; a middle group that get by for their lives, living on their last pay check, and then a very small third group that will control most of the money in circulation.

The confusion lies that it is not a fact of the universe that the amount of money in the world is finite. This is rather a condition that we as human beings have agreed to. A lot of people around the world have woken confused in the last few years to how they valued their own money in a confused way. Property prices falling, stock markets losing massive value, pensions going up in smoke.

Perhaps the greatest modern confusion, highlighted by the instrument of money, is how we have confused the need we have around the word leverage. When we are able to leverage ourselves into a million pound home with no money down, or we have increased our net worth through assets made up of leveraged balance sheets; when a country has borrowed with no way of paying back, with only a vain hope of leveraging their own economy to keep up with their neighbors; have we not become confused that the leveraging tool may one day not weaken and finally break? A love of power is blindingly confusing.

HOPE NOTE

Today out of the bottom billion that have lived
on less than one dollar a day,
120 million have received and are using micro loans
to produce products and circulating resources.

98% are paying back loans and interest in full.

120 million micro social entrepreneurs.
That is a very great amount of great people.

Micro Producers - What can they make for you?
Micro Distributors - What can they buy from you?

Micro Trading can bring us all to the clear brilliance of
who we are,
what we can do,
how we can help each other,
And where we can benefit ourselves and our world

Confusion - YOU

"It is human to have a long childhood; it is civilized to have an even longer childhood. Long childhood makes a technical and mental virtuoso out of man, but it also leaves a lifelong residue of emotional immaturity in him" Erik Homburger Erikson (1902-1994)

So what made you confused ..... about you?

You were there, in your crib, hungry for your mother's milk. You knew already innately what to do to bring attention to this fact that your tummy was empty. You cried and your mother heard it. She knew the cry, different to the 'I am tired' cry and the 'I hit my head on the car door' cry. She comes into sight, ready to satisfy your need. You know what is going to happen next and you are ready to be fed. Thank you Mummy. I love you Mummy. I trust you Mummy and you care for me Mummy. Next instant disaster. Mummy has swiveled on her feet and disappeared out of the door again. Your life, even though it is a short one so far, falls apart. Your face contorts into total despair and your cry turns to one of complete anguish. Unloved, not cared for and abandoned. Your reality.

Only your reality. Your mother, though, heard that door bell, turned and left the room and is now signing for the package she had been waiting for, with your next size up clothes. She makes it as fast as she can but it is too late. The damage is now done. She comes back to you and soon your cry is gurgling into the middle of her breast. However the germ, the seed, the feeling left by the judgment taken on, remains and one day it will sprout.

You are confused and that is an essential part of your journey.

Confusion cannot be avoided by any of us. You were created, went into childhood and now confusion must be present. Confusion shows up in business, marriage, life, and clearly in understanding yourself. How you deal with it and how you then understand it and move through it provides the next critical junction to your ability to HEAR.

Our personality traits come in confusing opposites. We think of ourselves as optimistic or pessimistic, independent or dependent, emotional or unemotional, adventurous or cautious, leader or follower, aggressive or passive. Others confuse us even more labeling us industrious or lazy, fun loving or introvert. Some of these inborn temperament traits are gifted to us through our life, but most characteristics, such as feeling either competent or inferior, are learned, based on the challenges and support we receive in growing up, before we leave school.

How confusing was it for you to be told repeatedly by teachers that you were brilliant in one subject and terrible in another and that you needed to reach their set goals and study the subject you just didn't like or resonate with and that's why you didn't excel? Why could you not continue to be supported to spend more time on your virtues and talents instead of being set upon to crack the problem of subjects that just did not interest you? What indelible scars did it leave?

How confusing is it as well when you are training in a company and they send you off on courses that are designed to change your weaknesses rather than enhance your gifts and talents. You had irrevocable skill sets when you joined. That's why you got hired in the first place. Why not continue to increase your level of excellence in what you are good at?

So we have a choice. Batter away at the goal line of life and try to create a different result, or drop onto the learning line of life. It is this learning line of life that is both accessible at any time you choose, not just at that time in our teens when we didn't want to be at school yet we didn't have any choice in the matter, but throughout our lives. To be in environments, what ever shape they may take, where the learning line is celebrated and to go back to school the way you always wanted it to be. You can choose to do this at any time of life, even when you are seventy or eighty years old.

I did choose this path and along the way, when I was thirty-nine, I entered into a Masters Degree course at the University of Santa Monica in California. Located on Wilshire Boulevard, just as the road at the heart of Los Angeles lets you glimpse from your car the blue Pacific ahead, it is the small university which is held in good regard throughout the world of psychology and counseling. It was here that I became familiar with a study that had immediate deep resonation with me. I became aware of the startling work of Erik Erikson.

Although he was influenced by Freud, Erikson believed that the ego exists from birth and that behavior is not totally defensive. Based in part on his study of Sioux Indians on a reservation, Erikson became aware of the massive influence of culture on behavior and placed more emphasis on the external world, on such issues such as depression and wars. He felt that the course of development is determined by the interaction of the body (genetic biological programming), mind (psychological), and cultural (ethos) influences.

He organized life into eight stages that extend from birth to death. Since adulthood covers a span of many years, Erikson divided the stages of adulthood into the experiences of babies and infants, children, young adults, middle aged adults and older adults. While the actual ages may vary considerably from one stage to another, the ages seem to be appropriate for the majority of people.

Erikson's basic philosophy rests on two major themes. The first is the world gets bigger for each of us as we pass through our life, and the second is our failures are cumulative. While the first point is fairly obvious, we might take exception to the last. It is true that in many cases an individual who has to deal with horrendous circumstances as a child may be unable to negotiate later stages as easily as someone who didn't have many challenges early on. For example orphans who weren't given caring attention as infants have an extremely tough time connecting with others when they become adults. However, there's always the chance that somewhere along the way the strength of the human spirit can be ignited and deficits overcome, like I witness time after time in the most horrendous of post war countries in Africa's rural areas when we visit war victims. When I first was presented with Erikson's study it had powerful connection with my own awareness of myself and my own history and that is why I give you the detail and references of his study now for you to examine with your own life as your example. I am also giving you the opportunity to journal any thoughts that may present themselves solicited by the eight stages.

1. Infancy: Birth to 18 Months
Personality Trait: Trust verses Mistrust
Basic strength: Drive and Hope

The first stage of Erik Erikson's, centers around an infant's basic needs being met by the parents just like the story of a mother and the bottle. An infant utterly depends on its parents, especially the mother, for food, sustenance, and comfort. The baby is driven and as a parent you will notice that in your child's calls to you.

My three children all had very, very different cries for tired, hurt and hungry. You also witness great hope in all that a baby looks to accomplish in its first movement to toddler, and its hope with every mouthful on its spoon that the food is going to find its way into its mouth and not splattered on cheeks, or chin or floor!

Your own memory as a child and your relative understanding of your world and society come nearly always from your parents and their interaction with you. If parents expose a child to warmth, regularity, and dependable affection, an infant's view of the world will be one of trust. Should the parents fail to provide a secure environment and to meet the child's basic need, a sense of mistrust can result.

According to Erikson, the major developmental task in infancy is to learn whether or not other people, especially primary caregivers, can regularly satisfy basic needs. If caregivers are consistent sources of food, comfort, and affection, an infant learns trust and that others are dependable and reliable. I will be fed when I am hungry, I will be picked up from my cot when I wake at five in the morning. If they are neglectful, or perhaps even abusive, an infant instead can learn mistrust - that the world is in an undependable, unpredictable, and possibly dangerous place.

Through HEAR I bring forward the philosophy that the issue is how we choose to respond to the issue of our lives and our world that is the issue.

A baby's response is both simple and direct and a baby knows very clearly how to deal with an issue.

What do you feel from your own baby within?

_____

_____

_____

_____

_____

_____

_____

_____

2. Early Childhood: 18 Months to 3 Years

Personality Trait: Autonomy verses Shame
Basic Strengths: Self-control, Courage, and Will

During this stage we learn to master skills for ourselves. Not only do we learn to walk, talk and feed ourselves, we are learning finer motor development as well as the much appreciated toilet training. Everybody poops! Here we have the opportunity to build self-esteem and autonomy as we gain more control over our bodies and acquire new skills, learning right from wrong, and one of our skills which has helped create the term "Terrible Two's" is our ability to use the powerful word "NO!" It may be pain for parents, but it develops important skills of the will.

Surely you can verify the will of a two or three year old as they clearly do not want to concede to sleep. My own eldest daughter Arabella would take an hour and a half, every night to go to sleep when we lived off the Ventura Boulevard. I would walk her around the Valley blocks in Sherman Oaks and then if she was still not asleep I would hold her in the bathroom and listen to music. Maybe we were not courageous enough to let Belle cry herself to sleep! But then we had an excuse. Her mother and I were only adults and our wills were not as courageous as our child's!

It is also during this stage, however, that we can be very vulnerable. If we're shamed in the process of toilet training or in learning other important skills, we may feel great shame and doubt of our capabilities and suffer low self-esteem as a result.

The most significant relationships are of course still with parents and now elder siblings. Courage often is seen with playful interaction with a bigger brother or sister, and for parents do you remember the little courage package with a little rucksack running up to the door of your care giver for the day, turning back to you at the side of your car, only to say, "Bye Mummy."

Again what comes up for you if you can remember any of this time?

_____

_____

_____

_____

_____

_____

_____

_____

_____

3. Play Age: 3 to 5 Years
Personality Traits: Initiative verses Guilt
Basic Strength: Purpose

During this period we experience a desire to copy our parents and care givers around us and take initiative in creating imaginary worlds and play situations. We make up stories with Postman Pat,

Barbie, Legoland, red fire engines, toy phones and today even computers, and in real life may be with our family pet. We are playing out roles in our own universe for hours, even experimenting with the blueprint for what we believe it means to be an adult. We see children darting into mummy and daddy's shoes, trying to moving their tiny legs under the weight of leather and heels. We also begin to use that wonderful word for exploring the word, "WHY?"

You may have an issue with reading this in connection with your own three to five year old, but we also start to see confusion coming forward around sex. Not the action of it of-course but the feelings within. Since there is such energy on sex in life and probably your life, it does make perfect sense for it to be deep routed from a very early age. While Erikson was influenced by Freud, he downplays biological sexuality in favor of the psychosocial features of conflict between child and parents. Nevertheless, he said that at this stage we usually become involved in the classic "Oedipal struggle" where we have a natural tendency to be attracted to the influence of the parent of the opposite sex. Oedipus in Greek Mythology kills his father, Laius and marries his mother, Jocasta. We resolve this struggle through "social role identification." Amongst my friends that have grown up to be Gay and Lesbian many of them also highlight to this time when they connected most with the energy of the opposite parent and perhaps took on their traits, like an eldest daughter with her dad and then taking on his energy and later on in life liking girls, as dad did as well as the patriarchal energy that plays out in their own beautiful relationships.

Also if we're frustrated over natural desires and goals, we may easily experience guilt. I know that the children I have had around me these last ten years burst into massive tears if they think they have done something wrong and they carry massive guilt for minutes but not usually longer.

The most significant relationships are still within the basic family and our first friend that we can remember may have shown up! You will be able to access certain incidents now of this age.

What are your first memories of your life during this age?

_____

_____

_____

_____

_____

_____

_____

_____

_____

4. School Age: 6 to 12 Years
Personality Trait: Industry verses Inferiority
Basic Strengths: Method and Competence

During this stage, often called the Latency (when we get comfortable with children and care givers of our own sex), we are capable of learning, creating and accomplishing numerous new skills and knowledge, thus developing a sense of industry. This is also a very social stage of development and if we experience unresolved feelings of inadequacy and inferiority among our peers, we can have serious problems in terms of competence and self-esteem. This shows up most in exams, friends parties and fun time, sleep overs, and early sports trials. Also it is amazing that as children we sing and dance until we are eight and then we lose so much creative expression because we are told by someone somewhere that we are no good. We stop and may never start again. So much brilliance goes dormant in these years!

As the world expands a bit, our most significant relationship is with the school and neighborhood. Parents are no longer the complete authorities they once were, although they are still important.

We know the level of skill of our methods, whether we study as "A" students every week in school or cram for exams to squeeze a better grade and prove our reports wrong. Whether we remember shirking school and experimenting with our first cigarette behind the railway arches (which was very familiar to me, but why did English boys always start their smoking careers with French filterless Gauloise). We learn to push the boundaries by going to bed an extra ten minutes later. We negotiate brilliantly with our parents for extra treats and things we think we need. Even though we may not be child prodigies we do learn that we are also good at certain things and brilliance emerges to be irrevocably etched and directing many of our life decisions.

What were you good at, and what did you give up at this age that you wish now you had kept up but someone had judged that you were not good enough, and the talent was suppressed?

_____

_____

_____

_____

_____

_____

_____

_____

_____

5. Adolescence: 12 to 18 Years
Personality Trait: Identity verses Role Confusion
Basic Strengths: Devotion and Fidelity

Up to this stage development mostly depends upon what is done to us as children. From here on out, development depends primarily upon what we do ourselves and how we act out. And while adolescence is a stage in which we are neither a child nor an adult, life is definitely getting more complex as we attempt to find our own identity, struggle with social interactions, and grapple with moral issues.

Our task is to discover who we are as individuals separate from our family of origin and as members of a wider society made up of our school friends and communities. Unfortunately for those around us, in this process many of us enter a period of withdrawing from responsibilities, which Erikson called a "moratorium." And if we are unsuccessful in navigating this stage, we will experience role confusion and upheaval. We may look to substances to numb our feelings as we distance from wanting to hurt through confusion. Some start taking drink or drugs

A significant task for us is to establish a philosophy of life and in this process we tend to think in terms of ideals, which are conflict free, rather than reality, which is not. The problem is that we don't have much experience and find it easy to substitute ideals for experience. However, we can also develop strong devotion to friends and causes.

It is no surprise that our most significant relationships are not with our parents but with peer groups.

What did you believe your friends thought of you at school?

_____

_____

_____

_____

_____

_____

_____

6. Young adulthood: 18 to 35
Personality Trait: Intimacy and Solidarity verses Isolation
Basic Strengths: Affiliation and Love

In the initial stage of being an adult we start to seek and be sought by one or more companions and to explore intimacy leading to love. As we try to find mutually satisfying relationships, examining our mistakes with one person, with the hope of better results for the next, we also start to act out our relationship confusion with others. Some of us have difficulty in committing, preferring to be conditional in our giving to another. Later, when we do feel we have found the "one," we push, bear and open ourselves to un-conditionality first through marriage and friends, and then by being faced with the unexpected learning of being a parent, though this age has been delayed and pushed back by many couples who today don't start their families until later. If negotiating this stage is successful, we can experience intimacy on a very deep level. If we're not successful, isolation and distance from others may occur. When we don't find it easy to create satisfying relationships, our world can begin to shrink as, in defense, we can feel superior to others.

Our significant relationships are with relationship partners and friends, although we may also find ourselves acting out our relationships even with our sports teams and business communities. If we have been "unlucky" in love with our partners, and as we start to physically to be less able to drink as much as we did in our twenties and we truly start to realize that we are no longer children it is possible that we do start to confront transformation as we come out of this cycle, which often coincides or collides with our mid thirties.

Perhaps I was unconscious of the cause and effect of my actions that I was birthed into and existed through my early life cycles.

I learned to survive and then live quite satisfactorily with myself. Yet what I had packed into the back pack of myself weighed me down and the artificial support that I sought like business acclaim, alcohol and sex, were not firm foundations for the future of my life. Time for change and, thank God, I did.

What was your biggest regret that you have about the decisions you took after you left school to your mid twenties?

_____

_____

_____

_____

_____

_____

_____

_____

7. Middle Adulthood: 35 to 65
Personality Trait: Generatively verses Stagnation
Basic Strengths: Production and Care

Now work is most crucial. Erikson observed that middle-age is when we tend to be occupied with creative and meaningful work and with issues surrounding our family. Also, middle adulthood is when we can expect to "be in charge," the role we've long envied. The significant task is to perpetuate culture and transmit values of the culture through the family, caring for the kids and working to establish a stable environment. Strength comes through care of others and production of something that contributes to the betterment of society and our world, so when we're in this stage we often fear inactivity and meaninglessness. As our children leave home, or our relationships or goals change, we may be faced with major life changes—the mid-life crisis—and struggle to find new meanings and purposes. If we don't get through this stage successfully, we can become self-absorbed and stagnate.

Strong relationships are within the workplace, the community and the family. Did you ever have an emotional relationship with your work at the expense of your family? What is your relationship to the concept of work and have you looked at running your own business or have you always been content to be a "staffer?"

What is the greatest awakening you had about your self?

_____

_____

_____

_____

_____

_____

_____

8. Late Adulthood: 65 to Death
Personality Trait: Integrity verses Despair
Basic Strengths: Wisdom

Erikson felt that much of life is preparing for the middle adulthood stage and the last stage is recovering from it. Perhaps that is because as older adults we can often look back on our lives with happiness and are content, feeling fulfilled with a deep sense that life has meaning and we've made a contribution to life, a feeling Erikson calls integrity. Our strength comes from a wisdom that the world is very large and we now have a detached concern for the whole of life, accepting death as the completion of life.

On the other hand, some adults may reach this stage and despair at their experiences and perceived failures. They may fear death as they struggle to find a purpose to their lives, wondering "Was the trip worth it?" Alternatively, they may feel they have all the answers (not unlike going back to adolescence) and end with a strong dogmatism that only their view has been correct.

One significant side question to ask and be conscious of in today's world is when does "late adulthood" now really start. Governments are seeking to push pension age up a few years and riots are taking place on the streets of France and other countries because of this.

In Hollywood I was mentored and have worked for over a decade with the legendary film boss Frank Yablans. Frank is in his late seventies now and during our time has been as passionate about the business of screenplays and film distribution as he was when he was thirty two, head of Paramount Pictures, and putting out both The GodFather 1 and 2, China Town and Love Story. Today he mentors the next group of young aspirants, with as much direct expression as he did the young Pacino and Nicholson. A brilliant man, whose dad was a taxi driver from New York, can still remember the era when a good script, and not the special effects, was the basis for a hit film

I know eighty-year women, like Barbara Marx Hubbard, who have overflowing exuberance and excitement for life just like a four year old, and way more than many of our teenagers!

The significant relationship for this age though is with all of mankind—"my-kind." If you can be mentored by someone who is in this age cycle, and who was brilliant in his or her life, you should jump at the opportunity.

What would you like to see written on your tombstone in 50 words or less?

_____

_____

_____

_____

_____

_____

_____

_____

A Stage Before Your Time.

When I first studied Erickson, which was during my own seventh stage of life, I resonated deeply with his findings and with the signposts and criteria that he had provided. I also found the stages identified confusion. Purely through a sudden awareness of this clarity of identification, I automatically could lift myself from my own confusion that I did not know or hear I had before I comprehended Erickson. I started to remember and journal incidents during each stage of life, starting with the seventh, the most fresh in my mind and working back through the stages to my early childhood.

However to aid myself I have become aware of another stage or cycle. One that I feel is essential for compassionate understanding, which gives me the opportunity to recognize a level of confusion that I have seen in myself and which nearly all in our world suffer from.

I call the stage Karmic Placenta and I connect these two words together in a number of entries within HEAR. To me the connection is obvious and yet when I Googled Karmic Placenta there was no former reference, so if linking these two words is confusing for you the reader, it should be as you would not have heard it before. For me it points to a time when we took what was peripheral in the intent of our creator and made it central through the answers of generational minds to finish up as the hinge to the thoughts and actions of ourselves and our generation. A time that gradually laid the mind-fields of confusion within ourselves relating to our judgment of male and female, black and white and the Koran says this and the Bible says that and Jesus is pulled apart as far apart as one side pulls at the pages of the other side's good book. How confusing can a birth, a death and an ascension be? Or is it not the how this happened that was confusing, but on what value did we put the why? Why oh why are there sides? Why is there such competition to separate our souls?

Karmic Placenta comes gushing out of your mother's womb as quickly and as assuredly as you popped yourself out into her world. You were born and clearly into a setup situation. It may have been like many of my friends, a slum in Mumbai or Nairobi with your mother cutting your own umbilical cord with no light or clean water. Many of my friends had an opposite experience and everything in between. Your birth could have been carried out by a team of midwives and nurses, a doctor, a doula to comfort your mum, and even the necessary but sparingly used hanging-around dad, all in the poshest of clinics. The sheer heavenly grace of birth hides so much that is waiting to enter through the wings of confusion.

The example of births in abject poverty in an African slum surrounded by a nation of tens of millions in poverty is one that many would agree as a tough way for another baby to be born. I have learned to look at other less obvious examples, not because of a slum's terrible situation but because there is so much grace and faith that remains forever in the actions of those that live it. Also micro solar lights and clean water are now getting to so many.

Lets take another example. Everyone is a Fan.

You are. You have loved something from when you were little.

Sport makes many of us fans. One that statistically is the most played or followed sport in every country around the world is of course soccer, or its other confusing word, football. Soccer or Football. Confusing because USA television loves to confuse us with promoted titles such as World Series and World Championship terminology. When it comes to the National Baseball League or National Football Association, both at the moment are played - at the moment - by only North American teams.

Take any city and you will find Karmic Placenta confusion driven by generations of zealous fans and the rivalry of opposing teams and even their conflicting colors. New York with the Yankies and the Mets, and those that still hold on to the legacy of the old Dodgers as opposed to the new Dodgers that unforgivingly were abducted to Los Angeles.

In Australia you have a series of Australian football teams all in the same town, Melbourne and you can be classed with the establishment if you follow Melbourne, Geelong or Essendon, or with an athletic dynastic like Collingwood and Hawthorne, or upstarts like St Kilda. All that before Adelaide, the Sydney Swans and the West Coast Eagles usurped the party and confused the whole State of Victoria taking championships out of State on a regular basis.

Soccer is very confusing. In Spain and world sports it doesn't get bigger than Barcelona and Real Madrid, each representing the population of a metropolis, a differing culture and a way of life. In Italy, AC and Inter Milan. In Mexico Cruz Azul and Club Americas. In Mexico where 100 million people live, over 50 million admit to being a fan of one team or another.

There is little choice when caught up in the placenta goo of Karmic history, when the physical, mental and emotional arrive to drive your spirit into knots. I am not even going to start on the red of Manchester United, Liverpool and Arsenal and their fans feelings about foreign money being pumped into the blue of Chelsea and Manchester City and the coaches that may be hailed one month and gone the next. Chelsea have spent approximately £86m since 2004 in compensation for managers. Chelsea had eight managers in their first 70 years from 1905 to 1975, they are now going for eleven in nine years. Roman Abramovich, the owner, has now had as many managers in his nine-year reign as United have had since 1937. Chelsea have sacked seven managers since 2005 and won seven trophies. The average life span for a manager under Abramovich is eight months. Chelsea have had thirteen different managers as long as Arsenal had the same manager since 1996. Its a confusing statistic as Chelsea have won the Premiership title three times in eight years and Arsenal none. Chelsea had less than twenty percent of the ball against Barcelona in the semi final of the 2012 UEFA Championship Semi-Final and won. They had one corner against Bayern Munich in the Final, scored and were crowned Champions of Europe. Within a few months they had fired another manager because they went one month without a win. Sport is a constant window for showing how confusion can become crisis in the space of a few days. In 2013 Chelsea brought back Murihinio who they fired after he won them two championships and when he arrived back he said he was confused the first time around. Confused?

Karmic confusion has always gripped the great capital of Glasgow in Scotland, historically known for its Braveheart clans. Celtic were formed in 1888 by Irish Catholic immigrants who began emigrating to the west of Scotland in the 1840s and their descendants. Rangers, who were formed in 1873, have always been perceived as "the Protestant club" and Celtic "the Catholic club." Until 1989, when Mo Johnston signed for them, Rangers had never fielded a high-profile Catholic player. The blessing today is that religion and race have become receding issues in sport, although fans sometimes cannot help themselves or their historic roots. We all suffer from Karmic Placenta. At eight and nine I was called Monkey as my fellow school mates thought I had big ears, was a dwarf and yet had long arms. I didn't know that the Karmic Placenta was working through my physical genes, to help shoot me up to a dazzling six foot by the time I was twenty, which was a very late age to stop growing.

At sixteen I would play air guitar in my Eton College bedroom to Stairway to Heaven, playing on my record player, so I absolutely had to see the Led Zeppelin movie "The Song Remains The Same" when it came into the local town's cinema. Led Zeppelin together with Meat Loaf, Bob Dylan, Ziggy Stardust Bowie, and McCartney's Wings were postured all over my walls, although they had to compete with the legendary Farrah Fawcett poster that made every English school boy dream of California Goddesses or at least their Charlie's Angel.

The only way I could get to the cinema would be to escape school grounds during a gap in school schedule times. This meant my band friends and I couldn't change out of our school uniform and get to the movie and then get back to class with any time to spare. Uniform was long black cut off tail jackets, pin stripe trousers, a waist coat and stiff white collar. As it had been since the fifteenth century. So off we rushed across the playing fields of Eton, ignoring the duties of academia. We were Zeppelin rock fans. It was natural that a gang of young boys in Slough, where the film was playing, would look at us with scorn and resentment. They circled us with the rant of "Penguin, Penguin." The fact that I had rosy cheeks and golden locks did not deter the fact of the black and white matter for them. I was an upper class toff and they needed to make sure I knew this, and so I did with a bruise from them. The rebellious creatively of Zeppelin and the confusion of the bruise would stay with me.

There is clearly what we know we know about ourselves, and then there is what we don't know we know about ourselves. The

Karmic Placenta of history, of our history, of our world's history so clearly sets this up the opportunity for a new learning.

What residue of a former life in your past or even your ancestry do you sense you have had to deal with in this life of yours and that up unto this point in HEAR you have not forgiven?

_____

_____

_____

_____

_____

_____

_____

Whatever you have written in the above lines is now what you must address with forgiveness and compassion. You are holding on to something and it is confusing the heck out of you as you are not allowing yourself to "be."

Whatever you have written in the above lines have held you in a vice of the past, which also has you irrationally fearing your future. You have to forgive and that means forgiving the judgment you have on the other person(s) in the story and then forgiving the judgment you have on yourself. Throughout HEAR you will see reference to "forgiveness of judgment."

It's the judgment, and not what you think happened that needs to be dealt with. Deal with the judgment and the story will look different. If you judge your father for whatever reason for not loving you and deserting you, your brothers and sisters and even your mother, there is a vital exercise of releasing yourself from judgment that must be done.

You have a choice to either be separated from the love and worth of your own self or to apply fogginess and self-forgiveness, which is the remedy, the medicine of everything that holds you back today.

Breaking ground on the Well of Grief – 1980

It shouldn't have been this way. Death and injury had suddenly come all around me.

My generation was the first NOT to fight on a battlefield since 1066. I had come out of opulence. My passport said, "Place of birth – Hampton Court" and my schooling was Eton College. At eighteen those around me said I had the world at my feet.

The first that did it was my best friend of ten years who I would go on pony and shooting play-dates with. He was the victim of being the youngest of five children of a brigadier hero from World War II. The gun had been turned into the chest and the shotgun blast had been heard only by the butler, who did not raise the alarm as the young men of the house often would be shooting stray vermin from bedroom windows.

Then my first young teenage burning love. I would break her out of her Ascot convent school, where Monaco princesses had been schooled, and have her back before daybreak. For two years we were seen by the youth of London society as inseparable, two golden children in love, as we laid our plans for a life of promise.

I started University in the northern tip of Scotland in Aberdeen surrounded by oil riggers spending their money earned at sea on excesses of drink, drugs and sex. An innocent youth, closeted for most of my life in a luxury cotton wall, suddenly found myself caught up in bar room brawls. Lovers suddenly hundreds of miles apart and the nights were spent for hours in idle love chat until long train journeys brought us together. We would stay at our friends parents house near her school and then every day of our holidays we found a way of being together.

The week she started her university career down south she was brilliant and beautiful. At the end of the first week of new possibilities she lay across the backseat of a Mercedes traveling the countryside in the dead of night. A truck came over the brow, a driver swerved. CRASH. The impact was against the rear Mercedes door. All came out of the car without a scratch, except Joanna, her head crumpling down into her spine in that split second.....leaving her left for life without the freedom of the stunning limbs she had been blessed with. I did not have the tools of life to deal with this. I had been taught to internalize every emotion. Not to cry out. I was unaccustomed to crying.

My life had been spiraling out of control and I had acted out that had me isolated from those I had known. Darkness had conquered anything I held onto which had been good about me.

I too took my shot gun and dog for a walk and then far from the house turned the barrel in to my mouth.

So many of those I held dear was hurt or gone. Why not me? They were brilliant and acclaimed already in their achievements. I was struggling desperately to know who I was and what to do. Yet angels had carried their soaring souls away and left me. Was I like the kid in the Omen, seized without knowing it by the Devil?

The Mercedes driver, another best friend, committed suicide the following year, leaving an affluent Ascot family to remember fleeting youth. Other parents, the most successful in the country lost too as sons and daughters mis-programed, straying within the deadly minefields of their minds, blew themselves up on the unseen "Unworthy" and "Unloveability." Names that could have gone on as their ancestors to be Prime Ministers and war heroes, now left just a series of funerals with those left behind fighting to buffer feelings and the question too agonizing to look at of "who's next?"

Hellish demons raged around me, plucking even those set to achieve. Anthony was a year senior to me through nine years and two schools. I had looked up to his friends brilliance and measured my ability on how I could tackle the best player in the rugby team. I finally did it better than anyone else and so I became his partner on the sports field. Anthony, a flying rugby fly-half to my own tenacious scrum-half. We were at the heart of an unbeaten prep school year. After Eton Anthony earned a young soldiers highest honor, the sword of honor from the Sandhust officer's academy. I was very proud of Anthony Daly after we left school.

At twenty-three my friend's life was on a clear and fruitful path. As a young officer he commanded his small troop of gleaming silver shielded Blues and Royal cavalrymen, leaving their Hyde Park barracks and steered them towards their daily journey on their way to perform daily ceremonial duty at their Queen's Buckingham palace. Every day in the summer thousands of tourists from around the world would marvel at the sight of immaculately turned out horses, shining armor, and colorfully plumed helmets. Shortly Anthony's magnificent troop came into view of another set of eyes, an unseen enemy, deaf to the innocence of our world, with a thumb pressing on a detonator box.

A flash moment later horses and riders lay dead or mortally wounded beside a blown up Austin car that had been sinisterly positioned beside their daily Hyde Park route. Lieutenant Anthony Daly was the young officer of that fated London day and would not survive the IRA attack and nor would three of his colleagues. A bomb on a warm July day in the middle to London's capital, blowing up leaving carnage of horses, and cavalry men. Three hours later, with scared Londoners listening in another sun drenched park to a regiment band playing the sounds of Oliver the Musical another detonation exploded under the band stand. Another seven lives were lost and dozens of wounded.

What was the point? Minefields of mines isolated only in judgment and non forgiveness caught up in separation and a Karmic Placenta of generations before them. Who was hearing what?

Everyday of my life I would remember Anthony as I had received a thick top lip from Tony's left shoe during a passage football game in prep school that left its permanent memorial. I also remember this memorial because the school had me have stitches in my lip at the Swanage hospital without any anesthetic. The bump stayed for ever

More followed to their untimely parting. A friend riding his motor bike leaving a three day equestrian event, run over by his drunken friends in the car behind him. A funeral that we turned up for late for due to the drinking of the night before. Another killed thrown out of his Porsche on a darkened French highway. More with syringes in their arms, misjudging their own desperate drive from caring to apathy as black bags were zipped over their youthful aristocratic bodies.

Finally it was my time. My mind had told me this as I lay in bed. I walked out away from the house, onto my family's private land. No one would hear the shot and very few would care for long after. I could feel the cold nozzle of the barrel on my teeth and pallet of my mouth. The pellets would take my flesh through my brains.

I was so isolated from dad and from God. I judged both had deserted me and that I was not worthy of their mercy as I caused such suffering.

Yet life took another turn.

The moments of possessed disarray passed. Blindness and deafness would flickering be reversed. A faint voice positively introducing grieving compassion brought safety to me. Then my heart connected to my mind and victory of love conquered the remorse. I kneeled down in the undergrowth of my estate and cried out in anguish. I did not believe anyone could hear me.

The barrel was released but the crack of the shot that echoed through the woods shocked only rabbits and pheasants. I breathed in my next fresh breath and my mind was thinking differently. I heard new words.

It would not happen now and it would not happen again. What seemed certain over a few hours that day, became the farthest from my mind for my own life. A life would not be wasted. What could not be heard was heard?

Other hurdles would remain.

I was still to pay my own judgment penalty for venting my cry through acting out and through crimes against my society. My own life was spared but now I was given labels of "black sheep" or "a leopard can never change his spots. Even "Why doesn't he just go work a sheep farm in Queensland?" which was the modern equivalent of "banish him in shackles far away to the New World"

The demons had their man and they turned their back on me, thinking that my rampant self-judgment and confusion would keep me a prisoner from freedom and peace for the remainder of my life, however short that may have been.

What they overlooked were the coins left at the bottom of my well of grief. "Fruits of the Spirit" coins placed in this child of God that would occasionally glitter in the darkness as beacons that could one day guide me back to a peace filled journey.

However at a young age the coins were hard to find, and even tougher to dig out of the mind-field of my youthful mind.

Confusion - MY LIFE

When I am confused, I cannot hear.
Yet it is only later I hear I was confused!

I wish whatever it was that Confucius "Says" was sometimes a little louder or easier to hear.

It's so hard to be clear about confusion as confusion is confusing! Confusion is confusing.

However it is clear that confusion reigned in my life as I grappled with my world as a teenager and entering my adult years. It does for so many teenagers and seems to more in each new generation.

I will always remain sad for those that I lost along the way, seized by their demons, not to wake into the dawn of their own bright futures. I have witnessed confusion coming from a wealthy family than a poor one. This itself could be confusing to read if your family was poor.

Certainly a powerful father can leave a son judging he is not worthy, living in his shadow. For me my filter system of judgment was confusingly present early on in life.

Like my going to the elite all boys school Eton College with the last name Gay and waking up with a fully-grown eighteen year old naked forcing himself on me in my bed. We were so privileged we all had our own private rooms. He had waited till I had gone to sleep to carry out his masculine urge. Then screaming out and, after I was saved through the intervention of the captain of the House, I had to endure dealing with a chain of questions from housemaster, headmaster, doctor, and school peers. This inevitably led to a judgment label "Gay boy", which after a while I needed to change so I had strategically visible relationships with Claire, the choir master's and Lucy, the doctor's daughter!

The name "Gay" certainly had its shaping whilst I was a teen.

Like being a Latin scholar at the top of the school, being taught by the headmaster, and then intimidated by my own smallness into fear rather than passion for the subject, and plummeting through the grades to be near the bottom of two hundred and thirty boys in my first year. Yet a few years later, amidst terrible school reports, I confused my masters by then getting a 1 or A+ in the national exams because I received holiday extra tuition with Brimsley Sheridan, the teacher I felt secure with from my prep school, where I thrived in my learning three years earlier. Was I a scholar just because I could read and translate Virgil's Iliad as if I had written it?

What labels of achievement do we all confusingly live up or down to? Being told, and telling ourselves, we are dumb or smart, is a big one that can stay with us all our lives.

Confusion was that I was not my fantastic yet wealthy and successful dad and daddy was not my God. I became confused and judged disappointment with both. Confusion for me then developed as relationship confusion, with me entering the world after school as a young man. Who was I? What was my class? How was I to live?

As I turned twenty utterly confused, yet liberated from the confines of school, it was time for me not to hear anyone else at all. It became time to rebel from them, from my class, from my mum and dad, from everyone. I spent years rattling around, acting out as a youthful entrepreneur on the streets of London, trying to prove my worth. A series of risky businesses were started up. Venturing with silver helium balloons, historical bricks and kamikaze sushi in the day and veneering my heart with every buffer to feeling at night. Surviving knives and guns and then a crazed machete drugged gang in a Caribbean jungle hut. I lost more friends though and at night I became isolated regardless of who was lying beside me.

Yet hope did endure, as the fog of youthful confusion would always lift itself from time to time to reveal the dawn of the next inspirational thought and hope for myself. And so, after a crash course in "street smarts," my long-term career path came to me as I sat on a far off Jamaican beach. Cray fish were caught in the streams and lobsters by the reef at night, but I was not a native, just a young man lost, a long way from home. One morning it was enough and an idea arrived and stuck in my head. This was welcoming yet confusing, as I had no professional university track planned.

I went back to the UK and extended my love for high profile events and sports with the establishment of a corporate hospitality event. At the time sports venues were antiquated with their service and catering facilities and in fact England as a whole hadn't really caught up in the early eighties with the Americans who understood that service was king. So I cold called companies offering them half price facilities at Wimbledon with Centre court tickets and free champagne - at least that's how I sold it on the phone. Then, with success, I employed my friends from school who didn't know how to work either, and my ex debutant girl friends who were not making enough money as models, and we put up hospitality tents at sports events. The idea of entertaining clients caught on across the marketing desks of London businesses. Suddenly I was being written about in society magazines for my amazing event marketing skills. I produced May Balls at a Mayfair hotel for Thatcher's Conservative government and then the Foreign Secretary's reception parties, and hired the best English chef, Anthony Warrall Thomson, who brilliantly had brought micro portions into vogue at his Beauchamp Place, Menage a Trois restaurant.

With this highly confusing success to me and everyone around me, I needed a mass of tout tickets for Wimbledon, as my clients included Ford and Nabisco, the biggest sponsors in tennis, so I became the friend of the underworld carrying a confusingly large amounts of cash and a very, very large mobile phone. I entered the East and North London scene as an old Etonian Chelsea football supporter (this was not wise and very confusing when in business with Arsenal fans). Even though I was working with Britain's industry leaders, my inner confusion started to recognize its close ally, compromise as my life became gangster like.

Being successful at events led to our own venue. The London Arena was built in the docklands. Pavarotti and Pink Floyd performed and those were magical star-studded nights. Yet we forgot about the need for parking when we opened it, or access to the docklands at a time when the people who had lived in their East London homes for generations were confused as to what we were doing there. The London Times and the critics panned our venue.

Then, one night my partner and Chairman was shot as he got out of his car before a boxing fight. A gunman had been waiting and shot him in the chest. Frank Warren survived and the gunman is still free, and Frank knows who he is. Confusing indeed!

The next day our public share company tanked. My business partners had been having huge disagreements for months and I was on the way out anyway. On that fateful night instead of being at the fight, I was at a meeting near our office discussing how to televise a World Series Polo game. As I walked across the Covent Garden Plaza later I looked up at our office windows and saw torchlights, moving through the building about the same time the shooting occurred. This fact will always remain confusing to me.

A suspect was arrested but there was confusion everywhere and I was very scared for myself. One month later, with no money to my name, I found myself flying on a plane to far off Australia to stay for Christmas with friends. I did not know that I would not return to my homeland for years.

The plane taxied on the Melbourne runway and I arrived on a very hot December day. The heat together with a type of Christmas tree that I had never seen before, and shrimps on a Christmas barbeque made the first few days most confusing. Yet I surged inspiration and a knowing again that this was clearly not meant to be a short visit. I felt alive.

Australia. A country that could have been called "Passion" or "heck Charlie it doesn't matter who you are it's what are you doing." No labels from my new surfing mates, no self labels and absolutely deaf to any Aussie "Pommie" banter which considering they had an all conquering cricket team was not very evident.

Within a few days of arriving I met the top promoter in Australia, Paul Dainty, for lunch in Melbourne and I had created a job for myself, bankrolled to establish a new division to run equestrian events and sponsorships for his concerts. Three months later we were touring the amazing Fleetwood Mac and Phil Collins! The end of Fleetwood Mac tour meant the most alcoholic night of my life until then and a very confusing next day for everyone that could not remember the business deals we had structured.

However Phil Collins and his nightly sound checks throughout multiple dates in the same venues gave me an insight to sheer professionalism.

Sound that is confusing is not a good experience, yet your ear and my ear can hear brilliant music and know it to be so. Two and a half hours of Phil Collins night after night drilled into me a meticulousness regarding the high bar around clarity of sound at a concert venue. There is no confusion when you hear the first bars build around Gods own loudest whisper that penetrates you "In the Air Tonight."

Then in November 1990 CHER arrived and the course of my life altered rapidly again.

We met in Adelaide, where we had her contracted to perform first after the five hundredth ever Formula 1 Grand Prix. It was a crisis show as we staged it in a car park area at the course and by the time she went on, over ninety thousand Aussies were there, many worse for wear from Fosters beer, sponsors of the race. We had to take radical action to get CHER out after the concert and safely to the airport. Things got better and less confusing for her and all of us. For the next months as we zigzagged across the vast country, playing to sell outs, a bond was forged with her and her wonderful touring personnel. It became also clear that if I wanted, she would welcome me into her team where she lived in Los Angeles.

Confusingly I loved Australia and Australia was fabulous to me and yet I could not ignore the energetic pull that had encompassed me in an instant. I packed my suitcase again and traveled on.

I was received for who I was, with all my skills ideally shaped for the inner sanctum of a Hollywood Diva, and her Woman's World. Perhaps like the court of Elizabeth 1, I had been summoned and who could refuse?

I arrived in Los Angeles July 2, 1991, a city full of creation and childhood dreams.

These were again new beginnings regardless of the back pack of my confused pained body as I cycled in and out and around the Cs of my life. Life got faster, confusion became more frequent. Respect, disrespect, trust, mistrust, healthy living on beaches, blackouts in the nightclubs, excess money, not enough millions, idle tongues, gossip, television, record labels, ticket sales, high stress.

I settled in Los Angeles, the ideal canvas from which to comprehend how to live in compromise and limbo.

LIMBO

I want to talk with clarity in this moment,
But if I do I will be only lying to you.
As this moment on a tightrope of confusion
I don't see any safe ground below.
In limbo am I awake or asleep,
In limbo is it real or just a lie?
If I seek to speak or move forward
I don't trust my steps or the words I voice in the present.
I thought I knew how to do it, yet how can, in limbo, I be.
Do I control future steps or manipulate my past voice out of crisis?
Shall I cry in self-pity with shame or brush off decisions apathetic?
I do not know because I am in limbo being in limbo.
Can I hide the knot in my gut for that moment
For perhaps a week, a month, a year or this lifetime?
Yet what occurs as my sense becomes unmanageable?
Will I then spiral again into spinning self-reason?
When all I can see is my lonely reward
And realize the vile road blocks of illusion.
These fleeting moments of lustful disabling
That can leave only residues of regret.
I know how foolish this is in its action,
Yet the inevitable happens none the less.
So now I am in limbo and who will ever know I am to be
The person I know, when my heart whispers softly to me.
I want to be with you in clarity
Where I am connected without being held in place.
When we align and I'm grace filled without need.
But I fear in this moment I need to hold myself upright,
As if I don't I will fall as the fool on my face.
Fall as the fool as I do.
So the question is Do I hold myself up with control and attitude?
And what does it matter if I don't.
What happens if I move just to be in freedom of the fall
And not care anymore about my surroundings?
My dimensions say I can release myself.

And who know what's in store for tomorrow?
Because right now this ignorant fool is in limbo.
And I have no idea who I am to you,
My love, my children, my world.
Until such time my me turns to we,
Until such time my me turns to we
And then I may hear
what was questioning
in limbo.

What are you confused about right now?

_____

_____

_____

_____

_____

_____

_____

_____

_____

Chapter 16.

Compromise

Compromise. The bookends of life that we rattle between.

A question is:

Can we dislodge the one end that we chiseled for ourselves,
and then flow peacefully?

Compromise

A Trading Room - 1996

I wanted the money. I needed the money. I craved the money.

The appetite was that strong, fueled by string of successful ventures following on from my tenure with a superstar Diva. CHER herself knew the value of money when she won best actress at the Oscars and insisted a Bally's Fitness commercial in the same year, both only a few years after playing to a small audience in Vegas, down on her luck, a few years after having the number one television show in the country and I've got you Babe." Can you imagine the stress around a movie actress, up for an Oscar for Moonstruck, choosing to sell the merits of a chain of gyms to Americans. What did those Hollywood suits know with their answers especially since a couple years later CHER's own exercise video, distributed by Fox, was number one for over twenty weeks with over six hundred thousand units pre ordered! What a day it was when, with the heads of FOX watching on, CHER suddenly stopped taping, and turned to them giving them guidance to their marketing campaign. "Macaulay Culkin had his hands on his cheeks to promote Home Alone. Well, I can do this." She whipped around, bent over and clapped her hands on her famous tattooed bottom cheeks. "This is how you market my videos" She knew!

I had moved on from CHER to contract other stars to help design and sell their perfumes, and beauty care. I was desperate for the money and now bankers with the last name of a Godfather were bank-rolling my idea and my "dog and pony" had gone down well with their inner groups.

The sweat room had young broker dealers pitching the sizzle of the business idea and my stellar track record, all centered around Hollywood cosmetics, with a Chinese actress, a Latino TV star and the best pitch woman of US television who had pitched back to back two hundred million dollar programs selling a pillow and an Abflex. A few hours later and the share price of the reverse merger into the public shell opened up.

The boiler room brokers had done their job. My ten million shares spiraled from five cents to over four dollars each and the lead banker turned to me with a smile and said "Congratulations Charlie, today you are worth forty seven million dollars."

An idea in a company that hardly existed with no product made and no hopes of revenues for months.

The share price of Hollywood Cosmetics did not last and the bankers made their money on the trade and were long gone, and my paper value soon evaporated.

A couple of years later better paid brokers on Wall Street somehow came up with their own set of standards, practices and approvals to price AOL based on what AOL assumed the annual income per AOL member would give them. The very highly paid and respected banking firms patted each other on the back.

In 2000, a new company called AOL Time Warner, with Steve Case as chairperson, was created when AOL purchased Time Warner, one of the worlds most solid, predictable and portfolio-rich companies, for one hundred and sixty-four billion dollars. The deal, announced on January 10, 2000, and officially filed on February 11, 2000, employed a merger structure in which each original company merged into a newly created entity. The Federal Trade Commission cleared the deal and so on January 11 the shareholders of AOL owned fifty-five percent of the new company while Time Warner shareholders owned only forty-five percent, thus the smaller AOL bought out the far larger Time Warner.

After the merger, the profitability of the ISP division (America Online) decreased. Meanwhile, the market valuation of similar independent internet companies drastically fell.

Confusion, Conflict and Crisis reigned in brokerage houses around the globe. Everyone's share portfolios went into a black hole. As a result, the value of the America Online division dropped significantly. This forced a goodwill write off, causing AOL Time Warner to report a loss of ninety-nine billion dollars in 2002 — at the time, the largest loss ever reported by a company.

In 2003, the company dropped the "AOL" from its name, and removed Steve Case as executive chairman. Later Time Warner spun off ownership of AOL under the legal name Direct Holdings Americas, Inc. Case resigned from the Time Warner board on October 31, 2005.

The compromise of money and the lessons learned through the clarity of what is real and what is not. But how did I know what was real and how do you know now when we HEAR the answers that are not?

Compromise versus Compromise

When you read the word "compromise" do you sense it as a positive uplifting word with its interpretation for reaching an agreement, like a coalition of political parties or what family outing you are going on? Or do you see it as a negative word with your principles being compromised or finding yourself in a compromising position?

I write here in the world of the latter, knowing something yet acting out differently.

Compromise. A word set in confusion itself.

Compromise and compromise, the bookends of life in - Love and Light at one end - Fear and Darkness at the other - and all your life rattling in the middle.

How can we go from birth to childhood to confusion with such speed and certainty and then live in compromise? We ALL do to some degree.

You know what you are doing or being right now. It might be a business role you have in the office, every day having to be someone you are not, or selling something you don't believe in. You might be a President or Prime Minister and despite all your efforts and powers you just cannot get that Bill passed through the House and you settle for something just a little watered down, and then you smile triumphantly at the media as it passes into law with your legacy on it.

You might be in a relationship that doesn't work, but for the sake of the children, all else can be compromised.

Compromise - We nearly all do it. I don't know whether there is a Being alive that does not live in compromise, but that is for you to sum up between the bookend of your ego and your heart consciousness! Forest Gump in the 1996 Oscar Winning movie was written as a character that knew no compromise. He had no opinion either except when it came to his mother, to Jennie, the love of his life, and to God. Maybe the most impressive of many great lines in the film was said with frustration when we did see Forest get angry and Forest played by Tom Hanks said, "I may be stupid, but I know what love is. It's a box of chocolates"

Stupidly we have all learned - in our real life society - to live with compromise. Because of it we know that the internal gnawing at our soul and mind is bound to voice internal conflict and one day the thorn of compromise will frustratingly explode out and crisis will be there for all to see. Today it is in so many places.

The brilliance is that love always conquers fear, if we choose to let it, and whether we know it now or not, we each do know "What love is." There is nothing that we need to do to know this, nothing. It simply is our Being to know. The question remains when will we know how to be?

Compromise - OUR WORLD

What happened ..... to the rainforest?

What happened ..... to indigenous tribes driven from the rain forests?

What happens to the ecosphere when we buy their lands so we can build theme parks so we can have millions visit them?

What happened to man's respect of young girls, now child prostitutes, seized from the indigenous tribes that were driven from the rainforest?

What happened to so much that was pure and clean; to the fishes; to our oceans; to the ice caps, to fresh water for two-thirds of our population; to chickens and pigs that live in atrocious factory farms in Poland owned by the United States big businesses, and funded by the European Bank, all because of our over consumption and need for meat?

What happened to a child in school knowing what a potato or

broccoli is? What happens to your child in school?

What happened as we eat the foods we are not meant to eat because we have little money for anything else, even though we know we head towards the epidemic "obesity"?

What happens when seven billion of us eat every day, and then poop and have no regard for global sanitation systems? What compromises will be occurring when ten billion people inhabit this planet by 2050?

What happened from the moment we went to university and received credit cards and student loans and learned how to survive on debt throughout our lives?

What happened to color, to creed, to money, to your country?

What is happening to: (fill in your blanks, any blanks)?

What did we let happen?   Have we any idea of what we are letting happen as you read this?

Compromise - MONEY

Compromise is synonymous with the getting of money. Maybe there is no more greater motivator to compromise than money.

Today most of us are witnessing and experiencing the breakdown of centuries old answers around money and banking. The institutions and banking names we trusted are now literally upside down and sinking with more deaths and destruction than the tomb of the Titanic.

Many, many of you, will be saying your most compromising situation in life had money as the central character. What do people need to do to get the money, whatever the motive? Whether purely to support a crippled relative or greedily driven through the love of power and a need to win against a competitor?

We could write multiple books on the stories covering the extent to which business people compromise their own personal principles in order to create the result that will lift them in the eyes of their superior and lead to a promotion or an end of year bonus.

The justification is that, "they" are only doing what anyone else would do in their position, and that if they didn't do it, they would lose out". It's a dog eat dog world mentality that drives compromise.

Why does the lust for money trigger compromise more than anything else? (Except perhaps for sex). Even in your own simple home. One hundred and twenty million mortgages in the USA with "no money down" as the bait to tempt potential homeowners.

The history of money and compromise can be easily observed in the energy that shifts through the pollution of it. What was initially created in the energy of money with sacred energy and connection to the divinity of its sacrament to Mother Earth is not at all how we view it in this era.

Today in the midst of such economic uncertainty we have caused and allowed every possible compromise in how we have engineered the revaluation of money, stretching its worth to suit only our own devices and temptations.

Now money is called "Filthy Money", "Laundered Money." Money is derived from debt and the consequent interest that is charged because of it. Money has become submerged in a mean-spirited, terrifying, paralyzing energy. It carries with it all the fears, anger and greed, and what about those end of year bonuses!

Nick Leeson and the fall of Barings Bank in Asia. How many of his superiors, spurred by the greed of larger bonuses, egged him on? Both Berni Medoff and Enron. Able to accomplish their rise before their collapse because of the systems that banks and accountancy firms put into place and which for years passed the scrutiny for years of security commissions.

Jerome Kerviel, the alleged "rogue trader" blamed by French bank Societe Generale for the loss of nearly five billion Euros (then worth £4.1billion) in losses was accused of forgery, breach of trust and unauthorized computer use and in October 2010 he was sentenced to five years in prison. Monsieur Kerviel, only thirty-three years old, has been under investigation since SocGen unveiled the losses in 2008, which it blamed on unauthorized deals carried out by him. The former trader has always maintained that the bank knew about the risky deals. In his own book, Mr. Kerviel claimed that his superiors turned a blind eye to his trading while he was earning money for the bank, but intervened when he began to lose.

SocGen announced in January 2008 that it had been forced to unwind fifty-billion euros of unauthorized deals it says were made by the young trader. The revelation shook the financial markets, but was soon overtaken by the global subprime mortgage crisis, the collapse of Lehman Brothers and Bernard Madoff's Ponzi scheme. SocGen was fined by the French regulator for weaknesses in its internal controls and has since spent about one hundred and thirty-million euros on tightening its systems. The case has come to epitomize for many in France everything that is seen as wrong with Wall Street capitalism It is a sentiment echoed by Mr. Kerviel in his book, The Spiral: Memoirs of a Trader. He wrote that he was "at the heart of the great banking orgy," and that traders were "only ever given the same consideration as a cheap prostitute: a quick thank you for a good day's takings." Mr. Kerviel made millions from the London Transport bombings manipulating insurance shares.

Today financial tsunamis can hit at any moment. On May 6, 2010 an innocent four billion dollar trade made by a mid size Kansas City brokerage house sparked the biggest single meltdown on the American Stock market in history. In twenty minutes without any warning the market dropped ten percent. Over one trillion dollars was wiped off US equities. The fact that the market recovered through the day, left exhausted traders and regulators saying, "What happened there?"

What is happening here now is that human greed and the love of power is using the highest speed computers coupled with the highest speed broadband to analyze every trade and all market fluctuations as they happen, assessing their effect and then triggering computer trades immediately through "buy" and "sell" orders. The computers are positioned as close to the trading floor as possible to even try to gain even an extra one-thousandth of a second advantage over a competitor.

Gordon Gecko would see Flash Trading as the most advanced change since his Wall Street days. The question though is: is man's greed compromising the safety of the world exchanges and will Flash Trading take us one unexpected May Day to chaos or is it just a great advancement so that the traders can make yet greater financial gain for their clients and themselves? It is a very big question and the computers know their answer.

Also what happens if China pulls in the Unites States debt? How much massive compromise has there been to allow such debt to exist?

Compromise - YOU

Between confusion and the inner conflict exists a place that many of us live and learn to reside in, called compromise. Where are you as YOU move through from confusion to compromise? Do you in fact see it in your own life?

As you reach this page is there anything that leads to a sense compromise inside of you?

That you are living lesser than?

That you are living with limits around your belief?

That you let judgment and fear attack you for too long on your playing field of life?

If you are feeling conflicted around anything, perhaps check now into the bookends of your emotions and feelings.

Where is love now for you and how much do you care? Or where is anger and fear?

Did you do something, even today, that you know just is not what you wanted to do but you did it anyway for all the reasons that you always do it? Are you finding you are competing with the PROMISE of your own life and do your promises to yourself that you will never ever do this again, fail to prevent you from doing it again, and again and again?

The Gulf of Compromise. How polluted are you in the middle of it?

Compromise - MY LIFE

I have compromised repeatedly in my life.

There may be no more compromising a position than when a father separates from the mother of his children, and lives a life apart from the children that taught him about un-conditionality.

My past is chronicled in pages throughout this book. There were compromising positions aplenty. There were compromising actions in school, in business, in money, and often in sex.

There was a large chunk of my early life when I compromised in my relationship with God and Jesus.

I thank Jesus that in his death, he provided an eternal path to forgiveness of my compromise. It was up to me to choose that path.

I thank God that I awoke to understanding how to embrace compromise for what it is as it rattles between the bookends of life. Love and Light on one side and Fear and Darkness on the other. There is only fear when I fear fear itself and today as I have awoken in the middle of my life and I am traveling through the wood, I get to acknowledge compromise whenever it enters my awareness or tugs at my heart.

Unfortunately as I am who I am, I occasionally swagger unconsciously right into compromise. It takes consciousness to this fact for me to extract myself from the vice of the book-end. It takes compassion too, as sometimes it takes conflict or chaos to prod me out of the ignorance that compromise exists.

What is compromise to me right now? Today I am a father and I am not with all my children. I don't see them as they wake. I don't help put them to bed. I am not playing with them. Two of them are far away.

I am daddy to three precious children. My darling Arabella is the eldest born in 2001 and her brother Jamie Stuart both live with their mother in Idaho. Sahana the youngest born in 2008 is with her mum in Los Angeles. I have chosen to live apart from them. It was my choice. In the middle of the road of my life Daniella and I fell in love and together we bring up her two children, Luca who is the same age as Arabella, and Kai.

In theory I have five children therefore, twelve and under, but not in practice.

There is no such huge love than a parent has than for their own children. I love mine so much. My Belle Belle, the belle of my heart. Strong little Jamie (or James as he clearly says) who I am so convinced wakes up thinking why isn't his dad with him to show him how to swing a baseball and help him with his worries. Sahana, who is such a light to her Hungarian mother, Adrienn, a traveler from east to west, brilliant in her own endeavor to be the very best.

Their young faces are all around me as I sleep, beaming out from silver picture frames, and coming in and out of dreams.

They live in different states and I in different countries most of the time. Belle Belle who is a prayer warrior, said to me she knows all is OK. She told me too that she cries at times because I am not there. That was nearly three years ago. I have not heard her voice since, except in my dreams.

I have not been given the opportunity to speak to her now for so much of her developing years because her mum is disappointed with me. Despite Skype and Face Time, I have not been given the opportunity to see or speak to Arabella or Jamie for an age.

I did not know the cause and effect of walking away from their mother in 2007. I do not know how the children will be effected in their own confusion when we do re connect. God knows.

Recently I have been producing quite a few concerts and broadcasts in the USA. and so I have shown up again in the life of Sahana. Christmas Eve around the tree with her, her mother, and Daniella was a joyous moment, where compromise had passed and connectedness was the greatest present. The key shift was I showed up. I took on the responsibility of providing as much as I can for her.

Recently Sahana and her mum stayed with us in the Yucatan and it was lovely to have Sahana connect with Daniella's two boys, who I have brought up for the same length of time as I have been apart from Arabella and Jamie.

I did not ever hear or know of such compromise as being in love with the love of life, and loosing ones own children. Pain hurts.

I have looked for the question that will release me from the bookends that make compromise rattle back and forth. Every day I am able to trust, believe and hope, and of course awareness is nothing without my actioning. Yet I am the father that left.

I sense this self expression helps give me direction. In the past compromise had its way with me, and when it did latch on to my back I was unconscious of it. My ego and self will took me on paths that led to destructive actions. It's good to recognize compromise and since I do know it, I know sooner rather than later when it is showing up and when this happens other Cs can help me out.

Most of my life choices however show me that the standards, I know how to set, are not in compromise.

Being a father is an epic journey and has very different dimensions for me.

Sometimes I look in the Bible at Joseph's journey.

He was the youngest and journeyed far, having been lost to his own father, through being put into a pit by his own brothers. He emerged in a new scene, a city, taken there under the control of others. Joseph was maligned and misunderstood yet he did not hide his light and his natural talent of interpreting dreams shone brightly. His value to others for their own gain was first created. In the end Joseph's authentic expression became the chartered course. Joseph then became the appointed father of Pharaoh, whose nation was kept safe through tough times.

I now sense our Western world's compromise as we see less and less influence of the Father and Mother - as a unit - in families and societies.

With or without children it is important that the Father's influence is not compromised. I don't know what that looks like or how we shift, yet as I write this I sense a Father's importance in the future of our collective intentions and I am fearful as I see such judgment that exists in the world.

A judgment that fuels compromise to such a degree, that the conflict in our families, cities and nations is forcing us to boil over – a fast boil that in its aftermath leaves us burning in crisis and chaos.

Compromise needs a confusing summing up! There are three levels of my mind. Conscious. Sub-Conscious. Un-conscious. Ignorance exists in the divides and gaps between the knowing mind and the un-knowing. I, like you, and the rest of our world, have allowed myself to compromise within what I know and for me there is nothing more expensive than this ignorance signaled by un-consciousness.

However I live lightly with compassion existing as there is much that is sub-conscious, in the realm of what I did not know that I knew. In this space I actually enjoy so much trust, faith, belief and hope. Ultimately I believe that out of chaotic emergence comes forth authentic expression, buried through time in sub-consciousness, yet remaining healthy. I am witness to a re-discovered consciousness that is of service to all. But I still compromise and it hurts when I do.

Chapter 17.

Conflict

*'The only thing worse than the sight of a battle lost
is a battle won.'*
Duke of Wellington,
after commanding the historic defeat of Napoleon
at Waterloo in 1815

Conflict

Every conflict of interest can lead to a heated argument which can lead to a war. A war of words escalates. Opposition between us, our interests, our morals and values, our needs. Family feuds, sibling rivalries, split marriages. All started in the realm of creation, fostered only through passion and love with no inkling of conflict. Then, in the youthfulness of compromising and confusing times, we bring ourselves to unsettled fields of conflict, fields that we often see from a distance, yet are always unpleasant and painful surprises when we end up in their middle.

We started this book with a look at answers and where they came from. Every answer standing amongst zillions of answers that every person has given throughout time. Every answer often competing with another's answer. The Ten Commandments, simple and clear when spoken to a tribe on a journey as the voice of God, today compete with over thirty-three million man-made laws. Will. Ignorance. Deception. Personality. Belief in one faith over another, or one gender over another, one geography over another, or one age over another, or just one answer competing with another's bloody mindlessness - but that would only be judgment, because which one of us knows that our own answer is the one that is not bloody minded? Not me. You?

These answers did create one result. Conflict..... zillions of conflicting conflicts. Most are simple and dealt with clarity and consciously. Yet others are not and lingering conflict often turns into history changing chaos. Boardroom rivals conflict to break up brilliant ideas and divide shareholders. Countries are imploding right now just as tribes have done for centuries. Marriages, that have lost their central passion, conflict and die.

Now we are seeing acute conflict that tries with less and less success not to show itself as a public crisis, as it inexorably travels a path that ultimately rubs against truth and nature to explode, for us all to see. We witness our own eruptions, witnessing oil companies and their care for the environment, the big meat manufactures and their care of the small farmer and the animals themselves; the accolades and money given to the worlds finest celebrities and some of their own struggles with their own honor within their families; Wall Street traders and their care of their clients share prices. All these examples give today's youth a new yet dangerous attitude. Seeking independence and their own identity of not being a child, they isolate, conflicted with parents at an impressionable age.

Confusion and compromise inevitably leads to conflict, except for lawyers. The former Lord Chancellor of Great Britain, Michael Havers, who had raised to prominence defending the Rolling Stones after a drugs bust, and prosecuting the Yorkshire Ripper, Peter Sutcliffe said it well. The great legal mind of his generation, in a great play on words, said that through the conflict of his chosen profession, like every other lawyer, he had been able to first look to get "on", then get "on-er", before finally becoming "on-est". Who doesn't?

Immediate or habitually by building up through the layers of a life - and even perhaps before - we have inherited this place of self-deception from our forefathers. A place of historic conflict where we literally don't know that we know. This is the fundamental problem of conflict, and prevents each participating party seeing through the forest. Self-deception can be defined as "not knowing and resisting or ignoring the possibility - that one has a problem". Most conflicts are inflicted and then perpetuated by self-deception. So are most failures in communication, and most breakdowns in trust and accountability. Clearly, as long as the problem of not knowing one has a problem remains, so will all other problems, and positive flow will not happen. Hearing has become more vital than ever.

Conflict - OUR WORLD

Right now as you read this sentence there are over thirty armed conflicts raging somewhere in our world. Good people are aiming to kill good people. Many of them pray before trying.

One third of our world's population is at war today. This is also the case because we enable it, by spending over one trillion dollars every year on arms and weapons. Money spent on fuelling and compounding conflict. This money is spent on protecting ourselves from ourselves. One trillion dollars a year. A figure that would resolve every conflict we have within our world: every famine, every debt, every shelter, every person not receiving education today.

Those countries, like yours and mine, which are not at war, have massive civil unrest erupting, with marches in the streets, demonstrations being broken up by police, arrests of students, of pensioners, of teenagers, even deaths. There is no longer an identity kit to a militant, who does not wear a swastika or a red armband or a white mask. They are like you and they are in crisis.

We are all in crisis - The lessons of every conflict through time seemingly ignored by today's participants. We have allowed this. You have. I have. We allow our governments and businesses to sell "Killing or plundering each other" to profit greatly from it.

The underlying conflict of all is that, in a shadow of ultimate darkness, the Love of Power, which is only man-made over time, is trying to thwart the Power of Love, a timeless imprint.

However we all have the power to shift from this conflict of all conflicts, avoiding the next crisis and move ourselves immediately to the choices that can shift our world and ourselves.

What is our issue? When are we going to learn? How are we to lift ourselves? It is clear to me at the moment that the issue appears to be that we choose to respond to the issues in ways that do not avert crisis and chaos – we are struggling to die, rather than struggling to give birth. We cry for Syrian children gassed as we once cried for a generation of baby Jewish children.

Conflict - MONEY

How many wars? How many murders in alley-ways? How many arguments around the kitchen table? How many nights lying awake stressed by the red numbers on the balance sheet?

Conflict around money is spurred by fear, created by ourselves in our own lifetime and inherited from the baggage of our parents, forefathers and society's own distorted interpretations. It has taken us centuries to get away from the truth and create our current canvas which is contained by as large a gold crusted frame as we can imagine. We are stuck in the mindset that money is scarce and limited and that there isn't enough to go around. Even when we have it we fear that we won't get more and this drives us to feelings of greed and hoarding.

I have experienced wealthy people as well as many poor people. It is the wealthy that often have more conflict with money due to their fear of losing it and not maintaining their appearances. The poor in the slums circulate their resources happily and are prosperous of heart. They may even utilize the little money they have to give away just as their indigenous forefathers gave to Mother Earth to give thanks for the crops.

The first signs of conflict around money and the separation from its source energy came in the time of Julius Caesar as he campaigned to conquer Europe. Caesar discovered the gold routes of the Celts, a path that led from Ireland across England and the Channel into France and Denmark. The route originally allowed the gold to be carried along from sacred ceremony to sacred ceremony giving praise and thanks as Mother Earth and Heaven co-mingled to produce plenty and abundance. The Romans saw different. They saw not sacred realm but secular value. They conquered Europe and finally England and stole the gold. From that point in history until now conflict rages over money.

In Africa today a diamond mine is discovered on the borders of Zimbabwe and Mozambique and within hours the trained assassins and henchmen of the despot President Mugabe take over the field. Blood diamonds to the north with Sierra Leone, triggered wars spearheaded by children, conflicted and then oblivious to their life task. Conflict diamonds. Do you know the difference when you look at the ring on your own finger? So the core conflict around money is its flow and how confused and conflicted we are as people around it. It changes us. Because at its source money is energy, it must be able to flow freely. Energy cannot be contained for long periods. Hoarding creates a growing wall of anxiety around blocked energy. As we internalize this block, conflict is bound to materialize. It is inevitable.

We decide as a collective whether there is enough or not and we are conflicted often in this assumption both as individuals and as governments. The USA prints up money and the economy improves. At the end of 2010 they stimulated us with another six hundred billion new dollars. Around the world money is being printed and handed out in its billions. This may ultimately be seen to be a biggest gambling game of all time. Is this the answer or a step closer to a question that has not been asked Russia prints up rubles and everything becomes practically worthless.

Let us HEAR our own actions with money and our desire to obtain material things with money. Were you conflicted if you were offered a mortgage in the mail every week or a credit card from dozens of companies and yet you knew that you knew that your credit was poor or your chance of paying off debt was low? If you said, "No" to the above question, know that fifty-million USA mortgages were awash in 2009, when the property value was less than the mortgage owed, and wouldn't we all be conflicted if we believed that the people that control our world are a small group that control the debt of the world, its people and countries?

There has never been such a time as this when the conflict around money has been clearer and because of it we are entering an emergency time of "Inflationary Chaotic Emergence"

Conflict - YOU

"The psychological rule says that when an inner situation is not made conscious, it happens outside as fate. That is to say, when the individual remains undivided and does not become conscious of his inner opposite, the world must perforce act out the conflict and be torn into opposing halves."
- Dr. Carl Gustav Jung

Why do answers that you give one day conflict with who you are the next day? Do you repeat the same mistakes time after time? Do you attract the same qualities in your love life, partner after partner or do you find the same qualities showing up in your business life, regardless of location? It is time to look at what is inside of you and what are the shadowy results caused by your answers that may have been dipped in confusion and compromise.

Your shadow

There is the light and there is darkness and when the light gets lighter the shadow is cast with greater definition. We have known this with great certainty when we sit in a garden on a summer's day, or being in a great sporting stadium as the sun dips behind one of the stands, or as we lie on the beach on a hot cloudless day.

It is the same for you. You have your light and you have your own darkness, or you can give these two traits other words that resonate. Even if you are conflicted with this statement, if you were at confession and compassion for yourself, as you will be in a few pages, you would say yes!

If you were Dante you would say YES. "The dark wood where the true way was wholly lost" was not the "sun drenched wood." The wood of judgment is dark and full of shadows - your own.

"So justice is far from us, and righteousness does not reach us. We look for light, but all is darkness; for brightness, but we walk in deep shadows." - Isaiah 59:9

"Everyone carries a shadow," Carl Jung wrote, "and the less it is embodied in the individual's conscious life, the blacker and denser it is. It may be (in part) one's link to more primitive animal instincts, which are superseded during early childhood by the conscious mind."

According to Jung, your shadow, in being instinctive and irrational, is prone to project, turning any personal inferiority you may have into a perceived moral deficiency in someone else. Jung writes that if these projections are unrecognized "The projection-making factor (the Shadow archetype) then has a free hand and can realize its object - if it has one - or cause some other situation characteristic of its power." These projections insulate and cripple individuals by forming an ever-thicker fog of illusion between the ego and the real world. An example of this behavior might be blaming another for your own self-failure. The mind may avoid the discomfort of consciously admitting personal faults by keeping those feelings unconscious, and redirect their libidinal satisfaction by attaching, or "projecting," those same faults onto another.

It's usually a finger pointing at you that triggers the conflict, unless it is your finger pointing at someone else!

Like pointing a finger out from a hand
It's so simple to blame another
Or blame oneself for not being another.
Do you see how easy it is to give and how hard it is to receive.
Yet in the pointing of the finger is the very signpost to receive.
Please look at your hand when you next point a finger.
When anger or aspiration takes you to give to another.
For in that moment you have three other fingers pointing back.
Personal signposts guiding what feelings lie dormant within.

Jung also believed that, "In spite of its function as a reservoir for human darkness" - or perhaps because of this - the shadow is the seat of creativity. Liberating your full potential often involves identifying and integrating hidden, or shadow aspects of your creativity. Even a person that is aware of a particular creative talent may still suffer from conflicts with others in society. Consider a situation where you enjoy painting, singing or even playing a musical instrument. Even though you may be able to create interesting and beautiful compositions or write a new song, you may not feel that your work is good enough to base a career on. In many cases, this internal conflict will only serve to increase the power of energetic implants, as well as create energetic shells that squander vital energy and resources.

You may find that this conflict will cause you to choose a job that is unpleasant, or even develop a mistrust of others, especially those that see you for who you truly are. As may be expected, the progression of this cycle will only serve to confirm that you need to suppress your most powerful genius impulses.

On the other hand, these drives may be the very ones that you need in order to succeed at a level that will be recognized by others, especially those you hold most dear.

HOPE NOTE

You entered this section knowing
what you could hear
and the conflict you have with others and yourself,
which has led
to your current circumstances.

My hope is that it is not in others
that you will be able to hear.

It is in yourself.

You are doing great.

Hang in there, or in this case Hang in *HEAR*.
Let the journey continue.
You can do it.

Your next "C" will bring you to new horizons.

Conflict - MY LIFE

The sibling of Compromise is Conflict. It's a by-product, an inherited inner feeling that has caused vice in my heart. Where compromise lives, conflict nearly always shows up and knocks at the door. Chaos then rudely and loudly breaks that door down, just when we try to push the compromise and the conflict under the carpet.

I have known what I have known and chosen, on occasion, to act or live differently than perhaps what I knew in my heart was 'right.' When this happens it always results in inner conflict for me, bringing forward regret that I am not able to hear more.

In my youth it resulted in acting out in a fashion that gnawed away at my beautiful soul. It may have been as trivial as cheating on a geography national exam paper - I so disliked geography, and so did my teacher well knew it. Yet for a reason I will never know, my Eton teacher chose to give me forty eight hours before my exam, the exact map of a small area in West England that two days later sat on my table when I went into school hall to complete the A-level. I passed even though I had not bothered to complete the practicum portion of the exam, which accounted for a third of the total marks. I always knew I cheated.

Other times were dire circumstances like escaping from school as far as I could go. Later I learned that it could become easier to let the voices of conflict be buffered. Alcohol became a great buffer to feelings. Yet the greatest liquid spirits consumed with ice can also be setting someone up to be the greatest human spirits of life. Bill W, coming from the tutelage of the Oxford Group, birthed an open, economic-devoid society, which now has had over three million members. Alcoholic Anonymous came from a group that convened to work together guided by the shadow work of Jung and now it has brought millions to recognize the path of spirituality and "God as I understood Him." There were times in London, in Sydney and in New York as conflict turned to acute crisis, that I uttered the only words possible "Oh God, please get me out of this." Why is that, like playing snakes and ladders, that when we have suddenly plummeted into a personal abyss and do not see the bottom, that our final cry is "God get me out of this" or "God please, please help and I promise never to do this again?" The snake often know how to disguise itself and bite again. My youth's shadow showed up as relationship confusion, which I acted out as sexual agenda. I got bitten a lot. There may be nothing right or wrong and yet it is the conflict of my mind's own judgment that can linger, paralyzing me from hearing truth. The shadow enveloping me and then voicing that I have slipped.

My greatest conflict today is trying to convince someone, from my mind rather than connect from my heart and the essence of who I am. Most of the time I live an effective life, connected and in inspirational place of being, without being attached in any form to a result. However there are times recently when I have been on my stage of life, looking for a particular result around a requested need for money. I know I know better yet I do not however hear myself and as a consequence I can be frustrated later when I realize how I was acting. I also get conflicted when I am in the expectation of "what's in it for me" rather than just being unconditional. I have also found it tougher the more I have opened myself up to service human kind. Its a theme that I see also in charity workers as good people helping others so much that they are unable to help themselves, and they have so little themselves in their bank accounts and compete with each other for donor gifts.

There are times when I fear I may never see my darling Arabella and Jamie again. This is the ultimate conflict I breathe as it opens me to the question of "am I really on my "true" path with God's grace?"

I have moved through much in my life and maybe this lingering conflict is the ultimate curriculum learning of my life. No conflict has had me awake at nights yet holding on to past memories now has me gaze up from my pillow. It started as days, then months. Now it over three years. The pictures I have of them are old. They too are putting their heads on their pillows, as they grow through so many of their own experiences without me.

May God's grace be with them today. Who's their daddy?

Chapter 18.

Crisis Chaos

Each of us is here. Yet where is here for each of us,
When each of our realities is different?

Crisis - Chaos

Gulf Coast environment disaster, Banking Systems set to implode, Debt, Riots, Climate Change, Floods yet too little pure Water, Malnutrition yet unrelenting Factory Farming, Viruses. Wars. Trash. Fill in the gap of what is next. Crisis after Crisis.

Despite every attempt not to be here we are indeed here. We have had all the Habitual Emotional Automatic Responses for too long and it has resulted in this. For some of us the chaos and crisis happens only a few times in a lifetime, and we spend the rest of our lives in the tranquility of clarity. Others think they seem to attract crises into lives every day, so they do. A few have made a profession out of crisis and conflict management.

The inner conflicts give way to the inexorable force of an outer crisis. It can be triggered in a second, like the killing of Archduke Ferdinand in Austria that precipitated World War 1. The bombing of Pearl Harbor one sleepy Sunday morning that brought invasion to the door step of the vastly powerful United States of America. Our own views of a country such as Pakistan, that has a small fraction of its people unsettling our world with bombs or sporting impropriety, and then millions are misplaced through floods. We saw countless advertising and media support for Tsunami, Katrina and Haiti and yet the crisis of Pakistan asks a deeper question of our own crisis within the business of charity.

Crisis now may be coming as a land bound storm over a period of years like the current economic turmoil goaded and baited by unregulated unscrupulous actions and no one even knew this until they were in the middle of it.

It may be a war breaking out in a proud African country like Liberia, that never thought it would see wars within its own borders, with the fifteen years of chaos as children fought children and two despots used crisis, whipping up crisis for their gain.

It may be weather cycles and not necessarily from global warming which scientists are now questioning as to its validity. Others point out that our weather pattern may be closer to 1000AD. Our generation just is not used to it and that's the crisis for our modern transport reliance. A crisis of emissions is however clearly man-made, as is our consumption of fossil fuels.

It may be just your child staying out for the first time until after midnight, or losing the keys to your car. Crisis in the home.

It may be no money in your bank account.

Crisis can come in a second and how often can we say we are prepared to experience the chaos that follows? When it comes, Chaos and Crisis are in your face and totally unavoidable. It is the unavoidability of chaos that actually gives hope at the same time, because chaos has to be dealt with. We cannot ignore it. We all see today the chaos in money, in politics and in the environment. Some are seeing chaos in the lack of education or dirty or no water; some are responding to chaos in education, and others in dealing with disease like HIV AIDS and Malaria.

There is a tiny boy who I know called Isaac. He is playing on a dirt patch with some friends today. He has been playing soccer all day. The sun is up and there are bright smiles on all the boys faces as they chase the ball, which skims across the grassless surface, throwing up sand dust all around. There is a throng of other children watching and across the way another game takes place with the most athletically-abled one-legged soccer players trying to score against a one armed goal keeper.

Isaac has suffered a lot in his short life. He has already come through a war relating to black and white, to a war relating to African Africans and West Indian slavery ancestored Africans, a war relating to diamonds, a war relating to the despot ideologies of two dictators, and a war that dims his memory of parents slaughtered by child soldiers the same age as himself.

Isaac is proudly wearing a blue soccer shirt with a number 11 on his back and the words DROGBA. The shirt is an import from Taiwan, with no official connection to the English football league, that was given to him by Isaac's amazing care giver Doris who runs the orphanage. Yet unseen on the touchline there is a menace that is as great as anything or anyone yet experienced by Isaac. A menace whose attention is now watching the brilliance of Isaac as he swivels away in celebration after crashing the ball through the dirty goal posts and past the diving opposing goal keeper.

There is a chaotic situation in Africa right now that arises from the very presence of creation and passion and brilliance. The successes of Didier Drogba, the great former Chelsea striker, (the scorer of the goal that crowned his team European Champions) and others like Michael Essien, have spearheaded a generation of great African footballers gracing the soccer stadiums of our finest European teams. They are paid a fair wage through their contracts, commensurate with league averages. The wages are therefore huge and everyone in the world knows they are. If a penalty awarded to Ghana with the last kick of extra time had not hit the bar in the quarter final of Africa's first hosting of the world's most watched and richest sporting occasion, we would have seen an Africa nation in a World Cup Semi Final, a tournament that grossed $3.1 billion in license sales to FIFA. There is so much money in soccer and everyone one of us knows this.

These brilliant African players are following in the foot steps of pioneer players from the continent like George Weah, the first African player to be voted world soccer player of the year in 1995. We savor the brilliance of a free kick from Drogba to win the FA Cup final, and also to contribute the cluster of goals that helped Chelsea top the league, and for the first time in their history land the Double. I personally have been a Chelsea supporter from birth, having been christened at Chelsea Old Church and spending my first school years playing on the Sloane Street football fields of the Chelsea barracks. I am therefore thrilled today to see their Russian made success.

Yet with all of this creation of African hope and passionate brilliance in the authentic expression of these immense ambassadors for their countries: Ghana, Ivory Coast, Cameroon, Nigeria and South Africa there is now the other side of the coin. A very dark shadow looms. It does not take the guise of child fishing slaves in Ghana, or child soldiers from Liberia and Sierra Leone, or genocidal tribal warfare from Rwanda and the Sudan. It does not take the scant disrespect of womanhood from tribal customs. Nor is it cloaked in the convincing ideology of religion or colonialism. Yet it is rooted in the confusion, compromise and conflict of all of these and the crisis emerges.

It is the darkness and the shadow projected as a direct result of the light and brilliance of Drogba, Essian, Eto and Adebayor and all the other gifted athletes that are playing soccer. In one bona fide continent-wide trial for the Qatar Academy of Soccer in 2010, over two million child footballers turned up in over a dozen nations for just twenty three places. Millions of children coming out of families of eight to ten children carrying the desperation hope of tens of millions.

Unscrupulous men have found an alluring, expectation-filled exploitation no different from any other child slavery before it. The promise of great riches to a mother care giver of eight children in the slums of a capital or rural orphanage is too much to resist. There are no questions as she signs over the life of her precious treasure to be turned into a footballer that could give her wages like the great players that are emblazoned on the backs of every child around every street corner. No advertising is needed just the gentle assurance that the child has promise and that this future is the only one worth working towards.

Now in the back allies of Paris are illegal children sent over with thirty day visas. The heroes and hope of their own homes, rejected by the European teams, just not making the grade and unable to confess to their failure to anyone. They are the soccer beggars. Fortunately for Isaac, the eyes of the touchline menace pass him by, judging Isaac maybe just a little too old or too slow or too small to make the predetermined grade.

So the question remains how can such creation and childhood that manifests the confusion, conflict and crisis emerge with choice and clarity? When is slavery going to have its own chaotic emergence? What guise will it take next? Has anyone any ideas how to question these answers to answer these questions? Yet even in the toughest of tough spots we must. Divine order is to show itself even on the football field and with worldwide slavery. Out of this chaos, because of every one's liberty that has been plucked, we must choose to find ways to bring it to an end. One hundred and twenty million micro social entrepreneurs out of the bottom two billion have already gathered under their own banner of freedom. They are free in their own world. It will happen if we choose not to abdicate the challenge we face for it to happen.

Its so very hard not to be attached to an outcome when in chaos and crisis. However everything is working in divine order. Releasing oneself from the expected outcome you seek may be the very way to moving out of chaos. It is becoming obvious to me that our questions only become pivotally meaningful only after our answers have failed and we have been hurtled into chaos. The problem is we hold on to the old ways with everything we have so we don't face the massive one issue that we never ever want to face. Yet we have so many pointers to say it will be OK if we just have the courage. How many of us would have loved to meet Abraham from the Old Testament and confront him with, "You put your precious son, Isaac, on the altar to sacrifice! How could you?"

Crisis / Chaos - OUR WORLD

Years have gone by since the tragic hurricane Katrina hit and drowned the city of New Orleans, killing over eighteen hundred and causing a massive crisis of, and a global case of grand failure in, governance, leadership, and public management.

Criticism of FIMA and The Red Cross was huge from every direction. I remember Oprah, standing on the first tier of the New Orleans dome, home to tens of thousands of refugees. She pointing her cameras at the devastation and saying, "We cannot ignore this. Our media cameras will leave within a few days to cover the next story, but we must never ignore this. We can never forget this"

How many of us have ignored and have forgotten or just have got caught up in our own problems.

When we saw the Twin Towers fall. We felt inside the massive loss of life crumpling in the mighty wake of debris, we said to ourselves and surely you did too, "We must not ignore this ever" Yet have we chosen to ignore this also?

When the transport bombings happened in central London and the Boston Marathon. When we hear of mass shootings in schools.

When Princess Diana died suddenly and we felt. We did feel. We felt everything inside of us, everything. Our personal well of grief utterly exposed, we could HEAR. Yet how long did it take for the wound to scar over again with the shadows still within?

Now as chaos and crisis emerges all around us, how many of us still choose to ignore, as in a trance, apathetic to the implications. Are you?

Are we approaching the Tipping Point? Indeed is there a Tipping Point that we will be given the grace to see and hear, or are we too deaf and blind?

Is our crisis still not clear to you and our world? It cannot be yet, even if we do know the "What is the Crisis?" and even though we are saying to each other, patting ourselves on our backs as we speak, that "Yes we know we must end world hunger and slavery, and our constant bombardment on the nature of our planet."

The issue, which is the crisis itself, is that we have NO idea HOW we are to accomplish this together. The crisis is not the "What is this Crisis." It is far worse than that because we all know the "What."

The awful crisis is the "How are we going to do it?" Collectively as we look to choose a future worth living, we have no idea how to move out of the chaos of the day. Neither our orgy of energy consumption now compounded by criminal control and price setting for electricity, gas and water, nor our complete ignorance or disregard for the unhealthiness of our nutrition.

Do you believe in climate change and if you do what crisis is necessary to bring this point home? Do we have to witness one hot summer day with waves crashing over the tops of our homes, as our children play for the last time? Is it possible that there may be a day when we will not let ourselves be?

Warnings are disregarded as we are destroying the fabric of society. Religions have so positioned themselves with their own clear answers,, that they leave no room for questions, questions that matter so much more than their own agenda answers?

Surely Hamlets position "To be or not to be, that is the question" has become the most relevant sentence of this, our generation. If you are a believer in Christ's second coming, will this day bring chaos to your world or an invitation for you to have ultimate clarity? Does this day mean judgment and righteousness within the walls of a church, as resides now with religions hunting as prejudiced gangs, or an opening never before witnessed for compassion and forgiveness in the true mirror of His reflection?

There is always rampant judgment at the same time as chaos and crisis. Many paralyze themselves and fear their next step and so do not make a step at all. This crisis may only be averted by your own step, and then the foot print you leave behind.

There is a well-circulated joke, which highlights perhaps some signposts to avert disaster and crisis.

A religious man is on top of a roof during a great flood. A man comes by in a boat and says, "Get in, get in!" The religious man replies, "No I have faith in God, he will grant me a miracle." Later the water is up to his waist and another boat comes by and the guy tells him to get in again. He responds that he has faith in God and God will give him a miracle. With the water at about chest high, another boat comes to rescue him, but he turns down the offer again because "God will grant him a miracle." With the water at chin high, a helicopter throws down a ladder and they tell him to get in, mumbling with the water in his mouth, he again turns down the request for help for the faith of God. He arrives at the gates of heaven with broken faith and says to Peter, I thought God would grand me a miracle and I have been let down." St. Peter chuckles and responds, "I don't know what you're complaining about, we sent you three boats and a helicopter."

What crisis are we still ignoring today? Water, food, God wars, or systems relating to health, energy, social and family values. Yet the crisis that hit inside our own homes through a combination of the state of our environment and our own individual lack of money seems to be awakening us to truth at the eleventh hour. If you conclude still that we are not in crisis, here is another question.

Why would the American Museum of Natural History find it necessary to write, "This mass-extinction is the fastest in Earth's four and a half billion-year-history and, unlike prior extinctions, it's mainly the result of human activity and not of natural phenomena?"

Extinction for those that are now extinct is a crisis that has no way back. It is good to be human..... until we are not.

"To be or not to be." This is the question.

Crisis/Chaos - MONEY

Are you in crisis around your finances today? Is chaos everywhere with credit card companies, car loans, mortgages, and more importantly loved ones haranguing you for answers and berating you for the decisions you have taken?

In hindsight who knew? Who knew that generation-old pension plans, providing security for your older years after decades of weekly toil, would evaporate without a single involvement or wrong doing on your behalf? Or that the shares you had invested in suddenly plummeted and there was nothing your broker could do even though he was the one who convinced you of the "good thing" in the first place?

Who knew, as we have stated through HEAR, that we could not hear the value of money? Who did bait us all into "no money down" mortgages" or investing in shares that had excessive multiples? How many letters did you get enticing you to say yes to a promise from a credit card company to buy you your television or a holiday for you and the family. What chance did you have?

Which regulator did not look at the blue chip accountants firms who were conned themselves into allowing our self-promoted conservative banks to value the same asset or paper as nineteen other banks and then proudly tell the world and media of the profits that the bank had made as they paid out the bonuses?

Governments appoint their regulators to get them out of their mess based on past performance, just like any other basic job appointment would be decided upon. Yet what past performance do we know to hold on to, and what do we need to release from the past way of doing things so that new economic ideas can emerge. This is a crisis in itself.

The USA economy and the money value of its dollar gives the world another pending crisis. It is now reliant on sovereign debt support from China, the Middle East, Russia and South Korea. Everything is bogged down and American people are becoming frightened. If the Cs of circulations and co-operation were more evident rather than the Karmic Placenta that still governs through personal gain and survival of the fittest, the problem would quickly go away.

However companies that don't yet grow anything, or support the land values or take care of basic human needs, now have the cash. Facebook, Google and Cisco have tens of billions each and growing in their cash wealth. The gulf between the have and have not grows as does unrest.

We are today seeing crises like never before. There is a perfect storm still brewing out there and we have not addressed the core symptoms, choosing to throw band aids at the gaping wound.

There was a perfect storm at the time of the fall of the Roman Empire, a time when everything that had been central to the goodness of the first Caesars had become peripheral in the depravity of Nero and Rome at the time of its fall.

We have seen it with our own disregard for the flow of money in its pure energy, allowing fewer and fewer businesses and institutions to control its flow. We are choosing as a world to stay in the poverty and scarcity that grips at us with ever increasing pressure of the vice with debt as our constant go-to solution.

There may not be a better way to break down blocks to being able to hear accurately than an economic crisis. This sentence may sound very insensitive of me if you are in the middle of one of the worst times of your life, yet there is so much to learn from the voice you now hear inside of you.

Rapidly moving forward through the rest of the "Cs" ahead will both surprise bankers and change money forever.

Crisis / Chaos - YOU

You are here for all the reasons you may or may not know. It's a very tough time for you if you are in crisis and we won't look to linger over why. You are in crisis, you are in chaos. It took you a while to get here, maybe a lifetime, or it took just a split second. More than likely if you are able to start HEARing you are starting to be honest with yourself that it has taken a while.

Well, you are here, and I am not looking to put a fixit band-aid on your predicament. It is probable that in the middle of crisis you may not want to or even be able to hear.

However please do the one action I lay out below and then I ask you to be brave and convicted, take your next breath and move on. We will be with you and there is an upswing ahead.

What can you do now?

First, and importantly if this sentence does find you in chaos, I ask you to do one thing.... just one... .find the eye of your storm, where there is no tempest, but eerie silence and breath. I will pray with you now that the waters will quieten and that you are to embark into the tranquil, peace filled waters of the "Cs" to follow.

What to do next?

How many of you have had chaos or crisis in your board room or your own bank account in the last few years? Please learn and take on the deeper implications as you move forward towards your next peace-filled day, which you are certain to have. Believe HEAR's journey that will bring peace, but release yourself from knowing when. If you need to know that you know when the crisis is going to lift itself from around you, you will be anxious and constrained in actually moving freely to the fertile ground that you cannot see yet, which is ahead of you. It is fresh ground that will give you the opportunity to grow and gather your strength again.

Crises are born out of natural and human made disasters, catastrophes, revolutions, and rapidly changing emergencies. We don't want them but they happen. The immediate surprise of the situation, however much it was foreseen, may also lead to surprising results. We all know or have heard stories of amazing heroism that happens in these moments. I have witnessed people that would not be labeled by the institutions or authorities as being able to deal with a situation, actually take on the lead when a disaster hits. They react fastest and effectively with a calm assurance. Something comes over them that gives them such clarity in the moment. Your own surprise management can be the best approach to managing or coping with crises and crisis-driven emergencies in and around you, and often it is the very crisis that propels you forward into authenticity, and you prove to yourself and to everyone else, that the answer really is in you. You just had to be given the question to let yourself out!

If you are in crisis right now my purpose is to help navigate you through the crisis without avoiding anything and then support you to stay out of it in the future as you become aware of what put you in it. This will prepare you better for the next set of circumstance that could be a concoction for a future conflict that can lead to another chaotic experience.

It might be the most painful experience and you may do everything you can to defer or avoid a pending crisis, but once you are in it, never ignore it.

As Executive Director of the Sole of Africa, I had the fortune of connecting with one of our Ambassadors, Oscar Pistorius. Oscar had both his legs amputated before he was one. Yet out of this divinely orchestrated crisis he grew up to run like the wind as the "Blade Runner." He became world famous and we all admired him. His successes and quest to earn the right to run in the regular Olympics became front-page fodder for the international newspapers. He did run in the London Olympics getting to the semi final of the 400 meters, before starring as the poster boy for the Para Olympics, where he won gold for the third Olympics in a row.

Then, after smashing records, winning medals and gaining global fame, he shot dead his model girl friend. Crisis hit Oscar and South Africa in an instant. I cried for him.

The shadow can envelop any ego and mind in a moment, and if abled by drugs and alcohol, any one of us can wake amidst the havoc of self destruction.

Crisis / Chaos - MY LIFE

A Stranger to Self - 1992

The knife's blade pressed into my neck.

It was the middle of a sadistic game in a little seedy apartment in the northern tip of New York's Manhattan. I didn't know where I was. I had gone with a pretty girl I had run into at an after-hours Manhattan West Side club. The alcohol and drugs of the night had taken me away from any self-caring. Starting so innocently backstage with a shot but with hours of helpless consumption, and then cravings. I just craved another snort of cocaine and the girl, in either order.

But now a hundred points of panic hijacked my head as I felt the first cold dirty blade on my skin. I had been in this precarious predicament before on other far away continents around the world, but they had been sudden. Muggings that had had no foreplay in unlit streets or caught up in gangland feuds.

This was different. I saw menace looming. I was surrounded by a group that only an hour before had let me barge into their car, so I could stay close to the girl. She had been at the concert given by my employer, an Oscar, Grammy winning superstar.

Since arriving in July 1991, I had been thrown into the mix of an extra ordinary person. Most our activity was around music as at the end of the day, and over five decades of performing CHER was and is a Rock chick. We booked the tours and then to save money I also tour managed. It was what would happen in the night after the shows that was so unpredictable.

One side of me presented the light, handling the energy and movement that happens around and through a Diva. The other side of me would look to the excess of stimulants to release me from the pressure of the daily chaos around the Diva, and, more importantly, to trumpet my own self-significance. On the road, when she went to bed after a show, this was the window for my self-significance to be aired. It usually entailed the band members ending up at 4.00am in my suite raiding my mini bar. This was one of those nights, except I had got lost from the band.

Now, through the smoke haze of that drug hole, we lay around in semi-unconsciousness, my novelty worn off even to the girl who was out cold. In a moment it was not fun and this was the second time drugs had brought death to my door. The first in Jamaica had me fend off crazed Jamaicans wielding machetes in my home. Now only a few hours after the back stage security of Madison Square Gardens, I was isolated at the dead end of life.

"Two grand might buy you out of here," the dealer said, and then we might go visit your bank wall."

Danger had descended on my life during the previous twenty-five years since my eight year old escape from his school into the wilderness of the Dorset Hills. In those instances of extreme vulnerability, when what was to happen in the next second could no longer be governed by control or thought-out manipulation, a strange sense of stillness and peace descended. It happened again as if I was being pulled by the back of my expensive collar by an unseen yet power filled hand.

I pulled my neck away from the piercing pressure of the blade and in one moment lifted myself on to my unsteady feet and turning to go into the tiny bathroom looked back and said, "I'll give you five hundred after I have used your lavatory."

In an instant, I had closed the bathroom door, forced the tiny dirty window open and perching on the second floor ledge threw myself, corkscrewing to the ground below. Picking up an aching body, with my Armani trousers ripped, I limped into the street. Lights shone in the murk of that earliest urban November dawn. I heard screeching brakes. Then another door opened and I was pushed into the back of a New York yellow cab.

A few hours later in my luxurious mid town hotel suite, 1 lay in a bath, a wet bath cloth covering my nose, with my heart and head thumping, bruised legs, but with a neck that was intact. "Oh God get me out of this. This is the last time. I swear. I'll do anything you want just please let me live."

It wasn't the last time. It was the third last time! Yet this time I scared myself and that would stay with me. The bookend of compromise that was chiseled from a glorious finale of "Turn Back Time" and a packed back stage with children charities taking pictures with CHER and us all being euphoric after a great night had within hours led into the abyss of self loathing and isolation.

Yet the sweet sounds of hearing were flickering through the personal haze, and the glimmer of Amazing Grace still lived inside this lost and wretched soul.

Crisis and Chaos. What to do?

There are pages in this book that may find you confused and uncomfortable. Crisis may occur as you decide HEAR is not for you.

However there are many pages where it is evident that something emerges in the light of HEAR to take you from this chaotic situation.

Thank God for chaotic emergence.

I thank God that instead of the alarm bells that would inevitably go off in chaos situations, I now aim never to avoid a good crisis when it arrives, even though I recognize the pain of its arrival.

I know that a deafening peace fell around me as an eight year old lost in the hills of Dorset; at twenty lost to myself, to my father and so nearly to this world; at thirty-four lost in dark wood of judgment; and at forty-eight as I reached my ultimate questions after the crisis in Mozambique, and then the questions brought forward by the questions.

I believe in these breathes in between time, in a place of "no time" I heard God's whisper. In the following moments I witnessed the fertile ground that became only apparent as my situations changed emerging me out of chaos to a beautiful vista.

This is so very easy to say and yet so hard to experience amidst a swirling storm prior to this time when I struggle to hear and grasp the lifeboat containing trust, hope and belief.

In my youth I was ignorant of this understanding and yet intuitively would function increasingly within this mode at a high level of operation and now I am shaped by chaotic emergence.

I have an innate knowing, which brings joy to me even in the eye of the storm. I have witnessed His amazing grace saving a wretch like me.

I witness chaos today, even when others are unconscious of it.

I know too others witness chaos in me at a time when I am unconscious of it.

You know your chaos point. Do you yet know your choice point?

Do we collectively yet know our choice point? Will our clear awareness be stimulated by our wars over the most basic of commodities – not food but water.

At this ultimate chaotic choice point, will our faith in the ability for the planet to heal itself be finally strong enough to put aside past judgments of each other, releasing ourselves from the struggle to give birth to a peaceful society.

Thank God that I have not had a crisis point yet of faith, and so I say "Thank God for His mercy and grace".

Chapter 19.

Choice

Choice.
To be applied on every page,
any sentence, any word.

If you are reading this with your head on the pillow of your night,
how did you choose your life to be today?

Choice

The Hinge of Life Of all the prosperity or success I may have in my life, five percent will come because of my contacts and ninety five percent from my attitude.

This is where everything rests for absolutely every thing.

Choice.

"Nothing can stop the man with the right mental attitude from achieving his goal; nothing on earth can help the man with the wrong mental attitude". Thomas Jefferson

What is our choice at any of millions of choice points? Choice starts at creation with a brilliant business idea, an inspiration, a hearts flutter, a creative impulse. How we act next governs most of the destiny of the idea and its future success. Some of us act in only one exact same way when confronted with our own million choice points. Is this a choice or a compulsion?

"In the long run, we shape our lives, and we shape ourselves. The process never ends until we die. And the choices we make are ultimately our own responsibility". Eleanor Roosevelt

In Childhood the choice of identity versus inferiority, of industry versus laziness.

"Life is a sum of all your choices".
Albert Camus

In Confusion choices constantly fly in and out of the mind. Am I great and brilliant? Am I worthy? Am I loveable? What do I need to do? Who am I being?

"The time comes in the life of any nation when there remains only two choices - submit or fight. That time has now come to South Africa. We shall not submit and we have no choice but to hit back by all

means in our power in defense of our people, our future, and our freedom".
Nelson Mandela

In Compromise. Shall I stay ignorant to the truth because it serves me to live in compromise? No one knows anyway.

"Some choices we live not only once but a thousand times over, remembering them for the rest of our lives".
Richard Bach

In Conflict. Shall I judge or blame someone or blame myself for not being like another?

I can choose to believe I am a divine being having a human experience or a human being having a series of spiritual experiences. This differing choice of understanding can move heaven from out there to being inside here.
Charlie Stuart Gay

In Crisis? What choices do I have in the second of chaos.

There are always two Choices. Two paths to take.
One is easy and its only reward is that it's easy.

We choose the life that is most useful, and this choice habit will make us most content.

If we are holding on to the past with judgment and prejudice, this restrictively governs our ability to hear what is present - Equally if we fear the future or live in expectation then we are also not free to choose.

The future is not a result of choices among alternative paths offered by the present, but a place that is created–created first in the mind and will, created next in activity and action. The future is not some place we are going to, but one we are creating. The paths are not to be found, but made, and the activity of making them, changes both the maker and the destination.

We all mostly live a "Need" Life. Yet if we hear accurately all the time our life would be directed by the flow of "Choice." Shifting your choice from dwelling in your history and moving towards your destiny is not a matter of chance, it is a matter of choice. It is not a thing to be waited for, it a thing to be achieved. Now. Today

When we are open in this very second to choice, all can be chosen to be good.

"Excellence is not a singular act, but a habit. You are what you repeatedly do."
Shaquille O'Neal

Choice - OUR WORLD

This is a very simple page with only a few words to describe the choice we are confronting.

We are either responsible or a bit-player within the problem that faces our world today.

The Answer is in us. The Question is in us.

We can be ignorant to the issues that our planet cries out every day to tell us. We can say, "God get us out of this" and then repeat our unconscious actions in a few days time and test the universe's response.

We can take no responsibility and say, "Its OK now, and if it's not, then our kids can deal with it. They are brighter than us anyway so I am sure they will find a solution in the future."

We can distance ourselves from God and Jesus, saying they have disappointed us and the Holy Spirit is nowhere to be found.

OR

We choose to recast - from the tragedy and drama into the most inspirational love story with an ending or a new beginning that Hollywood could not dream up.

We choose to believe you can, we can, I can - make a difference. We become a gathering group, a healing community stimulating a peaceful revolution.

We can choose to believe that we are the generation that has been gifted the opportunity of choosing the destiny of our planet.

We can choose faith and we can shine a light on what is good. What is good in all the religions of time? What is good in you and what is good in me? We can shine a light on our connected faith.

Can we help each other hear so collectively we can choose a future worth living?

Choice - MONEY

"If only I had enough money I could choose the life I had always wanted to live"

"I need more money to live how I want to" are statements so many people in the developed world utter or think every week. We can continue to always want or need all our lives and where does that leave us?

There is a choice around money, its energy flow and how we communicated about it and interact with it. We have a choice to change our relationship with money.... if we choose to.

Chaotic Emergence is without doubt bringing us to a heightened awareness regarding the "real" value of money today, what is does and what it is not doing for our well being.

We have a choice still to be baited by the financial houses to continue to think with error that a pound or a dollar can be owned through multiple pieces of paper by twenty banks and then validated by accountants who have lost sight of truth, and also ignored by governments that rely on the money flowing to them.

"I am not going to take this anymore!"
"I am not going to take anymore!"

We have a second choice to be like Peter Finch, the only posthumous best actor at the Oscars (followed recently by a supporting actor for the Dark Knight, Heath Ledger). We can all stick our heads out of the windows and scream, "I am not going to take this anymore"

If debt indeed is the issue that governs and controls us and restricts positive flow, what would happen if we choose to act differently around debt? Could we collectively say, "We are not going to take this anymore." If we chose to confess to our own compromise, conflict and crisis, tomorrow we would have compassion, clarity and conscious connectedness. If everyone whose mortgage is awash right now or who is seized by interest accruing debt was to network and bankrupt themselves en-masse, the world could reawaken through chaotic emergence.

What would happen if we all declared that the way money was valued no longer had a value to us and we all declared bankruptcy at the very same moment all over the world? It happens all the time - to countries and key industries such as cars and planes and banks themselves - and the governments excuse them and do everything they can to ignore their errors and print up more money for them. It may be disturbing to think this as you read it, but what would happen to us if "We, the economy" bailed ourselves out and debt was eradicated over night.

England's great football team, Manchester United, knows the cost of debt, as their books in 2010 showed a record loss of $137 million on a record turnover of $455 million and a record operating profit of $160 million. What that means is that the person or persons unknown who controlled the owners' debt netted $174 million in interest fees in one year. For that to happen many people in the know and in control had to sign copious amounts of paper and contracts and agree to let that happen. The motivating factor, apart from making fortunes far away from any football field, and gauging honest fans of every penny, seems to have been to keep their star striker, Wayne Rooney, happy. They succeeded.

Right now we each possess power to choose how we wish to act around money, to let it flow through and around us. We also have a choice to utter "We the Economy" are not going to take this any more. If we did we would also need a new expanded attitude.

We can also choose to be like Jabez.

The Prayer of Jabez comes from the Bible. In 1 Chronicles 4:10 *"And Jabez called on the God of Israel, saying, Oh that Thou wouldest bless me indeed, and enlarge my coast, and that Thine hand might be with me, and that Thou wouldest keep me from evil, that it may not grieve me! And God granted him that which he requested."*

The prayer is composed of four parts. First, Jabez asks God to bless him. Second, he asks God to enlarge his territory or increase his responsibility. Third, he prays that God will be with him and stay close. Lastly, Jabez asks that God keep him from harm so that he will be free from pain.

We can choose to hear words such as, "So I say to you: Ask and it will be given to you." We can choose to ask, yet we don't because we shrink and become afraid of the response we will get. We're afraid the person we're asking will say no. My friend Marcia Martin explains why such a notion is foolish: "What I point out to people is that it's silly to be afraid that you're not going to get what you want if you ask, because you are already not getting what you want. They always laugh about that because they realize it's so true. Without asking you already have failed, you already have nothing. What are you afraid of? You're afraid of getting what you already have! It's ridiculous! Who cares if you don't get it when you ask for it, because, before you ask for it, you don't have it anyway. So there's really nothing to be afraid of."

What happens around Money and YOU can today flow from Choice. Your choice. There are always two paths to take. One is easy, and its only reward is that it is easy. Ever since the fall of the Roman Empire we have en masse taken this route that leads us to scarcity, shame and guilt. We simply must bring ourselves to choose to return to the divinity and positive flow of money, to release our controls, our own personal attachment and as we do prosperity will flow through us.

"The most vital issue of the age is whether the future progress of humanity is to be governed by the modern economic and materialistic mind of the West or by a nobler pragmatism guided, uplifted and enlightened by spiritual culture and knowledge." - Sri Aurobindo

Choice - YOU

So it's really up to you. Not any one else but you. Your life and how you live it is your choice. What you choose to contribute to the well being of others, close or far, is up to you.

Do you continue to accept what it is you have been taking any longer? Do you take door one, two or three? Do you go left or right; up or down; do you eat meat or not? Do you exercise or not, are you gay or straight? Do you stay at home or in the neighborhood you grew up in or do you pack your bags for promised lands? Do you ask for help or do you keep it all bottled up, forcing your own giant emotional cork in it? Do you see the bottle half full or half empty? Do you drink to dull the pain or drink to pain others? Do you save or do you spend? Do you think yourself too old or too young? Do you shrink so others feel more secure around you or do you propel yourself forward with blind confidence? Do you travel to see the world or do you not let the world see you; do you speak in tongues or do you just have faith or no faith at all? Do you argue or do you meditate your thoughts? Do you serve or are you served? Do you think you go to heaven or do you go to hell and do you think these even exist?

Do you choose through choice or through need?

Do you say, "And" or do you say, "But?" Do you say, "Can" or do you say, "Can't?" Do you speak or do you stay silent?

Dear reader, what do you fear?

Everything you do in life, every choice you make, has a consequence. When you do things without thinking and hearing inside, then you are not making a clear choice. Instead the choice of need is making you.

Choice - MY LIFE

"If I could turn back time" - The encore started up and the cheers of hearing the familiar opening chords of CHER's brilliant hit single got the arena buzzing with thousands dancing to a universal mantra "If I could turn back time."

She had first brought it to the world, through a legendary video made famous by being banned by a fledging television channel, MTV. In 1989 US television executives were confused themselves to the messaging CHER gave to their audiences, as she performed to US sailors on the USS Missouri in a fishnet body stocking under very revealing bathing suite. Since then the song had become the encore for us for two concert tours, the Heart of Stone Tour and the Love Hurts Tour - both aptly named as CHER had, like all of us, her own relationship confusions.

I stood in the wings of the stage, with band, dancers and backing singers hovering around the great Diva, as she took her bows to her adoring crowd. Her soul had already traveled in this current magnificent life, a few decades with number one songs and number one television show in the massive USA market place. A life that then was playing in a rock band called "Black Rose" with a short lived boyfriend to no one listening and a career in a crisis. A life that was then propelled by advice from Francis Ford Copella to go to Broadway for "Five and Dime Jimmy Dean" and then a first film script and Oscar for Best Actress for Moonstruck. CHER's mantra then, and as she continued to progress through to now, has been "Snap out of It" from Moonstruck or "You just have to Start" from best selling exercise videos rather than "If I Could Turn Back Time."

CHER = No Limiting Beliefs

From the stage of another, my life continued, from being in the wings of others to becoming my own. I was to journey on, not held back by time as I finally reached a fork in the road of life, so clearly Dante's words "In the middle of the road of my life I awoke where the true way was wholly lost."

When choice dawned and Door 1 was passed by, "God get me out of this" and "if only I could turn back time, even by a couple of hours or days!"

Door 2 was ignored this time as it no longer served me to live lesser than and be 'Uncomfortably Numb'

I came to Door 3. The door set up with the foundation laid through eternal times for me to enter and live a HEAR and HERE Life.

Fathers Day, 2013

So many babies born, so many fathers, yet where are you?
Father, Father. You are so many night times farthest away.
A Way not for me.   A Way from me, from Meee.

You were there, born new, crying in my arms.
Was I going to hold you? First moments I feared, yet your touch
made us one. Close to me child, my child, you are Meee.

Magnificent I saw my baby grow, celebrating the extraordinary,
Lost in tears with the ordinary. You fell and I ran to pick you up.
I was preoccupied, yet your innocence would bring me back.

Your mother and I moved farther apart, and I released my paddle,
Drifting away from her, I did not even notice your fingers clinging.
Your voice did not know then how to shape "no daddy" No.

I heard nothing as she screamed her anger as I charted my course
Leaving chasms between us. Now I have left. Its over but its not.
Your whispered voice forming how to say "no daddy" no. No.

So many babies born, so many fathers, yet where are you,
where am I?
Father, Child. You are so many night times farthest away.
A Way not for me. A Way from me, from Meee.

Out of the whisper, the words were etching my heart,
imprints on my mind. "No daddy"
Finally crying aloud, because now I know my daddy is not showing
up for me.
Why did you leave me? Why did you leave me as my world falls
down .... "No daddy"

Skeletons. Once the dress up of my parties, now skeletons of trust,
Letting us all down, fragile , crushed , carrying all my pain
Skeletons broken, crumbling, dust scatters in the wind.
Who let me down? ...."No daddy"

Now years pass, who's father's day passes today.
Who is my father? Who am I?
I see paddles floating on ocean of tears,
but no figure comes in a boat to grab it

This father's day ... No ... No daddy ...
Yet like our first touch, our hearts still say "Yes"

You may not be here, my father, and this father's day is hard.
For me, for you.
You may not be with me my child and this father's day is hard,
For me, for you.
My fingers still beat your pulse on my heart. Pulse still sounds.
Yes child . Yes daddy

You are my baby born, so many thoughts know where you are so
am I.
Father, Child . You are so many lights in my dreams.
Near to me. A Way for me, Love for You. I Love you.

HOW IMPORTANT IT IS TO HEAR AND BE RESPONSIBLE TO TAKE ACTION FOR WHAT WE HEAR?
Leonidah, 17, Slum Child

Leonidah is a brilliant girl, prosperous of heart, brought up in Kibera, the largest slum in Sub Sahara Africa with 1.5 million people living in it. Today Leonidah, this "slum child" is a young friend of mine, who mentors others through the "Girl Effect", a global program supporting girls supporting girls. Leonidah is guiding the future of these girls in Kibera and towards the hopes and dreams of their futures. She and her friends are the new wonders of our world. This is what she wrote, in the midst of that giant slum, when I asked her to contribute to HEAR.

Introduction:
As they say words are powerful. They are a great tool to make or destroy a listener. I think we should be responsible to take action for what we hear simply because what we hear can be of great influence towards what we do and to whom we may become. The influence can be both positive and negative. That is why the media today has great impact on the society. For example when

they advertise on the use of tobacco we are always advised and reminded that smoking is harmful to our health. This leaves the ball in our court, whether or not to smoke which will determine how responsible we are towards what we hear and the actions we take.

The Expected:
Many are the times when we are expected to follow what we are told. Just like a sieve does: separates fine grains from the coarse ones, we should be fast and keen to take in what is suitable for us and leave out what is not. They say the tongue is one of the smallest organs in the body, but can be poisonous at the same time.

Many legendary leaders have been able to be of great influence to the society due to what they said in their times of reigns. We live by their words. They've inspired and nurtured many. People like Martin Luther, Mother Teresa.

Conclusion:
Therefore it's up to us to know what is best for us and what isn't. This way it will be easier to follow and act responsibly to whatever we hear despite the fact that whoever says it is a child or an elder person. It's our choice at the end of the day!

HEAR
.... the passing wind!
Ever heard of the passing wind?
I blow far and wide,
to help you unwind,
in clear and confused minds,
... am just but a passing wind!
They all listen to me, young and old,
I am a tale to be told,
a treasure to tightly hold,
rare to find just like gold,
... am just but a passing wind!
I cry out to be heard,
this is no task too hard,
to them that have and never had,

always glad when me you guard,
... am just but a passing wind!
Important it is to hear,
because you have an ear,
to find me I'll be here,
since am your best peer,
... am just but a passing wind!
To them that take heed of my words,
will forever get rewards,
today and the future we go towards,
we shall be holding hands,
... am just but a passing wind!
By Leonidah Mwamto (17) for HEAR

HOPE NOTE

Because you have a choice, hope breathes.
Like a breath, why don't you take a big gulp of air.
Close your eyes and breathe out slowly.
As you do, focus on the choice you now have.

You can always choose differently
To what has been chosen in the past.
Breath now your fresh intake of life's air.
Travel on dearest child. You are loved.

Chapter 20.

Confession

Self forgiveness of a self-judgment is the key to
your freedom.

If you don't judge, then you wont be judged
and all will be.

Confession

Is it time to confess, and when we do what will happen?

How does *"Don't judge lest ye be judged"* speak to you when you only apply the flow of its words and feelings and judgment in a direction towards ..... only yourself?

When you do not look at others in any context whatsoever. You reside solely in yourself and cognitively soulfully, and compassionately you know that you know that, when you have judged in the past, all it has accomplished is to leave remnants of judgment that remain as unseen residue around your own precious heart.

What do you feel now as you look at yourself, without pointing a finger or blaming another or importantly not blaming yourself for not being another?

Throughout this section of Confession I am asking you to do only one thing. Look only at yourself and admit to yourself those things that you have judged yourself as being or doing or acting as.

I want to also suggest to you here that, "Confession" leads you to the doorway of self-forgiveness and that self-forgiveness of the Judgment itself is the actual key to freedom. (I don't say forgiveness of others as in fact that is easy if and when you know that everyone else is doing the best they know how in any given situation. We will look more at this in the next Compassion section.)

Yet how hard is it to confess? This ranks up there with "How hard is it to ask for help?"

We also have to get over the misconception of "evil and wrong-doing" that the current energy has associated with the word confession. In many Christian faiths and practices, confession is similar to a criminal confession – an admission of one's guilt. In Catholic teaching, the Sacrament of Penance is the method used by the Church by which individual men and women may confess sins committed after baptism and have them absolved by a priest. This sacrament is known by many names, including penance, reconciliation and confession.

Often we have seen through history, a religion forgetting or ignoring the good word of "judging" and doing just that by looking to insert its own dogmatic authority. This was done with such force of righteous judgment, forcing confession through witch-hunts (remember Joan of Arc died as a heretical witch). Then there was the Inquisition which introduced and spread terror and torture with intense brutality for hundreds of years, as divine souls denied their captors of earthly satisfaction through non-confession. When Henry VIII decided to deny the Pope and the Vatican and ceded his church away from Rome, Sir Thomas More could not deny his faith even though the English clerical court pressed him to confess his sins and his silence led to his beheading.

How expensive is denial?

Denial is pushing something out of your awareness. My sense is that there is nothing more expensive than ignorance, and if you chose to be in denial or to ignore what you know then it has a way of coming out from the closet, or forcing itself up from inside your well of grief, and finishing up slap bang in front of you.....and until you address it ...and it is not ever pretty.

How Liberating is confessing?

The simple answer is "try it and when you do go as deep into it as possible. Like unraveling an onion, some layers will come off easily, others less so and you may cry!"

There have been millions that have been asked and maybe asked of themselves "Are you an alcoholic?" and nearly everyone through a Habitual Emotional Automatic Response would loudly and defiantly say, "No." Today more than three million A.A. members in one hundred and fifty countries hold meetings in church basements, hospital conference rooms and school gyms, following an informal structure. Members identify themselves as alcoholics and share their stories; there are no rules or entry requirements, and many members use only first names. Bill Wilson, who set out the structure, believed the key to sobriety was a change of heart. The suggested twelve steps include an admission of powerlessness, a moral inventory, a restitution for harm done, a call to service and a surrender to some personal God. In A.A., God, as you understand him/her/it, can be anything from a radiator to a patriarch. Confession is alive in the rooms.

Confession must exist if we are going to shift from being part of the problem to becoming the solution in every circumstance both in our homes, businesses and world.

Confession of simply recognizing what we have judged about ourselves and disconnecting this from anything more than the judgment itself, and not the act that may have left the residue of self shame, guilt or disappointment - will free us.

Right now there are many disappointments that may prevail, especially if we remain in the confusion, compromise and conflict of aspects of our lives. Yet if we do not express these disappointments clearly to ourselves and others we are allowing the energy to remain, festering inside of us, and this is bound sooner or later to come out in actions that are not going to be to our greatest benefit. Confession followed by a huge amount of compassion will release this and give us ultimate freedom.

In the words of Jesus, *"Don't judge lest ye be judged,"* confession is liberating as we sin no more (by not judging) and go from here (this second into the future of our lives). However those who have followed have at times self-servingly and erroneously let religious leaders manipulate His truth for the only convenience of themselves alone and taking what was central with Jesus and making it peripheral and what was peripheral with God and making it central.

Confession leads to a space opening, which allows for us to hear more clearly what is ready to come into own world. It releases the negative self-talk and energy that prevents what is good coming forward.

Confession - OUR WORLD

The issue of our world is now not the issue. It is how I, you and we choose to respond to the issues of the world, which is now the issue. How do we confess to this? Let us look at one issue and how we are dealing with it. Climate Change.

My friend John Symes who wrote "Your Planet Needs You" helped me see five perspectives:

Serious Change

Independent scientific opinion is all but unanimous: climate change is real and we are the major cause. Europe has just gone through several cold winters in a row, the East coast of the USA now has violent and volatile weather extremes, and all over the world, it seems to be getting both wetter and dryer.

All this makes for the cause and effect to be very hard to commentate on, and there is a school of thought that the temperature of the last fifteen years has not risen and in fact this is a natural cycle which last saw in 1000AD.

However all these implications take us way beyond its first confusing media title "Global warming." - Carbon emissions are out of control and we continue to compromise, even though we say we are not. The risks we are taking makes sea levels rise, environmental chaos, unstable weather patterns and disruption to the food chain as inevitable consequences set in.

Past The Tipping Point

When Arctic sea ice fails to re-form in the winter and the frozen tundra of Siberia starts to thaw there is reason to believe the rate of warming will only accelerate. Perhaps we can no longer avoid these changes, merely minimize them through prudent action.

Our Greatest Opportunity

Evolutionary biologist Elisabet Sahtouris wonders whether global warming is nature's lesson for us now, and poses the interesting question whether this can be the crisis that finally drives us to global co-operation and sustainability.

Can we confess, be compassionate over what we have done in the past and then move with clarity and deeper consciousness to a place of co-operation?

Can we?

And Still They Deny It.

The loudest voices still arguing the human cause of climate change are far from independents. Often it is industry lobby groups which fund the activities and research of those who seek to confuse, keep us in compromise and cloud the issue. He who pays the piper calls the tune!

Yet he who pays the piper simply poops every day along with seven billion humans and his poop along with everyone else is causing destructive effect. The tune has to change.

Let's Plan

It's time to turn our attention to the difficult questions: How will we cope with millions of people displaced by sea water in Bangladesh, the Thames Estuary and most of the United Kingdom or Manhattan? How will we protect our agriculture from temperature effects and water shortage? How will we adapt our lifestyles to head off the worst scenarios? How do we clean up our oceans? We have nearly seven billion people to sustain. We will have ten billion to feed, who will also be pooping, by 2050. God took six days to create for us what we needed so we could exist. How long does it take us through our peripheral goals and needs to dismantle all that is central to our existence?

Do we confess or do we deny? Do we live or do we die?

Confession - MONEY

Confession is also so very tough when it comes to the subject of money. For me the notion of the Karmic Placenta makes us stumble as we do what our parents did. This innocent ignorance compounded by the absolute needs that drive our personal lives to provide provisions for our family, or the weekly overhead for our business, prevents most of us from stopping long enough to be at a ready enough place to enter confession when it comes to our own relationship with money.

We mainly decide to linger in ignorant compromise, most often not knowing that lying to ourselves is what is happening, because we don't have a clue what truth or lie is. Yet do we dare now to move forward regardless?

We risk, yet can we trust to risk for long enough?

In 2009, Iceland, the country, went bankrupt. It had taken risks to be something for a few years that for thousands of years before it was not. The "Why" of this has thrown up many questions and finger pointing as monies invested mainly from Europe was lost forever. Many very innocent people were devastated, losing life savings.

At the time of crisis, the banks in Iceland had valuations of ten times GDP of the country. The banks had been allowed by the USA and European financial markets and regulators to build their house on cards. When the crisis hit, because the country was so small and only three hundred and thirty thousand people lived on the northern tip of climatic survival, there was nowhere to ignore the truth.

The central European and USA banking institutions and their governments could excuse and indeed have excused the risk, the ignorance, the incompetence of bankers and their financial instruments. If it had happened to themselves, and it has, they have been quick to produce their own band aids and try to maintain business as usual. It's tough not to as they have the value of your currency and the levels of "Austerity Budgets" to deal with. They have had a hard time looking at themselves as this would mean they would be self regulating and the hardest body to confess to its own shortcomings are the regulators that are seeking confession from others.

Chaos descended into every home in Iceland. Crisis arrived wave after wave, week after week from 2009 to 2010. I was fortunate to support women empowerment circles in Iceland when they woke to the mess of their economy, witnessing the confession of this strong and noble race. Led by their elected Prime Minster, Jóhanna Sigurðardóttir, we have heard them repeatedly recognize the question "How do we trust each other again?"

In 2013 Iceland's issues are long forgotten and bankers around the world now only have greater issues within their own banks. What was peripheral through the issues of small Iceland has now become central in the banking systems of London, New York and Tokyo.

What next can we confess to regarding money? We must take the deepest cut in order to emerge with an authentic expression. It is the only way the space will be gifted to allow positive flow to be unencumbered.

What can you confess to around your own experience with money?

_____

_____

_____

_____

_____

_____

_____

_____

_____

_____

_____

_____

_____

_____

Confession - YOU

Demon or Angel? Worthy or Unworthy? Loveable or Unloved?

Are you an alcoholic or an addict of any description? If you answered clearly "No" and you are not then....

Do you repeat the same mistake over and over? If you answered clearly "No" and you are not then...

Are you in denial of denial itself? If you answered "Maybe" clearly in your own mind and you have, then...

What can you confess to on this page? I confess that I did this to (another)

_____

_____

_____

_____

_____

I confess that in my own life I stop myself from being the best I can be by doing

_____

_____

_____

_____

_____

_____

_____to myself

If you left the two sections above blank, I would encourage you to take a few inner breaths, allow denial to drain itself from your consciousness and then pick up a pencil and write for a few seconds. These confessions now will be precious to you later.

Confession - MY LIFE

I confess to everything ... that I can and I am able to today.

In the middle of the road of my life I awoke.... and ever since the dark wood of judgment has been felled through confession.... importantly not of the incidents of my life ...but of the judgment that I held on to around the incidents within my life.

There were a lot of incidents. There always are in a life well travelled. When the backpack of life had taken me to the precipice of life itself.

Don't judge least I be judged. How hard can that be I say to myself? Its turned out to be really hard.

For years I confessed to nothing. What me? To my parents, "My sister did it, mum. Honestly." To my masters, "Me, no I didn't take the cane from your study, the one you were going to beat me with" or, "No I didn't cheat on my biology exam" or, "Me, why would I have been in the convent school at midnight or in London at a rock concert?" Before I left school I would get caught. We always used to say how unlucky we were that so and so was walking his dog when we were hidden behind the train bridge arches having a cigarette. Masters always seem to have a sixth sense or are just in the wrong place at the wrong time.

But after I left school, free to my own devices my ideology was "I have nothing to confess to. I am always right and if I have made a mistake I don't have time to waste. I have to keep running away."

There were days in my early twenties when the judge in the courtroom or the local police would have a clear opinion and I would confess to my guilty misdemeanors, but their judgment of my youthfulness would allow me to be free to pervert the rules laid out before me.

If I confessed then I would be saying something was fundamentally wrong. I would have to let down my guard. I would have to be open to what others would say or do because of it.

How could I confess that I was driven by things I thought I needed or craved, by relationship confusion, by insecurity? Who Am I?

How could I confess that I had lost my identity? How could I confess that I was trying to harm my own father, through my own isolated action? I thought that he had forsaken me at the hour of my greatest need? How can I confess today to what I know I know I can confess to?

How can a knot, tied so tight through the generations of time, be loosened? Where are the actual physical, mental, emotional threads of this karmic knot that can suddenly be unraveled with the courage of confession? What is the question that can lead to the words of authentic expression?

There was a day when all roads came to the middle of the road of my life and between chaos and clarity lay confession and a central heart of compassion.

There was a day when I caught sight of my self in a dingy Hollywood mirror. My Spirit was about to look down at myself as I plunged into the abyss of a weekend of drugs and disrespect. Yet that night my Spirit, My Jesus, My God entered through me and ever since my eyes have looked outward as one and my heart has been full.

Sleep became Awake. Darkness became Light.

Twenty years later, a generation from that night, I feel pain. The pain of a father. I cry for the children. I confess as a Father that I had no idea what would be in the future, when I saw their little faces peering from the window as I entered the taxi taking me to a Virgin plane for Africa that first time. I had no idea it would come to this.

Yet awake I am, and because I am in the world, children are here. I keep faith, trust and belief that our Father has their paths well written.

The greatest curriculum of life is the simplicity of these words. *"Don't judge lest ye be judged"*

The toughest lesson in life for me has been not to point a finger at myself, less three fingers point back to another, and the easiest judgments for me is "I am upset because two of my children are not with me. They reside in the back pack, and every day I try to unpack them but, until now, I have not."

Yet without this confession, the heart and truth of compassion cannot breath into its wonder.

Chapter 21.

Compassion

Whisper care
and you will hear your heart change your life.
Act care
and you will change your world through service.

Compassion

*'Out beyond the ideas of wrongdoing and rightdoing, there is a field.
I will meet you there.'*
- Jalal ad-Din Rumi - 13th Century Persian

What we have to choose to be the central response with all our actions is .... COMPASSION. This section is vital as without it you cannot journey on to the answers to be found in the questions. I strongly encourage you to reread it and then dwell for sometime in quietness on your own life's journey and discover and then feel compassion within you.

From this section onwards if you carry compassion as being the bed or foundation that you lay anything on, including confusion, compromise, conflict and crisis, then all can emerge for the highest good.

With all that is happening in our world as financial markets collapse, as lifelong politicians try to make sense of stemming the tide of economic collapse, as climates radically alter agricultural patterns, as marine biology is devastated by over polluted waters and oil spills, as unrest descends into the streets, it is time for the greatest flood of compassion to be the medicine for all. Can it be chosen to surround our every act and thought?

If it is we can move through to clarity and a flourishing destiny. Without it we will come to our knees, blow after blow taking the very life out of us. We must shift from the right and wrong of our answers to a field and rather than convince we must choose to connect with deeper and deeper consciousness

The Mayan people have suffered much over centuries and now the lands they still possess in the jungles of the Yucatan in Mexico are being taken from them so that underground water theme parks can be opened after the dynamiting of the Maya legacies still found in their ruins and cenote lagoons and pools.

I visited the jungle a few days after the erroneously portrayed December 21st 2012. The Mayan history had become a popular subject. Their temples and pyramids are as impressive a tourist attraction as The Egyptian pyramids. Their decimation by the Spanish and the Mexicans is written in the history books. In fact many say the Mayan race had disappeared.

The global media and Hollywood films had interpreted ancient a Mayan Prophesy, for-telling that the world would come to an end. This would occur at eleven eleven Greenwich mean time on the morning of the 21st. After over five thousand years their calendar cycle was to end.

As a result events took place in spiritual epicenters around the world. Everyone looked to sky. The media reported in their papers and web sites that nothing happened, that there was no great shaking, or mass exodus of people being taken into giant vortexes of light , or that our volcanoes all suddenly erupted.

Yet something certainly did. Compassion evidenced through a united Holy Spirit was clear to all that assembled or turned their attention to this day.

The elders of the Mayan counsel that sat in my office in Los Angeles on December 18th and then with me in the Mayan Jungle at the turn of 2013 New Year told me, "We have told our peoples to do nothing, help is on its way." Their faith is in Jesus and the Holy Spirit in all of us showing up as a compassionate humanity.

Compassion Central.

Compassion is clearly central to everything we sense as good. It is evident when we are at a heightened awareness for others in our actions and in our hearing. When we choose to reside in it, compassion is central to all peoples in the world in our actions toward each other, and there are no walls of righteousness, colors, genders and creeds.

Compassion is God-ing, (which is God in action in you) beyond the stretching to breaking point chord of expectation. "If I give to you, what are you giving back to me" does not exist in compassion vocabulary. In the morphing of giving and receiving resides a field of Compassion, where all is what is. It is central to the teachings of all religions, regardless of their tracks over the last few thousand years. Jewish faith holds compassion or rachamim (connected to womb) as the corrective course of justice. "That which is hateful to you, do not do unto others," is a Jewish Golden Rule in the Torah's third book, Leviticus that has stood the test of time.

'Compassion is that which makes the heart of the good move at the pain of others. It crushes and destroys the pain of others; thus, it is called compassion. It is called compassion because it shelters and embraces the distressed'
The Buddha in the words of His Holiness the Dalai Lama

In the various Hindu traditions, compassion is called DAYA, and, along with charity and self-control, is one of the three central virtues. The life of Jesus embodies for Christians the very essence of compassion and relational care.   Christ's example challenges Christians to forsake their own desires and to act compassionately towards others, particularly those in need or distress. Jesus assures his listeners in the Sermon on the Mount that, *"Blessed are the merciful, for they shall obtain mercy."* In the Parable of the Good Samaritan he holds up to his followers the ideal of compassionate conduct.

What is central to the centrality of compassion though is *"doing to others what we do unto ourselves'.*

So just as with confession, it is insightful for us to move from the understanding of judgment towards others and bring it upon ourselves, so it would befit us to look at compassion the same way. It is a natural heart feeling for us to be compassionate to another who is suffering, both through sympathy and empathy. Yet the key shift occurs when we shift compassion inward to our own selves. This becomes simple when we learn to become automatic in "Giving" doing the very best they know how in every situation.

We will judge the Nazis, the London transport and 9/11 terrorists and Kenya's shopping mall assassins. Yet If they knew how to do any different they would have certainly acted differently. That's why the ruin of us is not their acts of atrocity, but us holding onto the embers of judgment. It is the judgment that is our mortal wound.

Compassion - The Hope of Our World.

When we can no longer bear the suffering of sentient beings, we unleash our full potential to help others and ourselves. The minefield of our minds, the dark wood we are lost within falls away with this flexibility. The veneer around our hearts evaporates and we sense all that is good. Vitally compassion brings with it conviction and bravery for our own actions, guiding us from the heart rather than from the force of our minds. Critically we are able to HEAR clearly in a state of compassion. We are able to reach within our own well of grief.

The greatest gift of Compassion is that it gives ourselves the opportunity to be ourselves. No greater gift can we give ourselves.

Can you breathe compassion into every part of you?
Breathe in the word "Do Nothing"
Before you Breathe out hold your consciousness for a second in the space we call "No Time"

Then Breathe out "Help is on it's way"

Compassion - OUR WORLD

Knowing that every generation before us has done the best they knew how and if they had known different they would have done so, enables us to hold compassion for what has happened to our world. Yet of all the Cs this is by the far the hardest to hold on to. We all slip and as we do compassion slips from our senses. Later we then even have to be compassionate about the slip up.

What can a fisherman in Mississippi or Louisiana be feeling as he experiences an atrocious man made disaster from the British Petroleum company in the Gulf?

Or as a Jew you visit the concentration camp sites of the genocidal whim of Nazi Germany.

Or you are a mother of a young man plucked from his Israel youth by the bomb of a Palestinian brother. What would you feel if you faced your son's killer? At the same time somewhere else is a Palestine mother, with a son killed by Israeli troops.

Legacies that we must choose to never ignore.

The farthest sense from all of this is likely to be, "Don't Judge lest you be judged" and we are angry and we are upset and we are unforgiving. What did he think when he had spent his twenty seventh year in prison with his crime being the color of his skin? How could he not judge his captors that had with all their strength held on to the superiority of their skin? The Mandela of Compassion. After twenty seven years incarcerated Nelson Mandela formed "forgiveness councils" knowing that without forgiveness and compassion between fellow South Africans, his beloved nation could not prosper toward their future

'Men of peace must not think about retribution or recriminations. Courageous people do not fear forgiving, for the sake of peace.'
-Nelson Mandela

And so it has come to pass for the sake of our planet that we must all choose at this time the path of Compassion. It may be unbearable compassion. A compassion for this amazing planet with all it has given us and still is capable of providing for us for our well being. Until now unconditional in all that it has given up as we ignore the threat of extinction of species, for the using up of all natural resources, for the pollution of our water and of our air, and the conflict we have with each other over such separating matters as the color of our skin.

Unbearable compassion for ourselves as we know that this planet is not looking for us to save it and we propel ourselves forward at this its eleventh hour. Often I hear "What can we do to save this planet?" Yet I believe the planet does not need us to decide whether we can save it, it already knows it can save itself. The planet is looking to see whether we choose to live more freely and consciously and yet if our energy stays in ever increasing conflict and chaos, there may come a crisis day when the planet literally lets out a series of belches and suddenly burps five billion off its surface. Natural order would soon be returned by the remaining one and half billion conscious of mercy, grace and their new responsibility.

Compassion - MONEY

How can we possibly connect money with compassion? Authentic compassion? By achieving this we would feel the free flowing circulation of the energy that was central to its founding existence.

How can we be compassionate about wealth creation when we judge that the desire to get money has caused so many atrocious acts, murders, extortions? How can a rich person be compassionate toward a poor person when they ask for a loan, not just when a beggar who is an alcoholic scowls at you as you walk past? By achieving this we would free ourselves from the deadly vice of "I do not have enough and must hoard what I do have."

How can villagers in Liberia be compassionate to General Benjamin, the genocidal former child soldier, who massacred their kin because he was driven by payment in diamonds?

How can you be compassionate with the banks of our world that today have brought our countries to the brink of collapse? How can you, a single mum, be compassionate about money when it is in short supply and you cannot give to your children what you want?

Of course there is a way. The way we do all rush to connect compassion and money is through our individual and collective giving to non-profits and charities and in churches through the act of tithing. The USA gave three hundred and seven billion dollars in 2008, which made up two point two percent of GDP. Individual giving made up seventy five percent and businesses made up five percent. Religion circulated over one hundred and six billion dollars. In the UK, Comic Relief topped over six hundred million pounds since its first year in 1985.

These actions of giving bring each of us repeatedly to the portal of compassion. When we outpour to aid relief, given cheerfully, compassion flows through us, as in Comic Relief, or a television Telethon for Haiti or Katrina or Tsunami.

Worldwide the amount of money we give would have every person fed, educated and fresh water for all with social enterprise operating effectively to stimulate a thriving planet. Easily. Yet this is not happening and in fact the giving to Africa which has been staggeringly over two and a quarter trillion dollars since 1970 has resulted in many countries now being in worse condition than they were when we started yet. We have given and then given charity, some of which has been a band-aid to stem the flow of the crisis of today. A band-aid is like a compassionate product applied by a mum to a child's grazed knee, and can never be dismissed for the result that it will have today in the feeding of a child or an AIDS treatment or malaria net. What Midge Ure and Bob Geldof have accomplished since they conceived Band Aid in 1984 has been astonishing and outstanding. What happened during July 13, 1985 in Wembley and JFK Stadiums will resound forever in the planet's heart way beyond the last tones of McCartney's "Let it Be." I had dinner with Midge Ure, the day after I gave a speech to a business mentor group he is a member of, and we talked passionately about the issue of charity, how money keeps flowing into charity and the need for more continues and continues. Then we briefly talked about micro enterprise and the one hundred and twenty million women that are growing their money through social enterprise and letting you see your giving then returned by them with gratitude too and maybe even meaningful products for you to consume and benefit from.

Compassion is the act of giving gracefully. We are called to look deeper around how to deal with the issues of our world beyond our thinking that only the giving of money equates to compassionate help.

Compassion - YOU

You are doing the best you know how. If you knew any different you would be doing it.

Can you repeat this statement to yourself a few times and feel compassion well up inside you for yourself? As you shifted from creation to choice and then in the last section before this - confession, you seized the opportunity to look at your own judgments of yourself, you brought yourself to compassion.

What does your heart tell you about yourself?

What are you hearing that you know to be true of yourself beyond the reason of judgment, beyond the rights and wrongs that have labeled your life?

How much charity can you give to yourself today in service of yourself?

You may be feeling uncomfortable as you keep reading how I write about compassion repeatedly over these pages pages. It is critical though that you choose to "get" this and receive it for yourself.

How you can access Compassion

If you are having a problem accessing compassion then please go and undertake some "random acts of kindness" for family members or strangers. This will free up the opportunity for you to access the sense for compassion. By giving to others you will then be able to channel back to giving and receiving compassion for yourself. A flow that will be freeing as you forgive yourself for judging yourself as anything less than the brilliance of who you are.

Compassion does not come from only forgiving others. Its true centrality comes from accurate self-forgiveness of your own judgments of yourself, most of which were not real anyway! Compassion for others, rather than "doing" to impress them and/or expecting something in return, will inevitably result in you bringing yourself to the portal of clarity for yourself.

Surprise Your Self.

How to etch your heart forever

Be the world's most famous black woman with your own media "O" empire, which has put you in front of billions of people every day.

Know that you do not have any children of your own and yet you love them with an innate mother's heart, as your own grandmother loved you with all the care humanly possible. Know that many Caucasians have been giving aid for decades to the roots of your history, the African continent, yet also know what empowered you to rise up from your southern fields to be who you are today. Collaborate with many companies, selecting the toys and gifts that you fit into containers and travel down to South Africa, a new hope of freedom gifted by your beloved Mandela.

Have your production team, led by the intrepid Gilda, follow you into the first humble hut so that you can start giving to the children. In this tiny home you see a caregiver sitting on the ground with eight bright children all with grinning smiles looking up at you.

You love where you are. You know you are home.

Questions start. You say, "Why are they not at school?" She responds its because they do not have school uniforms. You look again at the children, their radiant health and hopefulness floods all around you. Everyone in the team is waking and hearing clearer. You find yourself saying, "So to go to school the children need to wear school uniforms? How much does one cost?" The caregiver with your grannies heart quietly says, "Six dollars."

In that second you hear what you did not know that you knew, and your life changes for yourself. The toys and all the fuss become meaningless.

You commit to empowering young girls in South Africa.

Your heart is etched forever. Nothing will ever be the same.

You open a first college a few years later.

What's next for the lady from humble beginnings as she looks to give a big "O" back to her world?

Compassion - MY LIFE

I slip. God do I fall on my backside sometimes.

I do not practice sometimes what I know to be true. I do not know it is going to happen till it does and it causes consternation to those that it affects and leaves a residue of regret for me. Sometimes it's my gender that looks to have a masculine force that takes me beyond reason to being unreasonable. Sometimes it is my fear of lack for myself that brings forward an agenda. A lack of love or a lack of worth.

I find it easy to give and be compassionate to our world, to homeless, to land mine victims, to refugees, to children with little schooling, to our precious animals. Recently this compassion has turned to home and my own streets and the compassion I have for our own circumstance as I witness the economic and natural crisis joining forces in a cry that is becoming wrenching. Yet sometimes I can be a real male tyrant.

Mother Teresa admitted in an interview with The Times newspaper that she sometimes had more evil thoughts than the worst of tyrants and if she stopped the compassionate work on the streets of India she feared she would see the Hitler inside of her.

Would you put Mother Theresa and Hitler in the same sentence? God's diminutive nun knew this of her Self and she confessed to it.

Journeying across the Cs of my own life there were many stretches of time when compassion was not the rudder to my actions. Because I was ignorant to self-compassion, I spent a span of years buffering myself from feelings I did not want to own. Now, because I am more aware of my own ability to respond, compassion is more evident and yet I still slip. We all do. It is usually such a small thing that rears itself up to show me that the big questions are still there to be looked at. Little things make for big lessons.

A few years ago I was scheduled to be a guest at a teacher training being conducted by StarShine Academy, which teaches teachers around the world to be better at teaching. The venue for this training was near Banbury in the countryside of Oxford at Broughton Castle. I was excited that Daniella and I would be enjoying this day together in a fabulous setting where *Shakespeare in Love* was filmed, and amongst my fellow humanitarians from the USA and the UK.

I was in London the night before as one of our community members, Dr. Derek Chase, was running as a candidate in the General Election in the City of Westminster. Daniella had texted me to say her mum was not doing well after an operation on her foot and that her youngest son Kai was also a little sick.

I was blind to the facts and remained on track to convince her that Kai could be at the child-minder's all day and that if her mum needed us we could turn the car around. I did not tell her that it was an hour and a half drive. I kept at her saying it was her attitude, her not caring. I shifted into victim mode and did everything I could to convince her to go against her intuition and instincts. As she kept saying no, I kept looking for another verbal angle to a point where suddenly I saw I had beaten her down.

The very sad fact was I kept this up as I was disconnected with everything that I hold dear and I caused Daniella grief. She cares so greatly and demonstrates this all the time. She cares for me. She cares for her children and mother. She cares for everyone she encounters. She cares deeply for this beautiful world that she is able to see and hear with such caring attention. I knew we were to be together when she asked me what did I want the most in life and I said to be cared for and to care for someone else at a level that I had never experienced. In that moment in Waterloo Station she had locked her arm in mine. Since then as we forged our journey as partners I knew and have always known the depth of her caring. Therefore to put her in a corner and pummel her with my own agenda only leads her to look at me in disbelief and bewilderment, and know my lack of caring in that moment.

Another sad fact is that when I see her show this face of disbelief it awakens me to my ignorance of myself. This only happens very, very occasionally and nearly all the time we are connected and in harmony. This very fact though makes this relationship, just like yours with your most loving partner, probably the one relationship where compassion must be chosen to be at the forefront of everything.

If we cannot care and be cared for by the single person we share our lives with, what hope is there when the world exposes our wounds and shadows.

On this day within a few minutes with all that I do know I was in a different place. One of compassion for my love and where I knew that a dark shadow of myself had shown itself in the intensity of the light of the situation. Love, teachers, castles, friends, time schedules: all great ingredients to let a shadow appear and it did and there is work to be done as there will be throughout this lifetime.

I went to the castle and surprisingly ran in to old friend, Martin Fiennes, who I had not seen for thirty two years since our school days. He is now the compassionate custodian of a part of England's history, Broughton Castle, and my heart was quickly filled to see how humanity connected the hearts of the organizers, Mhairi and Trish, together with simple people coming together to train to teach our youth together with the Lords of our land.

I went home to the compassionate caring embrace of Daniella and gratefully I was able to relight my light and I moved on to the next day.

The Choice of Confession and Compassion usually gifts us the light of our next dawn and enhances Conscious Collaboration.

Years later Daniella and I had traveled a great distance, across our Cs of life and in our trust and love for each other. Together we facilitated the opening of a new school in the Yucatan, Mexico, which Kai attends. His dad comes to stay with us and Kai spends his holidays being a French Canadian in Montreal.

Compassion. I am clear that we cannot have enough of it. It does not cost anything and if you can bring it to being central to how you are to let yourself be, all will be good in the world.

I would urge you not to question Compassion. I slip and so do you and if you arm yourself with nothing else from HEAR but compassion, your life will change.

If you recognize *'Out beyond the ideas of wrongdoing and rightdoing, there is a field. I will meet you there.'* Your life will change.

If you are able to live *"Don't judge lest ye be judged"* well, if you are able to do that, forget about it

Seriously if you are not judging you have compassionately forgotten about it, what ever "it" was. The past (the fore) would have been gotten and the "it" will not have hold of your present or future. It will be for-gotten. Therefore there will not be "I am upset because" as there will be no "because." Is that clear?

In sports terms a golfer or tennis player cannot linger and worry about the last shot. In tennis when Andy Murray eradicated the "because" on the court and freed his mind, he finally overcame the pressure of British sports history and won Wimbledon.

Chapter 22.

Clarity

Clarity only comes after a correct question

Clarity

An Elucid Tale

We all seek clarity and we are on a journey to discover it.

There is an epic tale told many centuries ago, that has stood the test of time, which may hold relevance to you today. Clarity can also be defined as 'elucidation' which is a term describing an experiential action - "an act of explaining" that serves to clear up and cast light on whatever it is directed towards.

An old, anonymously written, French poem of this name "Elucidation" was written in the late twelfth century.

A historic tale that tells the woes and then the triumph of an epic journey chronicling a question of clarity. The poem references for the first time the story of Percival or Parsifal, the Fisher King and the Holy Grail.

The Grail is thought of in Christian tradition to be the very cup or plate passed by Jesus at the Last Supper and in addition it is believed that it is the container that caught the blood of Christ.

One thread of thought through time is that it contains miraculous healing powers and that it has been kept safe since Joseph d"Arimathie, who Jesus decreed should be its first custodian, sent it on a passage through Europe to Great Britain for a line of guardians to watch over it. King Arthur and his Knights own history around the Grail was introduced in Percival, le Conte du Graal by Chretien de Troyes in 1180-1191.

There of course is much vaguery that lingers around this epic story and the symbolisms that are conjured up. Does the Grail still exist and like so many others, is this definitive historical artifact finally to reveal its Authentic Expression at exactly the time it has always been decided upon by its Source?

History has often repeated itself for all the tragic reasons of time and yet may this great story be the clear rudder to our planet's future. Here are insights:

Lines 200-212
I'll just tell you the essentials—
The men all travel together,
Along with the maidens
Who have returned to that land.
Through forest and countryside
They must to wander thus
Until God allows them to find
The court from which will emanate the joy
That will bring splendor back to this land.
Such adventures will come to those
Who seek the court
As were never before experienced
Or recounted in this land."

Lines 375-400
Finally, there is the last story:
Since I have embarked on this task
I have to tell about it,
And you'll not hear me put it off;
It is the Adventure of the Shield—
And there's never been a better one!
These are seven genuine stories
That all proceed from the Grail.
This adventure brought about
Joy, whereby the population multiplied
After the great destruction.
Through these adventures the court
And the Grail were truly found again,
And through them the kingdom was so replenished
That the streams that had stopped flowing
And the springs that had surged forth
Long ago but were now dried up
All flowed again through the meadows;
The grass was once more green and thick
And the woods leafy and shaded.
On the day the court was found again,

HEAR

Throughout all the land
The forests became so dense and deep
And so beautiful and thickly grown
That everyone who was traveling
Through the land marveled.

Taken from The Elucidation. Translated by William W. Kibler
Copyright © 2007 William W. Kibler
Translated for The Camelot Project by William W. Kibler from the
edition by Albert Wilder Thompson, The Elucidation: A Prologue to
the Conte del Graal. New York:
Publications of the Institute of French Studies, Inc., 1931.

The Elucidation and the clarity of it exposes us something unique
about clarity, its certainty in the moment and frustrating uncertainty as
it weaves into its future. For me "I saw it, I heard it, I felt it, I inspired
it, I am inspired by it", are all clear statements of fact uttered in the
moment. Do they remain clear to those I then retell in the wake of the
God-ing moment in my heart, or through the senses of sight and
hearing or do they too suffer a destiny of not being Heard accurately
as they are re-aired?

The story of Percival first came about with of course the clarity in
the moments and situations as they happened, and then the story was
told and retold. Common history tells us Percival had been brought
up in a forest by his adoring mother, her only treasure left after her
husband and two eldest sons had been killed in battle. She did
everything she could to keep Percival ignorant to the ways of battle
and of being a Knight, so he was raised innocent and even seeming
foolish to those that did meet him in the forest near their cottage.

One day whilst doing his daily chores he encountered three
Knights journeying through the forest, mistaking their shiny armor for
angelic skin. He innately knew that he too wanted to be like them
despite them laughing at his childlike questions and shooing him
away leaving him to run home to his mother. Their impact was clear
and like triggers they had ignited a feeling that was instantly clear to
him. His mother had been dreading this day and she tried everything
to stop him, but he was now such a strong young man and he was

possessed with the idea and so she finally heard inside and conceded to let him go to Kings Arthur's court.

There was a very great actor, Heath Ledger, who died a very untimely death in New York before going on and winning the best supporting Oscar posthumously in 2009 for his portrayal of the Joker in Batman's The Dark Knight. Heath catapulted to stardom playing the lead in the Knight's Tale which was based on Percival's early journey. His innocent portrayal of Percival made him an overnight sensation in Hollywood, yet ultimately he may never have been able to ask this ultimate question of himself.

Percival kept asking basic innocent questions along the way to court, which were taken offence to and as a result he kept getting himself into all sorts of trouble and scrapes. Yet he was naturally talented in swordsmanship and jousting and he soon proved himself, killing one of Arthur's worst enemies before being taken on and mentored by Sir Gornemont who taught him combat and chivalry, as well as how to curb his over enthusiasm. His sheer magnetic innocence and handsomeness won the heart of the fairest girl of the court, Blacheflour and he felt love for the first time. Proven now as a knight he decided to go home and give all his good news to his mother, but along the way an encounter took place that would shape the legendary story for ever.

He came across the mysterious Grail Castle, and arrived into the court of the Grail King, also known as the Fisher King. This noble lord suffered from a wound from a sword battle and lay in his great throne in severe pain. Percival was both bewildered by what he saw and unprepared to speak up and come to the aid of the distressed King. He chose to stay silent and got distracted by a jousting fete, where he could show off and prove his worth to a new audience. While attending the fete at the Grail Castle, Percival was also amazed when everything came to a reverent stop, allowing a procession to pass through the room. A girl carried a cup that glowed with a bewildering light followed by a boy who carried a white lance. From the tip of the lance fell drops of blood, as if the weapon itself were bleeding. Percival was astonished by what he saw. As they left the hall, he had to bite his tongue to stop himself from asking about it. He did this so as not to appear rude, as his mentor had warned him.

What had brought him naturally forward as a young man, the innocent child-like questions and the caring for his mother, had now been confusingly veneered from his mind. If his enthusiasm had not been curbed his questions would have been authentic and simple? What he had also forgotten was to be compassionate and chivalrous and to be attentive and ask the Fisher King "What ails thee oh mighty King?" Instead he was oblivious and he went to sleep. When he woke he saddled his horse and left. As soon as he rode off the Castle disappeared.

He learned from a grotesque woman that by not asking about the well being of the Grail King and Holy Grail, he had failed his more important test. If he had asked the one question of compassion and care for the Fisher King's wound would have been healed and all would be thriving in the land. She also told him that his journey home was for nothing. His mother had died soon after he had left her from a broken heart. Percival's grief could not have been greater. He traveled in search of the Grail Castle in order to help the Fisher King, and encountered adventures that proved his worth as a knight. Word got back to King Arthur about this nameless Red Knight and his many great deeds. However much of the land fell into wilderness.

For seven years he traveled through the lands which were becoming pestilent and diseased. Initially he traveled to look for the Castle and the King and he overcame the challenges of the dangerous road that he journeyed on. Seven years later, spent yet still committed to his constant search he eventually rediscovered the Grail Castle. The once great King was slouched in his chair with thorns and weeds all through the great halls. Just as the King, whose belief had vanished, looked to see out life with no hope, Percival was able to now ask the question that burned in his heart day in day out. "What ails thee oh mighty King?" a simple compassion question. With that, the Fisher King's wound instantly healed. Percival learned that this sovereign was actually his uncle and now Percival was ready to take his place as the next Grail King.

This story may be the very best story that brings us to the question of our own central clarity. It is a story that has profound impact at this time on our planet as we too have traversed out of the "dark forest" and now are becoming clear to the question of all questions.

We might stay in the forest as innocent children for the rest of our lives, our potential wasted. But then, if we are indeed the generation that is choosing the destiny of our planet, we feel the call of intuition, of conviction, of chivalry. We respond and our world is to be content. We leave the tangled forest on our own, and find our way to King Arthur's table, where inspiration and the promise of knighthood or being a grand Dame will be granted.

We go off to learn what it means to be an adult with caring responsibility. We learn from giving, from mentors and teachers that we seek out, or from books or friends or common sense. Once the fire for authenticity is ignited in our hearts, it is not easily quenched. We can never go to sleep. Percival's question healed the wound of the Fisher King. It was bound to and when uttered it completed a cycle of life and all was good and plentiful in the world.

Today the wound represents all the cultural humanity which is within each of us. It wasn't Percival's wound. It belonged to the sovereign of the land, which was referred to as the Wasteland.

The inherent message? When human values are prejudiced, perverted, neglected or wasted, the world is decimated, and by the hands of men and also women. We see this everywhere we look today - from pollution in the sea and in the landfills, to wars raging, to crime on our streets, to poverty and malnutrition, to a breakdown of family culture, and as a consequence of our ignorance, perhaps a hinging cataclysmic climate change that may not be salvageable. Today we create our own hell on earth, and only authentic expression in a state of clarity will bring us to a place of health.

The story of Percival provides an insight that the answer is to be found in us, expressed though chivalry, compassion and opening our minds and our hearts to hearing truth.

Clarity - OUR WORD and Everything Else!

How clear is clear?

Today, "What ails thee oh mighty world" is the only question we should have purpose to ask.

When we ask this caring question, we hear.

Out of chaos comes clarity. Money that isn't money; Icelandic volcanoes, Gulf of Mexico oil spills. Rioting in Greece; Overthrows in Egypt. Demonstrations in Brazil. More overthrows across the Middle East; Wars in Syria; Water wars rather than Oil Wars.

All seemingly chaotic and yet the very gateway to clearer thought. Politicians having to sit down, to connect over what they could agree upon, for change and compromise on their forceful manifestos. In Greece, Spain, Brazil and through the diverse voices across the Middle East crying out in Braveheart freedom, "We the People";

Anonymous no more!

In California, a governor that becomes clear that drilling should not be increased off the Pacific Coast Highway; and a volcano that simply informs us that mother nature just needs to cry out and the skies become clear of jet plumes.

All over the world the transparent messaging of the internet has swiftly fueled this ever increasing beat – "We the People."

"We the People" are not taking it anymore.

Chaotic Emergence brings forth an Authentic Expression that introduces clarity to an ever widening global audience. We connect to it through nature, signed by a planet's chaotic cries. We connect painfully to the clarity of our bank accounts and the value of our assets and money itself. We are connecting as tribes that were caught in the falsehood of black and white judgments compounded by religious divides. We connect to it as men and women in any combination of our love for each other.

Young men and women in the Americas said "No this is not right" when governments across North Africa prevented the voice of its peoples to be heard by closing down the state-owned internet.

These young people across the Atlantic, anonymous in their names, started cutting sim cards and were gifted satellites. Smuggling through Israel and Palestine, this young brigade of hearing questioners found ways for phones and internet to work and media to be circulated and brought out.

History no longer could to be written by those whose love of power, thought that they could once again vanquish.

Anonymous, the organization, was no longer anonymous. Its eighty or so founders shaped for their lives, and oh so young.

In the middle of the road of our lives, we awake, within a world that is truly lost. We say "enough" and we act. The wood becomes a field and we meet each other there, beyond the reason of right doing and wrong doing.

Authentic in our expression. The world is coming into good hands.

Seeking clarity and truth may be as simple as being open to the journey itself. Even Jesus, finding it hard not to doubt in the last seconds, uttered the lamenting question *"Father, Why have you forsaken me?"* which opened us all to the possibility of the ultimate journey.

We are connecting too to the clarity of our charity.

How clear is charity? How clear is service? I often refer to service as to the heart of who we are. Serving ourselves, receiving and then giving of ourselves to others. Children must first go to school to receive before they leave as adults from university to become doctors and lawyers and scientists and inventors. Service is clearly underpinned by receiving, learning, preparing oneself so that one can provide sustained giving of oneself in life and work and contribution. If we do not service ourselves we cannot be reliable in our giving.

The business model of charity is set up the opposite way. A way, I believe at the end of the day, is not solid in its foundation. I am clear about this. If you give as a donor to a charity you feel good and the charity can show you the good works it is doing. All is good. Then the charity asks you again for a donation. It has to. It is obligated to. It has spent your money on its good works and the money has gone and there is no expectation of a revenue stream to bring it back. You give again. They ask again. You give again. Everyone feels good. We all believe charity is good. It has to be. Right?

Then the economy falters. You lose your job, or your pension or much of your assets. The company you work for no longer has net profits for the Board to disperse a percentage to its good causes. The charity suddenly does not get your money anymore. Yet it has its overhead. Its staff have a livelihood. Its recipients still need feeding, the health care programs still need manning, the new schools still need building. The charity must find its money so it looks towards another donor. It competes with another charity, claiming its own efficiency records and clear need and results it can accomplish. It takes a donor from another charity and that charity suffers more.

The system of charity does not work and many fear being out of business today. When surely the dream of all us is that charity needs to look forward to being out of business. When the need no longer exists.

I am clear. I am lucid to this fact in this book. It is my fact and I own it. If you choose you can judge it and you can disagree with it, and the waves of all the Cs can wash over these pages. Charity must choose to ask the question of .....itself ......"What ails thee?" When it does its model will change and it will thrive.

We have seen the emergence, out of the chaos of famine and poverty. We now have one hundred and twenty million micro social entrepreneurs. Each one makes and circulates profit and does not rely on charity.

I love the service action of charity. It is simple and Christ-like. I admire immensely the brilliance of charitable organizations. We each have our own respect for individual favorites. I love de-land-mine organizations. I love the mobile clinics being set up by volunteer doctors taking time out from their life supporting shifts in your own hospitals. I love the dentist who is performing operations in a small tent with thousands lining up in an arid wilderness outpost. I love a charity that grants a dying child one last wish. I love charities that give a home to forgotten old Oscar winners. I love my friend Larry, who conceived how to set up a company to move over one billion dollars worth of surplus from your manufacturers to places of absolute need in the streets of our world.

However the business of charity, I do not love, and most of the people who are brilliant in performing charity also do not love the business of it.

The future of charity is for profit.   How confusing is that until it is clear? If we serve another, they will save themselves and serve another.

I know a man called Louis. He started a recycle business in Toronto in a small apartment and a van. Louis became the best at recycling and The city embraced Turtle Island Recycling, so much so that twenty years later Louis and his friend both received a massive amount of cash from a USA multinational.

Rather than write large checks to charity Louis took what he knew and persuaded the slum women of Jamaica who live on land-fills to start a social enterprise with Louis buying bales of materials suitable for recycling. They have a profitable business and it may be Louis has a profitable venture, doing good. He is serving his world well.

How clear is clear?

Clarity - MONEY

"Money does nothing to prove my Worth.
It is only a clarity around the Worth of Love that then reveals how I am to interact with Money"

Transparency is a massive word. Banks, Accountants, Governments and Non Profits use the word all the time. "We strive for absolute transparency in our books." A statement that we have seen, read or uttered all our business lives. Big words, but is it clear what that means when we remained in the self deception over our understanding of money, the real face value, and the accounting loop holes of "off balance sheet?" or the amount non-profits put into media and the administration of marketing before telling you proudly they are putting 91% into the field?   Big, big words.

We are forced in today's financial world to become clear again about money, the face value of it and the flow of its energy and as we come compassionately to our own place with money, clarity must be supported by the attitude change that we must choose to demonstrate from here on.

A change in attitude

The relationship we have with money starts to become clearer as we start to shift our attitude towards money. It does not happen instantly but over a period. For example winning the lottery does not often change our patterns around money and there are many examples of people coming into large sums of money which finished poorly. To hope for a true change of human life without our rediscovering of the true center of human nature is an irrational and unspiritual proposition. We will remain peripheral humans, being through our random lives, rather than Divine Beings clear in the center of what is true. If we are able to choose to change our attitude and hear what we know to be true then everything about us can be edified.

I used to think I needed money so I could build the stuff around me that would prove to others I was being successful. This was mainly evident in Hollywood Hills homes and got ridiculous when I moved into Casa de Lila, a seven storey house with two elevators on its own hill next to Madonna's old Bugsy Segal's castle - Both had three hundred and sixty degree views, overlooking the famous Hollywood Lake and Universal Studios.

As I was coming into the truth of my life, money was the hardest thing to move into clarity. After breaking away from my father in my early twenties (when I judged most severely his judgment of me when in hindsight he never did judge), everything I had done in life and business was off my own back and as I wondered through the excess of superficial success, money was like water through my hands. At the same time since there were times when I had it and then didn't have it and then had it again, lack or hoarding did not factor into clouding my decisions around it.

It's fortunate to me that I have been stripped at times in my life of money, that I have experienced the consequence of its loss and also the ease by which the flow can be opened up again with a clear accepting attitude. Now we witness the brilliance of its divine flow when we allow the clarity of flow.

In my early years its circulation was like a torrent at times and it circulated fast for not very worthy reasons. Yet this shaping gave me a clarity today when I am called to do holy redeeming work and I see the brilliance of the accountability of micro social entrepreneurs and their pride in circulating small sums amongst their circles and providing returns on investment for all concerned.

The very great Indian communicator, Sri Aurobindo said, *"the money-force has to be restored to the Divine Power and be used for a true and beautiful and harmonious equipment and ordering of a new vital and physical existence, in whatever way the Divine Mother herself decides in her creative vision. But first it must be conquered back for her....."*

An opportunity has fallen to us like no other.

It seems to be so clear that for the first time since before Nero and the Roman Empire we can gain clarity for ourselves around money. We are being given insight to the real value of money. We are revisiting the energy of circulation of its true resource. We hear "fair wage" for "fair trade." We understand the clear brilliance and accountability of circle groups within the swelling ranks of micro social entrepreneurs. It may look like "Austerity" budgets, yet to be clear first we must be prepared to feel. To feel all things both with joy and with pain.

Do we have it within us to recognize the central source that brings forward the pained voice we utter now as we inter act with money?

Clarity - YOU

Do you have it within you? The Cs of your life have now brought you to the lucid still waters of clarity. You navigated the storms, you got lost in the dark forests and woods, you strayed into thickets of gorse and you used all your might to knock down walls that were blocking your wrong direction, or at least what you judged to be wrong!

What?

You are awaking into the clear dawn of who you are. Abrupt as Dante in the middle of the road of life, you are awake. Awake to what is around you, what is inside of you, what is you.

How?

Now it is time to take responsibility for being yourself, ready to manifest beyond confusion and judgment. Your intuition and passion can be an ample concoction of life's abundant fuel, always able to propel you forward. Even beyond this stunning sight of a crystal clear portal. You gracefully and compassionately pass through and your steps are sure in the knowing of your truth and that you can just rest in clarity.

So the clear question for you is as you have travelled the path of the Cs so far, have you heard yourself authentically enough and asked enough questions of yourself, our world, and money, and of HEAR, to know who you truly are, and what your greatest legacy might be and how your next steps will be?

You are to be clear in your goals; in who you have attracted now around you, hearts and minds ready to support you in reaching your quest. You still recognize that tomorrow will bring more opportunity as at your threshold there will arrive unconscious shadowy orphans, long forgotten, with labels around their necks stating 'what you don't know is what you know and now is the time for you to know it.' Dealing with each shadow and each issue gifts you deeper insight.

It is now time for you; for you to become a creator, creating your business idea, your company culture, your own financial freedom, attracting the ideal partner, or simple living a clear and purposeful life.

Another story in the Old Testament gives us insight to how clarity of purpose saw a young boy emerge into the destiny of his life. How many of us would have given nothing for Joseph's chances after his brothers sold him as a slave? How could he come out of the crisis to become the father of all fathers, the father to Pharaoh, guiding a nation through seven years of lack? He did it through the clarity of his voice and vision.

Did your brothers or sisters plot to kill you? Did they throw you into a pit in the wilderness? Did you get sold as a slave? Where you falsely accused of doing something you didn't and then was thrown into prison? If so, so what? Without sounding callous and not empathic with your unfortunate plight, you still have a choice. Your choice, free of judgment to use your irrevocable skill sets in a brilliant way. Who knows you may finish up on a coin as the Father of a nation.

Where?

Wherever you are wishing now to direct your clear focus is wherever you will be traveling towards, and where you will end up will be guided by "this or something better for your highest good." Travel light now, knowing too that the shadows that lurk and pull at you along the path are mere messengers of what opportunities lie ahead on your road less travelled.

When?

Too many words are redundant sometimes. They can confuse the clarity of what you are trying to put across. A woman, Cindy Cashman wrote a book "Everything Men know about Women." It was very clear and sold over five million copies. It was so clear to the reader because it had zero words on every page. It just doesn't get clearer than that for those five million that found it accurate or humorous enough. Let us therefore be clear about "When" for you.

Who?

If not you, then who? If not now, when? I hope this is simple and clear.

How clear is clear?

Travel light "you the people" traveller.

Clarity - MY LIFE

I am clear when I go to bed and when I get up and I require no meditation or prayer work to know this fact alone. I have returned to the innocence of my child, shaped by all my actions of yesterdays for this second, for this day.

I learn from my adventures, and I encounter love and the pure light identified by the Grail. I learn how to hear inside and ask the questions of myself and others so that I can better serve them. By acting to serve, our world will automatically thrive.

Clarity for me did not descend in a second in 1994, when I went through my own personal epiphany. No, there were many times when my own heroic ego would jump in front of my caring heart. Thankfully, although usually at the time with great cursing, my shadow would make itself clear and in this I am truly grateful. I constantly have the chance to buffer my own mirror with my own questions of my self and travel on a little less afflicted.

I am called today to confront what can only be called Mystery, represented by the Holy Grail, and The Fisher King and encountered by Percival and all since who have quested love. Discovering it is not enough. Awareness is nothing without action and there is nothing more expensive than ignorance, which I define as truly knowing and yet being oblivious or distracted and therefore ignoring and being unable to hear the ultimate question.

I have to ask about it. I have to. I have to make inquiries. This is the only way to properly respond to Mystery, God's wisdom, ordained before the world unto our Glory. I relate to the inevitable not by claiming it, or controlling it, or describing it with guesses. I relate by approaching it, fearlessly, with an open mind and a desire to learn. I invite its question mark into my life, and insert it into all my conclusions. Just by recognizing its existence, I better fulfill who I am in this world that is only just able to explain itself.

I am hearing what I know I know,
Becoming aware of what I don't know I know.
And as I reclaim the innocence of my child
I know what willful cost is man's Ignorance of Belief.
I see now there is nothing more expensive than Ignorance.

Awakening, and clearer at times, I am navigating from the depths of the wood, swishing my soft machete of compassion, and felling obstacles on the path ahead. In this singular movement I feel clearer and sense more light around me.

You help me. I cannot do it without your support. I look into your eyes, sense your spirit and buff your mirror. This results in a clarity that budges shadows unseen before this moment. Then I see you wake to your own moment of clarity and I see more of my own spirit in your reflection and this is clear enough for me to be clearer and this stays with me as I travel on a little lighter.

The walls keep coming down and I see the face of God appearing in least expected places. Yes, I thought I was called to safeguard the helpless yet, as clarity dawned, I realized it was they who were doing no wrong, that they were the finest global citizens and that they were brave and noble and honest. It is here in the slums of the world that I witness the Kingdom of Heaven. Not some far off place in the afterlife but here clearly in this life. I am clear too that I am a child of God and have been since birth and the beginning of time. I am clear that each bludgeoning religion has separated us from what it believes to be 'somewhere out there', beyond our reach. "Are you saved?" has become a self serving question, causing judgment of fear, expectation and separation. For me there is never any question of separation if I choose in my loving heart for there not to be, just a re-discovery of what I didn't know I knew and a release through not judging myself lest I be judged. Compassion demonstrated is compassion enough and I am clear about my direct connectedness through the Trinity of God, Jesus and Holiness within. Fellowship with you in life, in the love of the Holy Spirit that resides so clearly in each of us, is so clearly good.

I am clear that I am a Christian being Christian when I am in service equally to myself and others,

God and Jesus did not say that They "were" or "will be" the way. They both said, "I Am." For me, without the need of religious rhetoric, I sense profoundly this simple direction given that allows holiness to glow within me. It doesn't get more simple than "Don't judge lest ye be judged."

Judging is holding on to the past or fearing the future. If I am in state of either then I am not in the "I am" and I have learned I am not being of service to myself and certainly not to others.

I have witnessed so much judgment on the walk across religious lines. What message is clear? Even when clarity is given from the most authentic of source expressions, it can so quickly become clouded by those that hear it however hard they try.

This is a judgment that I work on every day as I own it as my own. There are many that I sense who are being Christians who other self-labeled Christians judge as not one of them. Over the last few years I have spent time with two people named Michael. Both have tens of thousands be led by their messages of faith. The first Michael I know, Mike Bickle, leads the International House of Prayer, headquartered in Kansas City. He has been featured every week around the world on God TV, as he leads fasting, prayer and turning his audience to the face of God and Jesus as he knows them. His followers are evangelistic and judged by others to be rightwing intolerants.

The other Michael, Michael Beckwith, leads the largest growing inter-faith community in the USA and around the world. However the followers of America's traditional evangelical doctrine are very wary of what they believe to be Beckwith's "false" teachings.

Google searches also reference both as "cults" and "false profits," which is not unusual as many who gather people are labeled this way by others who do not like them.

I have witnessed both Michaels give much.

Bickle gives himself to what he believes is the call of God within him, giving direction for prayer and fasting and how we should know Jesus.

Beckwith gives without boundaries and I have seen him give considerably. I asked him to. He gave considerable support to Fuller Theological Seminary graduates who are Kenyan Bishops and who preach in the same Pentecostal tongue as Bickle. Beckwith gave his love and support and community money as they collected orphans whose parents have both died of AIDS in the slums of Kenya, and he did not give once but again and again, stating simply to me that they do "Gods Work." Yet his fiercest critics come from within the very religion that he gives to. I can apply this to all religious faiths.

We blow each other up over our opposition to either inter-faith or our focus to a single faith, driven by our personal fears and prejudices. We have not been able to help ourselves.

How sad it is that judgment of separation prevents the sweetness of convergence in the brilliance-wake of our fellow ships. How divine for you is the Koran, is the Guru Gita or the Bible? I walk as a Christian yet I have witnessed Godliness in Guru Mayi who has millions of Hindu followers. I have witnessed Holy compassion in Buddhist chanters, and in a profound Spirit swirling through Michael Beckwith's Agape worship. I felt it in Mike Bickel's praying, and I saw it in the soul of Dr. Billy Graham who may have reached more people in the name of Jesus than anyone since Apostle Paul.

Now in the Mayan jungle, I am witnessing Christ's Holy Spirit in the lives of the Maya people and their elders, without religious opinion.

What I hear in them, I witness in you or in myself. Yes Godliness shows up in you. You just have to be clear how transparent you want it to be through you.

What I hear through the work of striking humanitarians like Sophia Swire who operates Future Brilliance and in the past has funded over two hundred and fifty school builds through the success of her pashmina trade, is the Holy Spirit at work beyond religious opinion.

Good works beyond religious walls – how clear that is!

How clear then is clear?

When I look into the mirror I see how clear I am as I hear my heart voice to me.

I am conscious that tomorrow it may be different and the fuse box may be blown, the curtains drawn and I will be in judgment, and I will not be clear when I am in that place. Yet I am convinced that courage is bound to reopen all that is meant to be Holy in my next dawning or maybe the dawn after that!

I travel on, in faith, seeking my every next step to be towards Mystery.

How clear is Mystery? It is when you have belief, hope and trust in the clarity of its Spirit.

How I love Mystery! So lets take a break and connect faithfully with Mystery.

Book Break

BOOK BREAK TO HEAR YOURSELF
What are you hearing?

Be Clear and Conscious that you are here.
If you are rushing and need to do something
stop now and pick up HEAR later.

There are three sections ahead to help you keep clarity as much as
you can.

consciousness, connected collaboration, and circulation.

Book Break

If you need help or want to say anything
you can by blogging me
at http://charliestuartgay.com

Faith
I want to write about faith,
about the way the moon rises
over cold snow, night after night,
faithful even as it fades from fullness,
slowly becoming that last curving and impossible
sliver of light before the final darkness.
But I have no faith myself
I refuse it even the smallest entry.
Let this then, my small poem,
like a new moon, slender and barely open,
be the first prayer that opens me to faith.
David Whyte © 2007 Many Rivers

Chapter 23.

Consciousness

Let Go and Let God

Consciousness

Through Prayer and Meditation - 2004

I had been up close to an eagle in the wild once. I was one month short of my sixth birthday.

I was where I was meant to be. On the balcony of our Penthouse in Cumberland Terrace, overlooking central London's Regents Park. Goldie the Eagle however was clearly not. He had found a perch on one of our Greek statues, having escaped from London's Zoo and was in the middle of an adventure, eluding handlers and the nation's media for twelve days.

The blocking out of light, a tumultuous rush of wind from the powerful wings and the connectedness of that piercing gaze would remain with me. I have closed my eyes many times and seen Goldie. Or what my age old clarity imagines as Goldie. I have meditated and I have dreamt. I have soared alone and I have soared at times beside Goldie. There have been a few times that I have soared as Goldie the Eagle.

Now forty years later I had a sense I was seeing it again.

The gaze came from craggy features below long white hair. The body was still massive in frame, yet now stooped forward in its neck and shoulders. A huge dark raincoat protected the elements as for days I would watch him and see this combination of dark body and white plumes!

I watched as tens of thousands descended from their seats and made their way onto the field of America's largest stadium, The Rose Bowl, to be witness to his last entrance. As he had left his Anti-room in the tunnel backstage I had been the last to meet with him. He extended his powerful eighty six-year old hand and thanked me for all that I had done as Arrangements Chairman for his final historic gathering.

It had started over fifty years before for Reverend Dr. Billy Graham. He was not meant to be the lead speaker at a spiritual evangelical gathering, but his planning partner chose to back out, and left Billy to go ahead and gather California south-land followers in a tent on the corner of Washington and Hill. The media baron William Randolph Hearst heard about what was taking place and he instructed all his editors to feature the goings on and put the buzz out on this young preacher. The tent filled every night with seething spirit for more than three weeks and a living legend of our world was created out of this simple man who epitomized faith, belief and hope.

Across town at the other stadium in Los Angeles that I have produced events at, the Olympic USC Coliseum, there is a plaque memorializing 860,000 attendees over one of his Crusades in the 80's. Eight hundred and sixty thousand people turned up to listen to one simple man's message of conviction and compassion.

Helping manage over three hundred and twenty-thousand people at these final historic Los Angeles evenings over four nights and mobilizing nearly twenty-thousand volunteers, I was not in a personal place to really be able to receive kind words at that moment from the great Reverend. In fact when Dr. Graham requested to see me, I was not in the stadium grounds at all, as a call had come in on the walkie talkies that the equally legendary 1950s artist Pat Boone, (who dressed in white to Elvis's black) was stuck with his family on the 210 freeway a mile up the hill. Pat was a long time family friend of the Grahams and was meant to be on the stage when Dr. Graham was to make his final entrance but the Pasadena police couldn't figure a way to navigate his car down to the Bowl Entrance.

One of the perks of being a concert or large event promoter is you get to drive in super sooped-up buggies during the load in, which you need, as a stadium or a park venue can't be walked for a week with all the run around that one does. In Los Angeles I had secured from my production manager the top of the range, all weather, huge tire buggy. I quickly acted and with a police outrider, I sped around the traffic and on the pavement, picked up the legendary entertainer and whisked him back and onto the stage.

On my journey I was also called on my radio to come to meet the great pastor for my appointed time of one on one thanks. I had immediately told Dr. Graham's team that I could not be there to see him and pose for a keepsake picture of this proud point in my own history. However I knew I was doing my job to the best of my ability and that was honor in itself. They changed their plans and what I did not know was they waited for me to return! And after depositing Pat in his chair with eighty-thousand audience, Dr. Graham's close aides ushered me to him and as he was preparing to give his last great talk on behalf of his savior, he clasped his hands around mine and gazed straight through to my core. He said, "Thank you."

I told him that the thanks were all mine, which I meant. I was humbled by this humble man. I had seen unity as the mega Church hierarchy of the Southland in California had come together. Seeing any huge crowd focusing on something has always been an immense heartfelt experience for me, whether it be sporting, social, music, prayer filled or humanitarian.

Pastors praying together across dominational lines of today's church as rare as seeing a golden eagle flying in the center of London.

It started with man's ego like Henry V111 who ignored the silence of Thomas Moore, his Chief Chancellor, took his monarch led church away from the Vatican, divorced his wife, married his mistress and then beheaded Thomas. The cause and effect of this was havoc as his karmic placenta led children killed and killed and killed.

Then the church leaders started to interpret themselves. One speaks in tongues, the other doesn't, one thought Peter thought this and the other knew Paul was saying that. One is clear that women had been eradicated from the Word by men and another radical thinker is saying that gays can come into heaven.

Heaven forbid those poor billions of souls that walk this planet who have not been "saved." Saved from what? No, it is not easy to have bishops pray together. This did indeed feel good.

I watched then as the great man was golf-buggied out from the darkness of the Rose Bowl tunnel into an instant of thunderous sound and light. This was as deafening a sound as I have heard including a Brazilian World Cup final goal, a SuperBowl touchdown, a home produced Olympic gold medal, and Bruce Springstein's first chords of "Born to Run".

That last night with Dr. Graham I looked across at my production manager, Omar, who had been by my side as I produced, promote and managed super stars during huge concerts for fifteen years across the world. We had met because of the team we had around CHER, a super star of superstars, our skills and talents polished in arenas and stadiums across the world. He went from Cher to Miley Cyrus to Alicia Keys to Usher and JLo and much in between. Omar and I laughed knowing what we heard in that moment.

As I walked into the light behind Billy Graham I sensed deep connection and looked up at the heavens and said my own quiet prayer, uttered amidst a huge wave of sound.

"Thank you Lord, Thank you Lord Thank you Lord. What next?"

I thanked God for letting me have an inspired idea at twenty three years old. Sitting on a beach in Jamaica I went from not knowing what I could do with my life, to having an idea that would lead through may paths to the clarity of my life.

At twenty four I started a hospitality company taking thousands of corporate clients to the great sporting events every year in the UK. Because I needed a lot of tickets from black market scalpers, I became friends with North London families and this led me to help have the clarity to launch our own Arena venue and then promote artists. This led to Cher and Los Angles by way of Australia, and this led to expanding music and film horizons and then to producing at the largest stadium in the United States. The consciousness that said what Charlie does is he "creates and delivers live branded communities." A clarity that would stay with me forever.

For the next ten minutes as a tumultuous rain storm overhead descended from the heavens above, and deafening sounds swirled around me, I stood on the grass of the massive infield of the largest stadium in the United States, with every seat of the vast Rose Bowl filled, I was suddenly connected to a peace that was clearly familiar.

Two days later I became aware of a question that would bring me to The Tree of Life itself.

The phone rang in in my Santa Monica office and the person said "We represent Nelson Mandela's 46664 concerts and we would like you to be involved." The next Spring I walked on land mined paths.

If you were to utter a prayer right now in the quiet of yourself, what would your prayer sound like to be heard by the clarity of your Spirit within and to be heard by your universe?

Why Consciousness?

I have come to believe that consciousness is the engine room that stokes the rudder or propellers or sails that move us through our individual lives.

A state of collaborative, connected circulation of sense and energy sourced within each of us, interacting and interdependent with the collective energies of all things of the universe within which we permanently reside. The steering of this rudder is in part governed by the state of our physical, emotional and mental being.

The Latin definition, (which is often the finest source of reference - before man, scientists, religion and thinkers started to mess with its source meaning) is very simple to intuitively relate to. The Latin word "conscious" means "having joint or common knowledge with another."

The trilogy of Christ consciousness would relate consciousness to the connected understanding between God in the Universe, Jesus the body and the Holy Spirit that dwells mysteriously within each of us. Most Christians believe that we become a child of God when we are "saved" and are born again. My intuitive consciousness cries out to me that I was born a child of God and that the Christ consciousness within, has been a clear signal to this, even through the confusion and compromise, signed by feelings and judgments of guilt and shame. Every pointer since my creation and childhood lets me know that I know this.

If I was not believing I was a child of God, it was simply because I would refuse to acknowledge this fact, both in faith and through good works. I urge you that you never isolate yourself from the opportunity to choose this clarity, erroneously thinking and judging yourself that the Spirit of God has deserted you. It never ever does. This to me is a falsehood that only the self leveraging aspects of religion has promoted through time. The truth became half truth which is no truth at all. Remember earlier in the book, do not believe anything you have read unless it resonates with you, unless it is completely true for you. It is not for anyone to tell you, clarity lies in what you tell yourself in your own inner voice and God. God's confidence is in you.

One of my closest friends is a fine man in Dallas, Texas, called Larry Ross. He was Dr. Billy Graham's long-time publicist and spokesperson and is reputedly the first person Mel Gibson called when he looked to release Passion of the Christ. Larry knows his stuff. He even knew to invite me to be the Arrangements Chairman of the final Los Angeles Billy Graham Crusade in Los Angeles at the great Rose Bowl! Since Larry is a big man with a brilliant way of speaking, he always gets me at "hello." As I have stated before it is never easy having Bishops from different denominations pray together in the city of angels but ever since 1949 when he pitched his first revival tent in down town LA, Reverend Graham's simple message brought millions to know what he knew. It was an honor for me to work for a year with the Billy Graham Evangelical Association, Dry Graham and Larry Ross and their teams to bringing over three hundred and twenty thousand people to the Rose Bowl.

As I continue to explore a deep hearing comprehension of a "Child of God" and "the Kingdom of Heaven" Larry sent me emails reciting Galatians 3: 26-27, *"For you are all children of God by faith in Christ Jesus. For as many of you as have been baptized into Christ have put on Christ"* and backs it up with John 3.3 *"Unless one is born again, he cannot see the kingdom of heaven"* and if I still had not heard it he looked for the knock out two verses later with John 3.5 *"Unless one is born of water and the Spirit, he cannot enter the kingdom of God."*

Since Larry is a person of great action we also discuss James 2:17,20 & 24 *"Thus also faith, by itself, if it does not have works, is dead. But do you want to know, O foolish man, that faith without works is dead?"* You see then that a man is justified by works, and not by "faith only." We are not saved by "faith only" This scripture is a distinctive indication that verse by itself can be contradictory, when applied by itself, to the fuller meaning found in the whole.

In speaking now, Larry recognizes too the importance of fellowship and that a religion is indeed just a religion. It is not the Gospel. It is not Jesus. As I wrote this page Larry was enthusing from outside Dallas with his infectious tone down the end of my mobile connecting me with his new friends in Sri Lanka whose patriarch is a

Muslim married to a Catholic. "Buddy, did you know Jesus is mentioned twenty eight times in the Koran? Every one of us loves Jesus in our heart. Come to the Fellowship prayer breakfast in Washington DC next February!"

Traveling, I have also been fortunate to interact with some very conscious people, fine communicators from the East and the West who have been given labels by followers as people finding and living in a state of consciousness. I sense that the state we all seek is to be lucid and clear so that we can then hear ourselves and others most accurately. Our free flowing communication through our heart and spirit centers/chakras is a vein of consciousness. This is a communication portal that allows us to dwell in the state of clarity, the knowing that we know and it is here that we hear and see and have traveled from the darkness.

"Though seeing they do not see:
Though hearing, they do not hear or understand"
Matthew 13:14

How best do you discover consciousness, its state of thought inside of you and how you it connects you to the clarity of who you are? Simply..........SILENCE and allow Light to arrive on what it is you wish to see. Do not govern this, free yourself and your mind and then see and hear what shows up.

Before moving to the next page can you close your eyes and be conscious of who you are in the connectedness of who you are in the connectedness with yourself.

Hear your breath in your silence.
Let your breath carry you forward.

You may see the face of God and, contented, you will simply inherit the kingdom of heaven in this moment.

Consciousness - OUR WORLD

The consciousness you presume to apply to your world is to be THE deciding factor in the assumption that our world can survive with you on it. Past generations have been conscious of ushering something into the world. The great explorers, the great composers, the great soldiers and warriors, the culture driven by religion, the time of equality in race, color and gender, the industrial revolution, the medical innovations, the internet connection of our world. All ushered through the passion and co-creativity energy of former generations.

However in our world today rests one choice. It is not Tory or Republican, Labour or Democratic, or even a coalition of both, it no longer remains black and white nor to a great degree men and women - although this is still work in progress!

No, our generation faces a challenge that no other generation or forefather has faced. It is clear and it is now and it effects every single person in this world. It is the conscious, compassionate and clear choice of choosing the destiny of our planet. We make it through collaborative connection, of compromising through mass coalition and we agree to circulate freely our talent, our money, our learning, our resources. We do this through serving each other and our world. The result will be that our children and great grandchildren will face new opportunities not yet known.

If we are not conscious and remain ignorant and in a trance and do not rise up as "we the people" to this central and single challenge, then it is very probable that in a short period of time, that the planet will predominately serve itself in differing ways that the masses will experience in greater amounts of pain, starvation and death.

When attitudes change through conscious clarity and you and I become familiar in loving engagement as connected community, rather than acting out fearful actions through our habitual emotional automatic responses, then at this point we will hear and we will see the sense of who we really are. It will have meant that we had turned away from enticingly, convincing laws that just made things easier, even though we knew much was wrong and evil.

What does consciousness mean today for you and me as regards our World?

The simple step - Live Lightly on the Planet

Mankind has increased its collective footprint by more than double in the last forty years and together we now consume the resources of more than what our planet will be able to give us. What this means is that fortunately not everyone lives in America. If they did we would be consuming the resources of six earth planets; in the UK it is the resources of three planets.

We can Reduce what we use and buy.

We can Reuse by donating, selling (yes what is in the garage is a good start) and repair and invent ideas that give revalue (like turning old flip flops into brilliant products please visit http://www.uniqueco-designs.com

We can Recycle, so waste can be reduced and then made into different products. We can recycle food waste into water .

We can Circulate our resources and talents and money more freely, being of service and making a difference in other peoples lives and asking for help in our own (Craigslist and Gum Tree are great examples.)

Then there are tougher examinations and propositions that would require greater attitude changes to a level of deeper consciousness. Here are just a few examples:

We can fly and drive less - this is not easy and yet Skype and the Internet let us accomplish more in connecting for virtual meetings or factory to door internet shopping and we can do this. We can make every effort to save fuel and energy, and we can do everything we can to receive - receive water from the sky and purify it: we can all become rain-harvesters and we must campaign that our architects design vats under our shopping mall parking lots, and yes we can simply turn off more lights and did I say drive less?

We can question a lot more - why do we allow factory farming of pigs in Poland, compounded by our allowing this to be subsidized by

European community money for the single benefit of a USA manufacturer promoting to and providing for the appetite of an American desire for meat. Maybe it's okay to eat meat, the world loves meat, but we can question how it was produced, is it free range and organic, and do we really need to have it every day? Then like the Titanic, we may still let a huge issue take us into dangerous water satisfied that the answer was given to us. When we next go into Starbucks let us not just feel good that all the coffee is fair trade, let us also look at the label of the sandwiches with bacon and ham and ask "where is the free range label?" Yet we can be compassionate to them and still buy our Soy Chai Teas as I do every day. Yet my consciousness doesn't rest well with the factory farming and the images in the documentary "Pig Business" with Tracey Worcester and Bobby Kennedy Jr.

We can fill the web with ideas. You can be proactive and we can all "like" and "share" your ideas and actions

We can bring out the best in each other.

How can you be more conscious to support our world today?

Consciousness - MONEY

It will not be bankers, it will not be the Prime Ministers, Presidents and their collective Cabinets. It will not even be the small group of private individuals that inherently have controlled our world's debt. No, it will be you! Our consciousness collectively decides how we weather this financial storm of ours -and maybe all generations. Your heart beat adds to this collective coalition.

Sir Richard Branson who was patron of the Mineseeker organization that took me into the mine fields of Mozambique, became conscious as he heard himself through his encounters with his world, and what he learned from Nelson Mandela. He is conscious today that he has the responsibility of using his business experience, his connections and his money to make the world a better place. Experiences like Virgin Airline fuel conservation and Virgin Unite entrepreneur mentorship motivates Richard to circulate his earned wisdom gained from the Cs of his purpose packed life.

When we are conscious about the source of the energy and divinity of money, our woes will change. When you shift away from the shadow and fear of money, and direct yourself towards a true consciousness to what money's authentic expression coupled with a consciousness of the power of love rather than the love of power, then your attitude around money will have transformed and its divine energy can flow freely around and through you.

The planet's ability to thrive rests on your awareness on a variety of clear points and money is a central agent to them. I am underlining for you here in HEAR that it is "you" and not "us" or "we" or "they" that must take up the mantle as without "you" clearly assuming and embracing your role, it is very likely that "they" will not let "us" or "you" shift "their" attitude. When "you" choose to recognize the true value of money and change the way you think and feel about it, what was first divine and connected in its sacred offering that then became distorted and profane, may once again return to being a nurturing circulating abundance of energy and action-ment.

You are a consumer. You have it within yourself to shift this. Your forefathers already played their parts with the innovation from gold becoming money becoming plastic to becoming virtual. Now there is a freedom within the connectedness of conscious people to change the meaning of money and re-introduce its defined original intent. Do you want to embrace your own role?

What space can you free up within you today as you release your own judgment to what is in or not in your wallet? Your conscious attitude will determine the products and services of your future. And a simple first step is to bring forward heartfelt gratitude. Remain grateful for every transaction and you can recognize not only the law of attraction, but more, the positive actions you can take around your own experiential being.

Positive thoughts are good, but action is better, as faith without action is dead. The Prayer of Jabez, that we mentioned earlier, is a clear action statement. Jabez called on the God of Israel, saying, *"Oh that Thou would bless me indeed, and enlarge my territory, and that Thine hand might be with me, and that Thou would keep me from evil, that it may not grieve me. And God granted him that which he requested"*

Nine million copies of this single prayer made it a New York Times Best Seller after Bruce Wilkinson urged Christians to mantra the prayer for thirty days and watch what they could receive. He was then criticized for misinterpreting God's will by a confused modern day hierarchy, and he subsequently went to Swaziland for a number of years to work amongst an HIV community.

Another industry which is both attitude-shifting and not spared its critics from within and without is the Self Help industry. Mark Victor Hansen and Jack Canfield, co founders of Chicken Soup for the Soul, the worlds most prolific sales of a non fiction book series in the history of books, have supported millions of people to change attitude around money. So many have come out of their seminars and their entire lives have changed dramatically because of this one shift of attitude. Mark is a shining light on loving life. Mark wrote a book called "Tithing," he answered a call from Oprah to build tens of thousands of homes in Guatemala. He is honored by his country with the Horatio Alger Award, one of the highest honor of service to citizens of the United States. His dad had been an illiterate immigrant from Copenhagen. Jack could have been happy being a one room school teacher and yet instead he has spoken to millions of people. Jack defines the modern day language around Success Principles. He was also featured in the number one selling book and DVD of 2006, The Secret, which despite its massive appeal came under significant criticism.

I was an observer in the vortex middle of the "right" and the "left." In 2006 I spent the weekend in the next door bedroom as one of Mark's guests of honor at his sixtieth birthday and at the same time I was given an invitation to an enclave of the top American Christian ministers to meet in Virginia to debate "How can the mainstream media be re-embraced by the Church?" I didn't go but I did send an email with my own direction on the matter. "Read "The Secret", embrace what you do sense is good and apply your Scripture to it, as that is its source anyway." For me the simple prayer in the Old Testament, amongst the "begat who begat who begat" language, "The Prayer of Jabez" and The Secret are sourced at one and the same pure place. Both fell victims as what was central in their messaging became peripheral to their messenger critics. Does it matter your religion, your gender, your geography or your color and creed when you give your answer to how can you be more conscious in your own relationship with Money?

Consciousness - YOU

For you to be here, having reached the calm waters of your consciousness and beyond the turbulence of chaotic emergence means it is very likely that you now comprehend or are open to understanding why it is important to be conscious and how best for you to be connected consciously. Also why consciousness is a critical choice for you to continue to have clarity in your steps ahead, in obtaining your ideal scene around the relevance of your life and business decisions today.

If you still doubt this importance, and/or have trouble remaining in this conscious state, here are a few tips that you can look at when you have and don't have a clear conscious insight and outlook.

Problem Solving
Can you hear yourself amidst the problem?

One of the constant hearings in HEAR is "the issue is NEVER the issue. It is how you are responding to the issue, which is THE issue." You have to be conscious in your own ability to respond and then actually take the action of personal response-ability.

In addition, you are probably already conscious that most of your longer term problems are not being solved and weighing you down in the back-pack of your life. If there were people that diet would never put the weight back on, smokers that quit would never light up again and an old soul that has diligently turned up at AA meetings for ten years, would not suddenly have died from a binge fest.

You should look to choose harmony, alignment and balance as you consciously look to manage your own change. Shifting requires you to have multiple approaches towards the visioning, actioning and implementation of three of your states of being that stay constantly with you, awake or sleep, working or playing, alone or loving a partner and kids. They are your mental, physical and emotional states. Since this statement is a big one to take on board, it is also important for you to have expanded capacity to undertake and approach the issue that you face, and also compassion for your self in the face of everything that may come up from taking any and all steps!

Know the steps you want to take and be accountable to issues when they do arise.

Being conscious of the journey across the Cs of life, coupled with faithful belief in what is within yourself, immediately shifts a conscious approach to what is thrown in front of you. Now, instead of seeing what issues lie ahead and reacting with fear, anger and "I am upset because........," you are a manager of your own emotions, armed consciously to realize the massive opportunity for growth and movement. Never ever consciously avoid a good crisis! It's your chance to learn.

You can now choose to look at everything that is happening or you want to happen through the three life threads that show up as balance between what you judge to be positive and negative. The three states that are very clear for anyone to identify are Physical Manifestation, Mental Judgment and Emotional Feeling. If you have been applying yourself to one (like weight loss as a general example) and not given attention the others it is likely that the other two will make themselves known to the one that you have worked on and pull it back. In the example of weight loss, often it involves what you think of yourself, what you think of others thinking of you and what that makes you emotionally feel, that will trip you up a few weeks or months after you first drop the weight you wanted to. Ninety-five percent put it all back on again, despite the swaggering claims of the diet labels.

At the same time with your consciousness and attitude in full gear applying the one level that you have either worked on or suddenly wakened to witness in its grace-filled full glory of God brilliance, this can in fact shine its own light of success onto the other two and by doing so help them along their lines of positive flow. Again with the example of weight loss, whilst you are working the diet to give you physical success, you can also be shifting away from holding on to an over responsibility of what other people may or may not be thinking and what does it matter anyway if indeed they were. Why attach your reaction to their judgment. Why Judge least thee be judged anyway? There is also deep compassion and self forgiveness work around the feeling of shame or unloveability or unworthiness or whatever voice is inside that physical being of you.

You feel good on all three levels and thus one result inevitably comes about. You get to reside on the learning line of life, in pure joy and with an inquisitive nature, where there is no "I am upset because." "Because" evaporates, and since you no longer have to judge the "because," - this in itself gives you more time to being you.

Trustworthiness

In one of my poems, I write "There is nothing that I do that will prove me worthy. I am worthy simply because I am and so are you". If you are conscious of the trust of worthiness for yourself, your expression and your interaction with your partner, family, friends and colleagues, then lasting success surrounds you. Trust in this way buys you time, maybe hours in the day and even years in your life. You are not caught up in time-wasting exercises like holding on to the past, fearing the future, in spending laborious hours on how to convince and maybe over-convince in conversation. If you trust your ability to connect and communicate in an authentic expression of what you believe then you are most certainly going to be heard most clearly by who it is that you are interacting with.

The by-product is that you will have leadership qualities radiating from you, and that you will be instantly believable and you will have open communication coming back at you as you are trusted by others.

Instant discernment and reflective intuition translates to a better quality of relationship with others, attracting similar qualities in the people you have around you. As discussed with Consciousness - Money, your attitude determines much of your financial mastery, abundance and prosperity. Consciousness also equates to regulated diet, better regard about what you put into your body and how you allow it to support you in health and fitness.

Love Relationship

How great it is that consciousness translates to great opportunities for deeper loving relationships and if you are very blessed and your soul passionately entwines with another, then you are destined to have a full court experience of how to care as deeply as you can and be cared for during your life time. This is a huge gift for you and someone else.

The essential and integral ingredients for a loving relationship with another is to be in a place of co-commitment rather than co-dependence, where you are supporting your partner to be the best that they can be without an attachment for the outcome for yourself through the giving of yourself to another, also you have to be in a place of receiving their contribution of love and loving actions towards you. Conscious loving is underpinned by telling the microscopic truth to your partner, again without attachment as to how they will respond, where empathy, self awareness, trustworthiness, respect and support, are what we bring in to conscious commitment to each other every day.

When you come face to face with the possibility of this "love of your life relationship" you are traveling heavy, with the rocks of former times in the back pack of your life. Your aspiring partner is of course completely unaware of these facts and because you only know what you know and not what you don't know, you too have the inability to discard these rocks just because you have met "the one", the love that you have waited for all of your life.

It's therefore inevitable that the creation of this love so pure, will run its course through the Cs and suddenly a couple of rocks from both your back packs will clatter on to the table or into the bed and you will both have to face what these look like and how to deal with them. Do not in any instance think that this is not going to happen or you can avoid this. Do not look at this sentence and say to me and yourself that you are too conscious and clear and committed to your partner for this not to happen.

The more love, light and consciousness you have the ability to bestow into this cupid's mix, the more opportunity for the darkest of your shadows to show up, just when you consciously have come to the achilles heel, the spot where your rocks bang out and in an instant pummel your partner into a "wow, did that really happen?" Yes, it did, and with confession, compassion and then clarity and your ability to be co-committed, you will move on, becoming every increasingly more deeply conscious and this is the very best outlook you can give and receive with your partner.

Consciousness - MY LIFE

'Cowardice asks the question, "Is it safe." Expediency asks the question, "Is it polite?" Vanity asks the question, "Is it popular?" But conscience asks the question "Is it right?" And there comes a time when one must take a position that is neither safe, nor polite, nor popular, but one must take it because one's conscience tells one that it right.'
- Dr. Martin Luther King

I often say that I was given irrevocable skill sets in the first stage of my life, both consciously and unconsciously. They are now here to serve me and others in the presence of my life. I also gave myself, consciously, judgments in the first stage of life and later I judged others and myself unconsciously, unable to sense, see or feel the glittering coins at the bottom of our individual and collective wells of grief. Then I awoke. Ever since I have been conscious of one thing more than anything else. Being awake. This means it is also very painful to be aware of when I am asleep. This consciousness alone allows me not to take the safe, nor polite, nor popular path, but the path my consciousness tells me that is right. This can be hard, as I am immersed in activities around the world, bringing products I believe in to market, connecting fan and their creative messages, helping produce film and music ventures, working with ideas to help the world be better, and facilitating HEAR to those that may want to hear me.

I know how hard it is not to be in a convincing energy, trying to manipulate a situation or a deal process, rather than to be consciously connected to the needs of all parties.

I look to be conscious in the practicality of life and yet be authentic in the expression of what I wish to contribute. This makes me more effective as I do not get caught up in the drama of life, yet I stay present to what needs attention next. The key is to know myself and my own identity and be clear with others.

I have looked to also be clearer by being conscious about where I live and who I live around. Of course there is the consciousness to myself, and those that are closest to me every day. Now we live in a conscious environment as well, experiencing the Yucatan, home to the ancient Mayan civilization. We witness everyday simple villagers living in peace, love and harmony.

How can my skills and those of my family and team members help enhance the current lives of these beautiful people?

When I was young and growing up in the green fields of England I had no idea that my skills being forged then would come to help the villagers of the Yucatan. The impact of our shared diversity!

The Mayan was clearly immensely skilled and also clearly conscious of things history books can never now reveal. The laid out remains of their ancient communities constructed during a period that stretched from only a couple of centuries after Christ to the time the Spanish came to conquer, leave their legacy for us all to see today.

The Mayan of today wants still for nothing, but like his ancestor, waits patiently for help, which is on its way forged only by God.

What I have found out is not to abdicate the skill sets given to me in the first stage of my life. I have more confidence today in these skills being of help to others. They were given with purpose. Today I apply them in more conscious settings with meaningful output such as promoting creativity, micro-trade entrepreneur or sustainability.

Hearing my voice inside gives me greater freedom to express

myself authentically. This is enough.

Exercising consciousness, I am aware that the Cs are showing up all the time in different ways in everything that I do or seek to be. I recognize the courage required at times, when I need it most, towards a responsibility for being conscious in myself and for our planet.

I swab myself and others with compassion, the medicine of all.

I quest the Learning Line of Life rather than simply being comfortable on the Goal Line. This comes with an openness for continued personal learning and a hearing of others.

I check in with my attitude around intention, stretching myself into my Ideal Scene of Life. I receive help often when it is offered.

I surround myself with conscious people, yet know that my actions in the world, where others perceive darkness and foreboding, give me an opportunity to become more accurately aware of what I don't know I know, resulting in a greater ability to shine the light.

I am challenged by not having a spiritual by-pass whilst journeying through an issue, as I desire to seek this or something better for my highest good in each situation. Let go let God.

The first words God gave us referred to Light. *"Let there be Light."*

I love first words. There is so much raw clarity in them. God said. *"Let there be Light."* Light is goodness, light is all knowing, and light is everlasting.

Light also has an interesting property that it does not travel through time. Therefore from its "relative" perspective, it can exist at any and all points in the universe at the exact same time. It is omnipresent. Hence in the Kingdom of God a day is as one thousand years and one thousand years is as a day.

In the light of Christ consciousness I can reside as much today as when he said, *"Don't judge less thee be judged"*

In the light of most new dawns through the seasons of my life I can hear myself and those around me more accurately.

Its possible that I may write HEAR again, because simply there are things I know today which I did not know yesterday, made free because I have judged myself less today than I did yesterday. What does the future hold? It will be indeed interesting to hear that!

LEADERSHIP NOTE

Diversity

Even though we have looked to sustain a culture of shared values in our team, it is important to mould a team that has diverse qualities, as well as skills.

If all your team carry the same energy, personality and character, it is unlikely that you will have a healthy vibrant co-creative collaborative environment from within and also your client base opportunity will be restricted.

A simple exercise in identifying your staff's qualities is to ask staff members to identify their own as well as asking others to pin point colleagues qualities: It helps:

Identify as a leader what clear qualities you bring to the table and where your greatest assets lie.

Synchronize what qualities are existing in your team to recognize, celebrate and then mould together in clearer work detail. It also will support your own clarity around what you may be missing and need to draft in to complete and complement your winning team.

Introduce the collaboration opportunity in linking with joint venture opportunities with other companies.

Be compassionate to what is not in place. If as a leader your heart is open then you will attract what you are lacking. Help is on it's way.

Chapter 24.

Co-operation

Nothing changes for good without co-operation

Co-operation

The measure of our future can be based on the measure of our co-operation with each other.

Once we are conscious in ourselves with deeper insight and intuition, we start to trust ourselves with the outlook we have around us. This leads us to be attracted to interact with others which is a vital opportunity for us as co-operation through actions of connection and collaboration supports sustainable success. With new insight of consciousness and a clear vision, the outlook "Action" step of operating collectively, or co-operation now exists. These steps have a flow to them and each has its key role to play. If one is missing then all may be short lived.

Co-operation exists first with an agreement, an openness to work together, be together, love together, exist together for the betterment of a coalition, whether it be a relationship partnership, join venture business association or a political coming together across the divides of party beliefs. In the beginning we were clearly shown how to help create our world as all things were connected together. Our indigenous ancestry and habits clearly show this. We each just lost sight of serving this demonstration and started the downward slide of saving only ourselves. A service mentality has to be present, with positive co-committed action, as a service attitude supports each in the co-operative to be the best that they can be. Choosing to keep company and be connected also has to overcome individual tendencies of wanting to isolate in separation. When we interact with each other and fuse our brilliance and energies as close encounters, we speed up insights and outlooks. Relationship is clear with the way people choose to interact with each other based on their clear and intuitive experience. And since actions speak louder than words, each party needs to ask themselves what am I doing - and to whom? Collaboration helps people work together more effectively by helping them first find their own reasons and then their own ways to help each other. Within being open to continued change there must also be an attitude of all parties co-operating. It is clear that each brings only what they know they know to the table and not what they don't know they know. The opportunity to learn from the coalition experience, as we receive service from others, results in new awarenesses. The 13Cs are present, inter-weaving themselves through the action of co-operation, new fresh creative ideas, the childhood and confusion of new relationship, the compromise that all parties must make in their previous belief system to action this new co-operation. The chaotic emergence that can show itself with compassion and clarity sometimes minutes or days following what appears as impenetrable conflict and crisis. Then with renewed clarity arises the fantastic opportunity to be conscious of the greater good and agree to connect and circulate talents and resources.

Sounds like UK or Australian Politics! One cabinet minister in London said, "As we looked around the table at eighteen Tories and five Liberal Democrats, it was hard to imagine that only a week earlier we were tearing strips off each other on the campaign trail." The following weekend the new Prime Minister went on BBC television and announced that he was a "Liberal Conservative" as he welcomed Nick Clegg, the leader of the Liberal Democrats as the Deputy Prime Minister into his "Inner Cabinet as a co-operative."

How hard is it for a Black Democratic President in the White House to be in co-operation with the House of Representatives Congressmen and Women as well as his own Senate?

What if the USA woke one day and had a third political party with elected officials which would force a co-operative coalition, with no one party holding majorities?

Co-operation - OUR WORLD

Are we capable of BEing ONE human family?

Nearly seven billion of us, all unique in our individual ways, are converging in an awareness of shared anxieties, and fears and at the same time with united hopes and dreams and desires for our families and our world.

HEAR

HEARing each other is the key to being capable to connect, collaborate and cooperate, and this hearing requires two actions. The first is you and I having an attitude to hear. We consciously choose to hear each other's concerns, desires, requests, information. We do this and the result will be that we are able to truly understand what it is we must choose to re-act to and care for at this time and how we can go about this with our own authentic expression from what we know we know with our own resources and talents.

The great by-product of hearing another, is the shift that occurs in the other. The hearing of their voice allows them to feel appreciated, resulting in a fundamental attitude change in themselves from being defensive and fearful to being liberated as the opportunity for possibility is rediscovered.

I started HEAR with the words that the world was crying out in authentic expression and that despite the overwhelming threat to the way we currently live together, we face the moment when we can take up the challenge of choosing the destiny of our planet. This only, only, only and only occurs in our mass connectedness and through mass co-operation.

After experiencing the world premiere of Avatar, Daniella and I chatted with Suzy and Jim Cameron about the brilliance of the connectedness of the Navi with their indigenous lands and the network of trees. We chatted about the work that we have been involved with in Ecuador, spearheaded by the Pachamama Alliance resulting in the rainforest being deeded back to the tribes of the forest. Today big business IS starting to cooperate with governments whose leaders have taken on a greater responsibility for their people and less concern for their own power. Today this exists in Ecuador and so the Achuar tribe thrives in their natural habitat. Today Suzy and Jim's Muse Elementary school curriculum is starting to connect schools across the globe; their teachers working in co-operation and children sharing art and music through the internet in the slums of Africa, India and Central America with children in your own schools.

In 2013 Daniella and I facilitated the opening of the Tulum International School in Tulum Mexico. We had no idea we were to do this in 2012, and yet wonderful co-operative and skilled souls made it happen.

What will sustain our consciousness to co-operate?

This comes through Enquiry. We all, in our separate ways of practice are coming to the same conclusion.

There is more that unites us than separates us.

We are inter-connected. It is irrelevant whether the path to this conclusion is religious, philosophical, quantum science or just a good reflective walk on a Sunday. We are connected and through this understanding we can reach into a greater knowing. We can have ears to hear and eyes to see, beyond judgment in a sea of compassion for each other.

We had become so caught up with how best to look after ourselves that we ignored how to co-operate with the animals, the plants, the oceans and the fishes.

Old indigenous shaman elders have always found it paramount to cooperate with the animals yet they too perhaps have not co-operated with the new world, staying only in the old, and at their core remaining victims to what is happening around them.

Even the Bible created divides in man's minds between the Old Testament and the New, with certain religious orders remaining only in the Old, and choosing to ignore God's further direction, delivered through the experience of Christ in the New.

What can sustain co-operation is to recognize the value and resonance of every note that creates harmony for all. Harmony that unites old and new, black and white, men and women, Muslim and Christian, humans with animals and plants all living in harmony on the land and in the sea across North, South, East and West.

If we can create a score that has a melody that sustains us all in the harmony with each other – then everyone will indeed be in co-operation and the sound will be thrilling and enduring.

"The music of this Opera was dictated to me by God.
I was merely instrumental in putting it on paper and
communicating it to the planet"
Puccini

Co-operation - MONEY

If we have accomplished the journey through the 13Cs and we have consciously been able to change our individual attitude around money, then it is inevitable that the collaborative outlook will bring forward a new blossom. A blossom that will usher new understandings, new big ideas, derived out of the nature of its vibrant flow, and through our innovative attitudes.

This generation is already witness to it for within the very least the most has been given. There already is a new big society that was birthed by the big idea of an individual in Bangladesh and then co-operated by millions. We recognize the nearly one hundred and twenty million micro social entrepreneurs today. We are seeing poverty made history through co-operation, first with lenders, then with themselves and finally with a consumer through an establishment within a fair trade marketplace. The key to this success is this connected co-operation through a conscious attitude of support toward each other.

We have been fortunate to help stimulate a series of micro loan enterprise circles and the way this has occurred has been to:

Connect – Micro investment, micro production and micro distribution. We connect through micro-trade, micro social entrepreneurs in Africa and the Pacific Rim to vendors, stores, fair trade product buyers in Europe and the USA. The producers have brilliant skills like leather making, beading, wood carving, crop farming, fabric weaving and essential oil manufacturing

Co-operate - with field agents specialized in training and product quality control to co-operate with banks and their financial literacy agents prepared to visit women in slums who themselves have co - operated with each other to form micro trade and investment circles that will hold each other accountable.

Circulate - resources and lending money in small tranches and for the borrower to get into a habit of paying back fractional interest, whilst building a sustainable business, which then pays back the loan plus the interest. The loan can then be made to another recipient borrower and the interest can be allocated into capital, like a central weaving factory or food plant. In addition we now are witnessing fair wage and fair trade driving a larger segment of the global economy as an economic force of one hundred and twenty million micro social entrepreneurs that no longer need a hand out in charity - this is indeed a force for good. More and more people join this force's ranks every day.

If it can happen so effectively and with such positive results through the poorest of poor connecting together in good business practice, then why can it not happen in our own back yards?

It can. There have been companies like The Co-operative leading the way. When so many banks like Northern Rock and RBS were irresponsibly leveraged with only twenty seven percent liquidity on their books, The Co-operative financial services stated they had one hundred and twelve percent assets balance, adhering to the straight forward clear philosophy of only lending out less than it had taken in.

The Co-operative pioneered fair trade in 1992 with produce like bananas in its grocery stores and has a five and a half percent market-share of the grocery market in the UK and has a fifty million pound micro loan fund to stimulate traders to grow produce.

Peter Marks, the former CEO of The Co-operative asked me "How do I persuade Tesco to move into fair trade." In a sentence, I said, "Let them share in your twenty years of experience. Co-operate as The Co-operative in a way competitors could never imagine or dream."

The Co-operative has it's own label vineyards with South African wine growers and over ten thousand small rural farmers in Kenyan tea co-operatives. When I met Peter in Westminster, his daughter, Joanna, had just returned from working in school building program in Kenya and Peter had returned from his travels to Africa. Both had been truly and irrevocably touched and their hearts etched. This is the case all over the world with more and more of the world's finest businesses are connecting, co-operating and circulating their experiences and resources to help not only those in the fields but also their own peers.

As The Co-operative's own slogan states this is "good for everyone." Then even The Co-Operative slipped, and declared huge losses in 2013 and Peter had to step down from the helm. We all slip.

Beyond all reasoning of right and wrong there is that field. The field where HUMANS are actioning humanity surrounded by the lush green grasses of co-operation and connectedness.

The perimeter of the field can be boundary-less if we choose it to be this way and there is no limit to what can be accomplished.

Co-operation - YOU

Can you co-operate?

Szell: Is it safe?
Babe: You're talking to me?
Szell: Is it safe?
Babe: Is what safe?
Szell: Is it safe?
Babe: I don't know what you mean. I can't tell you something's safe or not, unless I know specifically what you're talking about.
Szell: Is it safe?
Babe: Tell me what the "it" refers to.
Szell: Is it safe?
Babe: Yes, it's safe, it's very safe, it's so safe you wouldn't believe it.
Szell: Is it safe?
Babe: No. It's not safe, it's very dangerous, be careful.

The above is the script from the movie scene featuring the great Laurence Olivier asking Dustin Hoffman's Babe to cooperate with his Nazi diamond smuggling character Szell in the memorable dentist chair scene during the pulsatingly brilliant 1976 film, Marathon Man. In the end to make sure Babe was co-operating fully Szell pulled a healthy tooth and exposed the nerve that forced Babe into authentic expression of massive pain.

How willing are you to co-operate right now?

Are you willing to be utterly open in your vulnerability and hear and be heard? Are you open to enquire and reside in the questions more often than your own individual answers?

Are you willing to combine your skills even if it means to hold the ladder, when the irrevocability of the talented other, is up the ladder?

Are you able to consciously co-operate with yourself, sensing your mind, body and emotions are in co-operative alignment and if not - to internally take the actions that will bring yourself right with yourself - rather than defuse your unconnected energy onto another?

Are you also able to receive in equal measure to what you are capable of giving and vice versa?

If you are ticking off the above questions with affirmative answers then you are awake indeed. Can you get up and action yourself and then we can see how able you are to remain awake. Perhaps set up a time to vision with your partner or set up a new business standards and protocol agenda at the office and see how you respond to all their interactions. Also if you ticked off all the boxes and you are Muslim, or Hindu or a Christian how willing are you to co-operate together.

How keen are you if you are an oil man from Texas and you are being asked to sit down with a greenie from Oregon to figure out how to completely eradicate gas and petrol from cars? If you said yep sure, then I ask, why is the clear air YES/NO petitions and bills in the California State get sponsored clearly by the parties that think they have most to win or lose by sponsoring their side.

If you are an ecological oceanographer and you are invited to be sponsored by big oil to work on how to make oil rigs safer and yet the government have said how important it is still to have drilling off your coast that you know will endanger the marine layers in your beloved ocean, will you look to journey to meet them where they are at? If you do will those around you judge you as compromising your belief?

"Is it safe?" could be the question an evangelical or Pentecostal or someone from any form of religion asks today as they consider a co-operative action with another.

"Is he/she saved?"

There may have been no more expectation and energy riding on this one answer through time. People expectantly have sought to control through selective religious persuasion, convincing themselves and others, that their way is the only route to reach the Kingdom of Heaven. Many have operated unlimitedly from love but are unable to co-operate. They are hindered by unrecognized tinges of fear for themselves and their chosen religion. What clear compassionate eyes can now be brought forward to behold belief, faith and good-works and the Kingdom within everyone?

What is central with God and what remains peripheral in you that prevents you from connecting and co-operating more fully? Do you do unto others as you would unto yourself, or are you selective as to who you chose to apply this clear direction for yourself? Do you judge forgetting that you are being judged because you judge.

How much are you co-operating with others?

Choose a person or a program and write down ways that you will look to be more co-operative in your intention and then in your interaction over the next ninety days.

How much are you co-operating with yourself?

How do you connect with yourself physically with your own health and wellness and what could you be doing better?

_____

_____

_____

_____

HELP NOTE

There are simple and effective ways of acting out
co-operation as well as giving and receiving support.
They all require action by you.
Hearing yourself and others.

Say hello to yourself in your bathroom mirror and give
yourself some encouraging words.
Be Mentored or Mentor someone
Join a Business Support Group
or Master Mind Group

Pick up the phone and simply collaborate by offering
your resources or help to some one.

Co-operation - MY LIFE

There was a time when I was a distance from co-operating with those around me and with my own life as it was. It was long ago, over three decades past. If I had not gone forward and co-operated with my life and thus entered a road less travelled, this incident may have left me at a C that I would never have travelled beyond or remembered past.

How Black is a Black Sheep? – 1979

It was the most beautiful piece that I had seen by far and I knew it was of massive value. The Maltese Cross, a legendary broach, with a stunning red ruby in the middle, four emeralds making up the cross surrounded by lines and lines of encrusted diamonds, all set in white gold.

My last year as a teenager had spiraled out of my control. I had lost the first love of my life. My selected friends were posh punks following a new band, The Sex Pistols, and hanging out on the Kings Road. I no longer had connection with my father or anything my father, stood for. Dad and I would have furious frustrated rows whenever we did see each other. I was running in a wild rebellious pack seeking a new voice and I was out of control.

My bitterness was directed at my own people, those closest to me. I had isolated myself at home and at school starting with impervious self-induced insecurities, which had led my living a life that was not me, and yet it was the one I was leading. A little fearful lie here, led to a modest ten pounds taken from my fathers money wad. My friends, some of whom were the children of the England's greatest historical figures, were fighting for themselves: attempting to find their own sense of identity, and many were failing, and falling from the glittering potential of their early teens. Thievery started as a game with a few. We laughed at what we took from Kings Road shops. Some took to feed the sinister monster of heroine.

However I took a different path. Now I acted out of sight, except I could not hide myself from myself, so I blinded myself and there was no one to stop me.

I followed the path of Sir Charles Lytton, the infamous Pink Panther, whose inherited name I was aspiring to live up to. It was a name that I was connected to because of my great Grandfather, Sir Henry Lytton. It also did not escape my mind's shaping that one of the most notorious London cracksman in the novel and BBCs hit series, Raffles, about an amateur gentlemen sportsman jewelry thief, lived at the Albany in Piccadilly, exactly where my family's London home was. My Hollywood hero was Steve McQueen and my youthful mind had traveled with him from The Great Escape to the Thomas Crown Affair.

I was also on the list of Debs Delights, the most eligible young men coming out of schools like Eton to be introduced to and escort the debutants of the year. Every weekend was another party. The gilded invitations would arrive, yet I was in turmoil.

What I was ignorant to was that both the famous Pink Panther, Sir

Charles, and also Raffles were fictional characters, ultimately safe in fertile writers minds. Myths like Robin Hood are enriched by story tellers and film makers over time. What I was doing was real and therefore a crime. It hurt people, although it made me feel better to think - whether accurately or falsely - that it was the insurance companies would pay. I would romantically convince myself of this.

The summer became a series of robberies from some of the most notable London family homes. Now this stunning Maltese cross owned by the spouse of the chairperson of the most famous Auction House in the world, slipped into my velvet sack. I was out of the building without pausing, euphoric for a few fleeting seconds as danger and success collided.

Yet within minutes, walking down Kensington, the weight of small stones increasingly felt like massive gold bullion bars. I went back to the Piccadilly flat, tossed the ancient gems and pouch onto my bed. I spent the night playing backgammon in a nightclub. I drank to become insensible to guilt. The next day, dressed in a tailored grey suit, I made my way to an old Swiss man who acted as my fence and bank. All I could do was to pass over the pouch. I did not want to see it again. I had to ignore any feeling. I went back silently into my pack of friends and drank a whisky, and then another and then the bottle to buffer any remaining feelings.

This compromised life was where I resided and I was journeying far away from the truth. I did not want to feel. If I did feel I felt pain - which I had no way of knowing how to deal with. A young man of twenty, dealing with these impressions had no one to speak to. There was no therapy open to me but the buffer of drink, the tonic of late night parties, and then the acting out which was not honest - neither to myself, nor to others.

An ultimate confession though occurred when my own father confronted me at the end of the summer, asking whether I was the culprit as the trail had landed at his doorstep. I looked at him and simply said "Dad it was me." From that confessional moment we learned to become united as father and son, realizing how far apart we had become. Remorse flowed and the healing began.

In only two years from that leaving day at Eton with its promise of future brilliance, my isolation from others, from God and from myself was apparent. Yet there were those that held their love for me. My mother and my father, and others too. However much pain there was, there was undeniable love. I did not know then that unforgettable light would be bestowed into me to help me emerge later from the chaos. Time was gifted to me. I was utterly vulnerable to my fate but an irregular intervention meant I was given no penalty in court despite pleading guilty to all charges.

It was a year later that a Knightsbridge judge said, "I am going to give you a chance to live a worthwhile life and do not let me see you here again." I travelled to become a son to a father I had hardly known who lay in a hospital bed from a heart attack in Greece. The stress perhaps too much to bear for a good man looking to be a good parent to a wayward son.

If the father had died, maybe the "Prodigal" would not have possessed the passion for life from that moment, and he would have pulled his own trigger. Yet the father lived, the father had been there for him and cared and fought for his son, and now the son would travel his life knowing the love of his father. It was to be an unbearable knowing that for a while longer I would look to deflect, destruct and destroy. Yet the love of my father had no bounds. Amazing Grace.

I traveled on from this pivotal place, across the Cs of life and through my innate quest for "caring," even before I comprehended the question of "What ails thee." It started with my support of other's own brilliance, as I gifted my given brilliance to them and then, within a dark wood, I would awake and cooperate with my Self.

How can a lost sheep become found? How can the prodigal son be so well received, or a leopard change its spots? Precious time reveals so much. In exploring this question maybe for me it was simply that I was not lost, that I was not yet ready to receive, and that the camouflage of an animal skin just served to keep me safe and shaped until one day I did not need to choose to hide any more - from myself or my world. Amazing Grace.

I have underscored the scripture "Don't judge lest ye be judged" frequently in the later stages of HEAR as it is everything when it comes to me cooperating more effectively with myself and it has nothing to do with you and never has. It was just how I judged it did that was the obstacle. A finger pointing is three fingers pointing back.

Everything is surmountable. I know this to be true as I have seen hundreds of thousands of the poorest of the poor create enterprise in the time it took you to read to this point in HEAR. All it required was hope and someone that cared enough to help them care more for themselves. Amazing Grace, how sweet the sound.

I have seen co-operation at the highest levels of dignity, trust, accountability and service as co-creating organizations, NGO's and conscious individuals come together in giving and receiving resulting in authentic expression and effective flow and circulation of talent, resources and money.

This is not something I need to hope for in the future - it is happening now and it gives me greater courage and conviction to both look more at my own capabilities and how more I can be responsible in this life time.

As I become clearer around co-operation with my own self I do allow more often a conscious movement of greater clarity to flow through my physical, mental and emotional beings and this does allow me to reside more often in a heavenly place of joy, love and unconditional service.

My father was sixty-six when all around me judged me as lost. When he was ninety-three I was in California and we were on the phone. There were increasing occasions after he journeyed his great life past ninety that I would call him and the phone did not answer. He was coming to the end of his life here. I was birthing Humanity Unites Brilliance at that time and had just held my first event at the Radisson hotel with an amazing group of pioneers as well as my friends, and nameless faceless heroes doing good works around our planet. Everyone one of us journeying through our 13 Cs.

The day after the extraordinary energy of co-operation that has inhabited that hotel room that weekend, I called dad and he answered the phone.

The conversation was short. He was excited to be moving on to the great adventure ahead as he called it. I strained to listen in co-operation to his every murmur, his every word knowing there would not be too many more. The voice I had yearned to hear as a child and then feared and disrespected in my youth. The voice that had always in fact encouraged me to live my life to the fullest as I traveled across continents. As I listened and said a few responding words, I heard his dying voice say, "Mum and I are so very proud of you, Charlie and how you re-created your life and made what you have out of it, but one question I have is, what religion are you son?" I had sat beside father as his only small son in our Dorset village church on Sundays in our front right family pew. For a quarter of a century I had then lost faith in our co-operative interactions. Dad of course remained constantly faithful and his joy was immense recognizing over time my own transformations, and we both enjoyed discussing faith and this great adventure, especially as his end came.

What dad was asking was a clear question that I sensed he had been considering about asking for some time. I said back down the phone, "Dad if I was Italian I probably would be for Catholic masses. If I was English I'd probably be attending a Church of England Anglican congregation. In India I would have loved the sweetness of a Hindu ashram and its meditative chanting. In America I have called many of the church or spiritual leaders my friends. When I was growing up you used tell me of the love you had for your Jewish associates. Dad, I have been asked this question by many. My reality is I just love Jesus, a Mystery of the heart of Jesus, and the experience of the Word in the Bible that are His words, and I try to live up to it as much as I can. Someone else can and usually does label me so who knows, dad, what the truth of a label by others would be. I love belief. I love faith and I love to experience what I know that I know to be my truth."

Dad responded "I love you son" and I too blurted the same. We both knew this would be the last time we spoke and we cried together. They were not silent tears as we heard each other.

A week later on an early Sunday morning I awoke to a phone call to say he had passed. When I went to see his body that he had wanted embalmed so that my sisters and I could say good bye, I did not get to say goodbye and I still have not, as it was clear to me his body did not hold his Spirit when I visited it.

Are we divine being having a series of human experiences? Seeing an embalmed shell of a human body reinforced my belief that the divine being had transitioned with enough.

How can one say good-bye if God is dad and dad is God?

Father, Child . You are so many lights in my dreams.
Near to me. A Way for me, Love for You. I Love you.

Man in The Mirror

A couple called me up in 2008 and asked if I could I come over and see what they have at their house. When I arrived at their Hollywood Hills home, Halima, who hailed from Afghanistan, excitedly took me to their bedroom, which was an unexpected initial request! I followed her and what I saw was piles and piles of new clothes. All over the room were trousers, shirts, sweaters and socks. Halima can wear the most beautiful designer clothes in the world, yet what I saw surprised me. She excitedly said, "Charlie, Wal-Mart had a one dollar an item sale in their stores so Jermaine and I and the family went shopping. We didn't just go to one, we went to a few Wal-Mart," I laughed with joy at what they had done and how they had done it.

Halima and Jermaine Jackson were living out their lives in the way Jermaine's younger brother, Michael Jackson, had made famous in his brilliant song "Man in the Mirror." Simple beautiful souls in action, circulating their God given resources in actions to help those with less worldly possessions than themselves. I imagined black Escalades driving around the perimeter sites of Los Angeles with Halima and Jermaine leading a Jacksons charge in and out of Wal-Mart. That would have been a sight to behold.

A year later Michael passed tragically with a massive amount of conflict, compromise and chaos all around him, but the Man in the Mirror will never die. Jermaine and Halima also remain champions to earth's causes. They came and spoke at an event for me and during a series of Christmases, bleak ones for many on low income, our group carried out a food, toys and personal care give away drive across multiple cities.

Take a look at yourself and then make a change.

Chapter 25.

Circulation

What goes around comes around

Circulation

Circulation takes us all through Chaotic Emergence to arrive at our own port of calling.

We see apparent chaos every day on our freeways around the world. Yet we always seem to emerge off them to our destination. We did lay a giant web of tarmac across all our lands so we could circulate. The freeways around Los Angeles demonstrate every day the chaos of modern day driving. The 110, 5, 10, 210 and the 405. It requires a maze of traffic to navigate the circulation of the city of Angeles. We need them all. One M25 gets us safely around a London metropolis, as did the North and South Circulars. Nairobi takes a day sometimes to get around and every town has a left to right or right to left web of tarmac. Every city has its web of tarmac.

Without circulation we do not get around. We do not get up with the sun. We do not move through the cycle of our life. We do not eat or drink. We do not poo and every body poos! We do not learn wisdom and pass it on. We have nothing if we choose to stop and get ourselves into an almighty road block. Nothing would have finally got past us and everything would have inevitably ground to halt, with a lot of angry screaming behind us because we have caused a road block. Everyone is the same. If we let everything in, every hurt and disappointment, and if we sought to control it all by putting a big cork on it, at some point we would just go pop and fizz or explode!

Fortunately the flow of Cs across all our seas today sees us witness greater understanding for the necessity of allowing life to flow life through us. Fortunately we have come to trust and believe in circulation. We know even if we are in the stress of today, that tomorrow we will be able to look at things differently and hear ourselves more clearly. Through HEAR this word has come up time after time, page after page - Circulation. It has to, simply because it flows through the book to give HEAR its own life and breath as sure as blood must pump through your body. The circulation from creation through childhood and from confusion, compromise, conflict, chaos and crisis to a choice point that leads to confession and compassion. The circulation of mind, body and spirit leading to clarity, consciousness and co-operation.

As you started to read HEAR you may have been refusing the slightest entry to circulation. Yet it is bound to have happened or is to happen soon. We are triumphant and joyous in circulation. We are faithful in belief of the circulation of our Creator. We believe in the circulation of our own creativity. We say, "What goes around comes around." With the Cs we can now deal with consequences that show up in between the going and the coming.

To hear we simply must be choosing to circulate the sounds uttered around us and from within us. To hear we can choose to be conscious of how our voices, messages and connections play themselves out through our bodies, our minds and our emotions. If all are in parallel then it is possible that we will be able to circulate our own spiritual selves with joy and love. At any time we are in or moving from or into one C or another - constantly. On any day we may have all Cs showing up, each featured are clustered around one aspect or another of our lives and actions.

Recycling and Reusing products. Circulating money around our world in Fair Trade and Fair Wage. Celebrating our individual talents and skills and welcoming collaboration gratefully through giving and receiving in unconditional measure. Everything healthy calls for healthy circulation. Clearly without it we will abdicate our capacity of choosing our Destiny. Each of our destinies and our World's. As night turns to day and the sun replaces the stars, so does circulation inevitably lead us along the path of the learning line of our lives, our world and all that is in it.

Circulation - OUR WORLD

Our planet's authentic expression is to circulate. If it is hindered in any way then it shows us, sooner or later, the errors of our ways. The air, the water, the winds, the foods, the resources, the people and animals, the creativity and inspiration, the knowledge. All must circulate. The seasons and the gardens, all demonstrate every day what must be.

As these elements circulate freely and healthily, our world moves and the sun circulates through our day with the moon its nigh-time companion. We thrive because of this daily shift.

As we circulate thankfulness for the grace that our world bestows to us every day, our hearts are opened and we are able to love our neighbor as ourselves.

As the poorest of the poor show the richest of the rich how to live prosperous, trusting and enterprising lives, our next generation will be freely circulating an energy and a connectedness with each other than our past would never have given themselves the eyes or ears to see and HEAR.

As our businesses circulate skills and resources more freely to each other, recognizing that this culture compels enhanced culture, leadership and sales, we will witness greater corporate usefulness.

And the bottom line of the bottom line is as we circulate love and resources across our world, in an authentic and vulnerable expansive energy flow that has peaceful harmony between giving and receiving love, then we will have learnt better how to live and how to care.

We see it all the time now and as we shine our light on what we see and what we hear, trusting this truth, then we are giving opportunity to others to be the same.

As we circulate serving one another then our world becomes what we dream it to be.

Circulation - MONEY - and Resources

We all have different needs, we are all at different stages of our lives and we live our lives with varied circumstances. Therefore the flow of money that each of us needs is different and varies to at different times of our lives.

Our attitude around the abundance of the flow of money must also therefore vary to suit the circumstance and we must be able to be conscious of this and allow ourselves to be open to the flow to suit the needs of our lives. Usually when we hear the phrase "circulation of money," it relates to the amount of money in circulation and the velocity of the exchange. Its flow often determines inflation rates as our attitude determines whether we sense there is not enough to go around or alternatively the advertising campaigns cajoling us to 'keep up with the Joneses' falls on deaf ears. However if we possess the attitude that there is enough money to provide for all and that all we require is a matter of circulation of real money with creativity and freedom, then our global economy would be healthy.

Today there are increasing signs of greater co-operation with the rapid emergence of social enterprise. Fair trade and importantly fair wage coupled with a more conscious understanding of both sharing resources, in profit allocations to staff, and the circulation of profit back to sustaining the communities that source, farm or manufacture the products we consume.

We are seeing business leaders and boards moving away from just giving though the historic feel-good charity mechanism. We are entering the age of the Social Enterprise, which is defined as a company whose primary focus is on providing a social benefit rather than just on maximizing profit for the owners; it is owned by investors who seek social benefits such as poverty reduction, health care for the poor, social justice, and global sustainability, through psychological, emotional and spiritual satisfactions over solely financial reward. We are seeing the emergence of community-owned organizations and co-operatives and these companies are becoming the ambassadors for sustaining business change in the future.

Simple young men and women are rising up and saying "enough!" Are you a Jamie Oliver dedicated to combating malnutrition for all children and even you? Are you an executive in a company like Patagonia in California that contributes one percent of all its gross revenues to environmental programs and only uses organic fair-trade factories regularly inspecting the factories in Asia? In Kenya I have had the honor of working as a fair trade director of Craft Link Africa. Craft Link links thousands of artisans and over sixty young Maasai women's groups now producing an array of beaded products with a world wide market. We sat with them in all their fine tribal clothing and multiple necklaces in the middle of the Kenya countryside. Huge smiles, weather beaten hands brilliantly sewing and beading. Then not one but three cell phones went off at the same time and out came the latest Safaricom phones. Smiles broadened.

What has a mobile phone to do with social enterprise?

The mobile phone which is owned by over ninety percent of Africans now provide them with daily pricing on grain and produce, guaranteeing fair wage for fair trade. The mobile phone is the most immediate and most secure way of transferring money. It can now serve as a wallet. The mobile phone is a classroom, connecting a Maasai classroom in rural Kenya to your own child's classroom or remote teacher facility.

Social connection, socially shared consciousness, and useful collaboration are all converging today. All at this time as strategies and implementation plans are being effected to even the playing field of education, of nutrition, of housing and energy and of fair wage through fair trade. Resources of money flows more freely than ever before.

Imagine a woman dying of HIV who has nothing. One day she is given some training and a tiny amount of money. Imagine one hundred and twenty-million people. Can you? Imagine that they are all like this first woman and they are micro social entrepreneurs. Imagine a young thirty-something from Essex outside of London, who when he was starting out precociously said, "I want to change the world through food" Imagine him doing that and winning USA's top television award for reality show of the year, beating out all your favorite shows, as he simply tells America about the epidemic called obesity. Imagine him providing necessary products to be bought and sold by healthy women with husbands and families living in homes across England. Imagine the wooden bread boards and salad bowls and spoons being made everyday by the social entrepreneur army in the slums of Africa. Imagine your money not going in one direction in aid, but circulating and growing in energy and value through trade.

Can you imagine this? I truly hope you can, because all the people featured in the above paragraph have been able to imagine it. They are not the only ones and they now have no need for greed or hunger and the world is getting better all the time.

Social Enterprise is changing our world's landscape forever and it is happening as you read this and as you imagine what you can do.

Circulation - YOU

There are more of you today alive than all the people who have died throughout human history.

There is such a mass of us circulating through our lives and on this planet. If we are to exist beyond the next few generations it may be essential more than anything else to practice how to circulate.

How you co-operate with yourself and your fellow human whilst you circulate your self between your consciousness, sub-conscious and unconscious minds determines your destiny.

How you co-operate with yourself and others as you circulate yourself in and out of the 13Cs also determines your destiny.

In HEAR you have been traveling your own 13Cs. I have asked many, many questions of you in the twelve preceding chapters focused on "You." If you are here in HEAR thank you for responding.

I said at the beginning of the book, if you are to hope to be accurate in your answers you must be willing to choose to spend much time on your quest for the question. I am sure there are questions that resonated with you and others that did not. What other questions lie ahead for you that will open the doorway to your own Mystery. This is your own quest as you bring yourself forward out of your own dark wood.

Ahead in the third section of HEAR I have set up steps for you to look at how to move from the questions to the answers, for You. My hope is that knowing and living your questions with the 13Cs you will stretch into being you for the sake of yourself, your family and our world. There is so much for you to give and of course there is so much for you to receive.

Today I would ask for you to look into the eyes of another, maybe your partner or friend. Just spend a few seconds looking into each others eyes. You will be giving and receiving whatever feelings come up for you. You will be circulating "You" with another "You."

As we are in circulation and we are in you, are there ideas you can birth and live with right now that can change our world? For example, what's in your garage? Is there a bicycle? Is there more than one? Is there a bicycle that has not been ridden this year or a kids BMX that your son has outgrown? Could you have a social enterprise idea and suddenly create "Bikes to Books" and have the bikes that your neighbors no longer have use of, picked up and put into a container to be shipped to Africa or India. You will cause some to be recycled for children in the slums, others sold and the money used to buy books for a new library in the school in the slum. John, a farmer in Calgary, Alberta came with me once to Africa and had this exact idea.

Every body poops. Every body eats, drinks and poops. It is essential we learn how to be conscious in the circulation of "food" "water" and "poop." Some one in Redwood California has found a solution. A microbe bacteria that eats solids and leaves clear water is an inspired idea.

What inspired idea can you have today? You are so capable so if you haven't been inspired why not spend a few minutes now, connecting with your own consciousness and come up with a social enterprise inspiration? Increasingly you are a more conscious consumer, demanding higher standards of farming, of growing, or rearing, of labels on packages, of the need for local co-operative growers. Increasingly with the little green bins in our kitchens with biodegradable bags you diligently save your left over food to circulate back to the earth, rather than still being part of a former generation that tipped everything into one dustbin to be taken to the land fill tip. Congratulations for sharing your mind and heart with the experience of this book and maybe navigating more clearly through your own Cs as we progressed.

What Inspired Big Idea can you share and contribute to our world right now and how could it work?

Tomorrow you will create, you will be called to the challenges of your business, your family, your world. How you respond to being able to circulate everything that you have and know will determine the course of your day, your year and your life.

How you choose to circulate all you have and know is to determine our world.

Circulation – MY LIFE

So I am one of you. We are people from all over the world converging under undeniable banners: Uniting through common purpose for a change in the world, reaching towards goals not scored by politicians and the United Nations. People with names. People who are anonymous. Activists, activators, lawyers, bankers, non profit workers, music artists, film makers, for-profit corporate responsibility managers and entrepreneurs, as well as every one of us – consumer citizens changing our purchasing habits, all converging with shared values as caring citizens.

I have been a Global Witness to this. I witness the 13Cs everywhere I look, everywhere I go, and even when every time I don't have the courage to go, then my ignorance still evokes a C.

For example I ignored the circulation issues, cause and effect of Sanitation. Of the world's seven billion people, six billion have mobile phones. Yet two and a half billion people do not have access to toilets or latrines. In the second decade of the 21st century, there are over 1.1 billion people still defecating in the open.

There was a day in Monrovia, Liberia in 2009 when I looked into a hole in a tin shack, built like cards about to topple over. The hole was full of poop and there was poop coming out of it. When I visited this lavatory it had just rained and it was on a small hill so all the poop was traveling down into Logan Town, the slum of all slums and home to the poorest people in the world after a genocidal war. It was one loo that looked after seventeen thousand people.

I have seen inside pf porto-johns at the end of a concert day and they are not pretty, but the next day they get hauled away to be pumped clean and put out for the next event.

In Monrovia the toilet did not get cleaned and it was not being moved. Every one of us poops and every one needs to care about this. We are working on solutions and I hope you can too.

Every day when I wake I know that I am to sail through the 13Cs of my day, and even though I know I am to journey this way, the C's can become choppy and a storm can be upon me with no warning.

Just knowing I am circulating through them gives me trust, faith and belief that the light will shine again.

Just seeing you and our world deal with the Cs gives me confidence in how to provide support in my own way to help you and our world.

Circulating from the Creation of my birth, the creativity of my own ideas and the creation of my every relationship means I am conscious, most of the time, of how to collaborate and circulate my own resources. Then there is the inevitable circulation from birth to transitioning from this mortal coil.

Over the last few years, I have found myself back in my nation of birth. I had traveled for so long around our world and I was back close to the Thomas Hardy countryside that I grew up in. Stonehenge standing on the verge of my mum's final home, Amesbury Abbey.

My mum is now past 90 and I have found joy in sitting with her, connected as her son, talking about the meaning of life, spirituality and Jesus. My dad had passed and mum missed him more and more after sixty years of marriage. Was she soon to join him again and importantly was there more purpose and meaning to her life in her nineties?

In our lives, my mum gave the love of the mother to me and my sisters through the circulation of our own Cs, just like every mum does.

I felt that she despaired of me during my life forming early twenties, yet I always felt her compassion and love and perhaps it was that kernel that kept me away from the darkest of despairing actions, when hope, trust and belief seem lost to me. I was able to circulate through the C's of crisis and reach more peace filled waters.

Circulation questions of life and death are asked by so many of our elder generation. With more people alive than have died throughout human history today, probably every C of this book is effected by such a statement.

Circulation too comes from me writing HEAR for you. By communicating as authentically as I know how in this given moment of my life, I am being present to and I am being responsible for the caring of life, and I become aware of more!

One of the great pluses that I have experienced from writing is that I am in the action of circulating. I am not attached to how you read this or even what you may do with anything you may glean from the experience of this book.

I have no expectation on you reading HEAR. If you have found your way to this book, I do have a huge desire that whatever you choose to know, you do choose to be part of the generation that takes up the challenge of choosing the destiny of your planet. My support to you, so you can activate this, is to aid your capacity to hear and express yourself authentically.

I hope that there is sense in the circulation of HEAR for you and that you may wish to circulate ideas that come up from it for yourself. That you embrace and action these ideas as I attempt in my way to do and that you look to share with others and serve our world as best you can.

I hope too that through this demo-culture demonstration of the circulation of the 13Cs, that it is clear how I look to circulate.

For myself I recognize there is no full stop. There is no "I did it" or "I made it to the end" as I see no end and if I did it would be a sign post to look inside again as I equate an end with a barrier to the true flow of circulation of what is core to myself.

There is however an end in sight to this book. We thank God for the questions posed and answers provoked.

I know too that what I heard to be able to write HEAR was purely to this point of my life. I will inevitable meet the 13Cs time and again on my travel and that there may never be a final full stop to HEAR.

For now I leave you just the opportunity that occurred after Jesus declared *"Father, Why have you forsaken me?"* The sins of the world were then forgiven through His resurrection and re-creation.

For you, whatever has been has been. A question remains. Are you to be or not to be? The Holy Spirit is live inside of you, so:

Re Create, Start and Circulate all over again!

Then once you are satisfied you have done what ever it is that you set out to do:

Re Create, Start and Circulate all over again!

Then when it doesn't work this time. Have a cry if you need to. This will pass and then you can have renewed belief in yourself, getting ready to recreate, then start and circulate all over again!

Never stop. Help is on the way. "How are you?"

SECTION 3

How Powerful are you?

Measuring beyond measure

Chapter 26:   RE-CREATE TO RE-EMERGE

I could have concluded HEAR at the end of Section 2 and the book may have seemed complete to you. However for me the "what" and "why" is not enough without a deeper examination and experience of the HOW. How each of us can move ourselves into action - Actually how each can live beyond measure!

Whether you the reader are an agnostic, or of faith and belief, having read this book I hope that you carry now a deepening desire to hear and then action what is central to yourself. How can you not look to re-create within your world of "How am I?"

Therefore I am going to attempt to give you "How to" ways, designed to bring you "out of your box" and serve you, whoever you may be and however you may think and believe you know.

Journeying the Cs, from that euphoric moment of simple creation, gives us new eyes to see and clear ears to hear and the opportunity to re-create and then re-create again and again, recurring as they must throughout our lifetime.

Embracing re-creation is vital. It allows us to live Live. It allows to shift into this live moment of our lives, not in the past scars or triumphs. Re-creation lets us be faithful in the freshness of our lives. Re-creation lets us re birth ourselves, releasing what did not serve us, and yet honoring what did, and bringing that forward with us to live Live.

Often when we hear the word re-create we hear a negative criticism. From school we heard "Go away and do it again" and we have to recreate the homework, or later "this isn't working, re-create it." The idea of moving into re-creating something was often viewed as a chore and boring. However I now view the chance and the choice to re-create as a fascinating and fresh opportunity to hear and use everything I have learned from my shaping of yesterday for what I choose to look at today to help impact my future.

From first conception, an idea appears brilliant and yet through time we experience the development of the creation idea through the lenses of some or each of the 13Cs. In addition we have collective input from friends, business colleagues, communities and cultures and we see what can now be re-created. The question is always are you open to receive and take on the input and re-create with the freshness and enthusiasm of when you had the original thought? Rumi stated "Beyond the reasoning of right and wrong there is a field, I will meet you there" and recreating means you and I just have another chance to jump into the field and meet more brilliant people like you. This is vital if we are to be innovative in ways to serve our planet's needs.

As you have travelled across the Cs of this book what have you rediscovered to be true and authentic about yourself? Have you received insights that perhaps you didn't have around your initial creative thoughts before other Cs cropped up to give you new ways of thinking - some of which had you shrinking rather than stretching into your life and ideas?

Let's look of some clear examples of the choice to re-create today. In the past others before us have created what in the moment was hailed as brilliance, until later when others point out that there may be a different upper path to take.

Inventions: The idea of creating the automobile was of course one of the most brilliant ideas in history. The idea of creating a V12 engine that consumed twelve gallons of petrol or gasoline was at the time brilliant. The idea of making petrol and gasoline the fuel choice of combustible engine shafts was brilliant, and the speed of these cars was utterly brilliant to many drivers. Yet we see all of this with new eyes today as we recreate better fuel consumption and less pollution with electricity, with air, with water.

An Inventor is a Re-Creator in Action.

After struggling to develop a working electric light-bulb for months if not years, Thomas Edison was interviewed by a young reporter who boldly asked Mr. Edison if he felt like a failure and if he thought he should just give up by now. Perplexed, Edison replied, "Young man, why would I feel like a failure? And why would I ever give up? I now know definitively over nine thousand ways that an electric light bulb will not work. Success is almost in my grasp." Shortly after that, and over ten thousand attempts, Edison invented the light bulb.

Are you prepared to look at something ten thousand times?

In business I was fortunate to create a company that tens of thousands rapidly thought was brilliant in its vision. Three years later the community had looked to add enhancements to the idea and saw it through different lenses as they sought ways to re-create their community messaging. I was probably given ten thousand pieces of feedback as to how the community should be directed. I too had journeyed through the 13Cs from the creation of the idea and once the community started to come into its own force and ideas, I looked at how to recreate my own role in the company, knowing that it was inevitable for the community to direct me. I had given speeches from the outset of the company gatherings about chaotic emergence and the need to co-create and circulate. I even set up the company so that I would not own it. Yet with all the barriers that we had intended to lay bare, it still took painful time for the community to embrace their ownership and for me to let go as its leader. Interestingly it started to emerge more when the President became a woman. She spoke and acted in a way that mirrored the community that had initially gathered and so the community stuck to her and then found their power. The community allowed me to buff my mirror through them and see my own identity more clearly and know better in the next moments of my life. I had new opportunities as I inquired how to create meaningful new ideas with re-created business and social relationships from many years ago, asking to be involved in what I know now! Re-creation often just layers new ideas and people on ideas already experienced and identified for their strengths and weaknesses. Re creation often turns something into a success!

Businesses are re-creating themselves everywhere. For centuries we have looked at survival of the fittest and winner takes all as the business mantra. Now we are seeing interesting joint ventures with major national corporations re-creating the work place with authentic expression for all, the environment, the workers, the consumers, and the business leaders themselves.

As an example the clothing and textile industry has been under massive chaotic fire for years accused of slave child labor, workers huddled together, forced to work for long hours making the clothes you decide to buy in your shopping mall store. As your demand increased for lesser priced, higher quality clothes, the situation got worse. Made in Sri Lanka, Made in India, Made in China, Made in Mexico carried a compromising tag, that most of us unconsciously ignored.

A few years ago approached to be involved in producing a concert on a beach in paradise, and launch a foundation and local social enterprise initiatives into Sri Lanka by a wonderful family that were introduced to me through Larry Ross, publicist for the Billy Graham Crusade. With thousands of artisans already supported by fair trade and the advancements of organic clothing materials, it was only a matter of time that enough people would question the answers to answer the questions and Authentic Expression would emerge. You, the consumer, have become savvy, putting pressure on the high street and the high street has answered the call with new eco-friendly and fair trade fashion lines. For this to happen and in the volumes of stock that it needs to happen with, the essential ingredient had to be factored in. The development of the eco-factory environment for the workers. Now this has been achieved.

The first one hundred per cent carbon neutral, one hundred per cent green, one hundred per cent ethical factory. It's situated two hours' drive from Colombo, the capital of Sri Lanka and has been funded and built by Marks & Spencer in partnership with a local manufacturer MAS, also a chief supplier of Victoria Secret and Gap. This working shrine to sustainability is producing one of the world's first eco underwear:

There are 'cool roofs', which reflect the sun. There are gigantic windows that magically let in natural light, but keep heat out. There is rainwater harvesting, which has reduced water consumption by fifty per cent, and Sri Lanka's biggest array of solar panels, reducing electricity consumption by forty per cent. And staggeringly, every single one of the workers has a view of palm trees and the natural lake with its lily pads, flocks of pelicans and the mountains beyond. Every single worker!

There are effluent treatment works that convert waste into drinking water, and M&S insists each of its factories treats its waste. Instead of air conditioning there is an ingenious system called 'evaporative cooling,' which uses seventy-five per cent less energy. The factory, making a high percentage of all M&S undies, (and if an expat asks for anything to be sent to them it is M&S undies) was opened in April 2008 by Sir Stuart Rose, executive chairman of Marks & Spencer.

Early in 2007, having watched an Inconvenient Truth, Laurie David's documentary about climate change through the eyes and actions of USA's nearly President, Al Gore, Sir Stuart came up with Plan A, because there is no plan B. It is a five-year, 100-point initiative to take the lead on environmental and ethical issues. Much has already been achieved: food carrier bag usage is down by eighty per cent; Seventy million coat hangers have been recycled (staff are now trained to say, 'Can I recycle your hanger for you?' as they wrap your purchases); Ninety per cent of food packaging is recyclable; fair-trade cotton sales are up one hundred per cent; and the 'Wash at thirty' campaign has saved over fifty thousand tons of CO2.

M&S already bans leather from India because of its ethical and environmental issues, inspects all its farms like its cashmere farms in inner Mongolia, and is committed to changing all its pork to free range. This building is a green testament and culmination of the brand's commitment to trading fairly.

They are very into 'empowerment' here. Women, who make up ninety per cent of the one thousand workforce, are encouraged to maintain a good work life balance, and to climb their way up the career ladder: A third of management are female. The factory has deliberately been built in a rural area, so that employees can remain in their villages.

We can build sustainable artisan village models around the catalyst of vibrant profitable factories that hold all the values of a Plan A because there cannot be a Plan B.

Samih Sawiris and his family were beer makers in Egypt with a factory that overlooked an idyllic coral coast line of the Red Sea. Now Orascom is one of the most significant companies in the world and if you visit his masterful resort, El Gouna, in the midst of a chaotic emerging nation, you will experience a sustained eco environment community with a power grid and water works sustained through the environmental programs of its developers.

Plan A is clear. What can you do to enhance it?

What is your "Plan A" business environment?

Millions of company executives today recognize the need to re-create the 'job." What is the job, what is the work place for the job?

What was retail last year is now direct marketing this year? How do we re-create the sales message that our conscious consumers now demand from us? What was traditional television advertising is now internet, social media marketing, and cause driven advertising. What happened to the power of the sixty second television commercial in between our favorite television shows? Now these precious and costly spots are fast forwarded by you as you command the digital remote in your living room. How do the advertising agencies recreate and how do you the consumer re-create how you want to receive marketing messaging so you can be informed in your choices? How do we recreate what clearly needs to be re-created? Recycling is fast becoming not only cool but big business. Now more often, biodegradable alternatives are being created. A program I supported in Boise, Idaho has women coming out of prison cleaning empty wine bottles collected from local restaurants. They lathe the bottles, cutting them into tumblers, then sandblast a company logo and sell them back to the restaurant or to the general consumer for profit. Most great ideas for recreating and recycling are simple.

As we all come through chaotic emergence, what are we able to HEAR more accurately in the world that then reflects more clearly into ourselves so that we rediscover the direction of our life's purpose? There are people that we meet that immediately impress us, individuals that have clearly recreated their lives. Lives that many, including themselves, may have judged to be in tatters and ruins. Each one now a radiant God-given example of what can be achieved. Each one able to inspire and help lift us from any shadow that might be holding us back.

Candace Cable, Joanna Owen, Jennifer Field, Amina, Kimmie Weeks, Louise Ashby, and Brad Cummings. They had no choice. 'God get me out of here' or 'it serves me to be lesser than' was not an option. They were awake to the responsibility of their lives, forced through unique circumstance. Disaster invaded Candace Cable's life in 1975. She was living her life as a blackjack dealer, working the casinos of Lake Tahoe. Her shift was over and she met up with her boyfriend in a bar where he preceded to drink too much. She asked him, pleaded with him not to drive and to let her drive them home. He was adamant that he was OK to drive and he did and she let him.   The jeep went off the windy lakeside road, Candace was ejected from her seat and her spinal cord was immediately snapped.

At the age of twenty one, she would never walk again. It took her a year to come to the recognition, even the desire of re-creation. A year when she wanted to kill herself. A year when she said every day "Why Me?" However, out of this tragic circumstance emerged a woman with the character and will to become one of today's most successful world athletes. Candace Cable became ranked number one in wheelchair racing competition from 1984 to 1990. She has won seventy-five marathons, including six Boston Marathons (1981, '82, '85, '86, '87, & '88) and has set world records in every distance throughout her twenty one year career.

Winning two Olympic medals in three Summer Olympic Games, Candace participated in the only exhibition event for the disabled. Additionally, she has won nine Gold medals in five Summer Paralympic Games. Since 1990, Candace has been competing on the United States Disabled Ski Team, winning three Paralympic medals on the Alpine team. In 1994, she switched to the Cross Country Team, and continued her distinguished career.

Candace is a very dear friend today. I utterly love her. Showing "limitation" as a state of mind, Candace speaks all over the USA about the celebration of human spirit strength. Using examples from her own life, she demonstrates how both able-bodied and disabled individuals face similar struggles to realize their fullest potential. She focuses on: re-evaluating our lives constantly, not setting limits on ourselves, keeping a sense of humor, staying physically fit to be mentally fit, and taking complete responsibility for our lives. From dispelling the myth that if you have a physical disability you cannot be a whole person, to finding solutions to life's problems through creativity and imagination, Candace can help you see "disability" is only a word.

In 2012 we screamed together as witnesses of the wonderfully empowering ParaOlympics Games. NBC had chosen not to pay the nominal fee to extend their Olympic broadcast contract to cover these extraordinary athletes overcome all their conflicts to compete at the highest level of human endeavor.

Candace and I sat arm in arm as USA women basketball players crashed into their Chinese rivals and overcame a huge deficit to win with the last score of overtime. How great is sport?

Other friends are the same and you know the same people as I do and if they are not these names below they are names you adore in your own life....... and if you don't have examples, you should, because their positive projection into your life is a massive gift for you in your future.

My first friend, the young love of my life that I mentioned in the beginning of HEAR, Joanna Owen, went from becoming disabled in a wheelchair for life at a tender age to being legal ambassador and re-writing the disability laws for the workplace in the UK.

Jennifer Field, rushing to a date with her boyfriend, slid her car into a tractor-trailer and became instantly a one out of ten on the vegetable chart. A chart used to assess the potential recovery of brain injuries. Jen's mum, Joanna is the great-granddaughter of Marshall Field, the great USA department store creator and like so many other mothers whose children have had tragic accidents, did not quit finding clinics and remedies. Joanna did not quit and Jennifer did not quit. Today Jennifer has a quite brilliant one woman show that she performs around the world.

Louise Ashby is today a walking menace to beep machines in every shop and airport. Why? Because she has over two hundred and fifty plates and screws in her reconstructed model face after a horror accident on the corner of Doheny and Sunset, five weeks after arriving in Hollywood to follow her dreams. Today Louise is an example of life re-created and through her own learning, is re-gifting her desire to help others with a vibrant life coaching practice.

Each of these courageous angels have chosen to turn the chaos of their human misery into a life of cooperative divine ministry. They awake, as Dante did, and walk their triumphant journey to remove those living in this life from the state of misery, and lead them to the state of felicity.

All the thousands of women that I have been blessed to meet who carry the HIV virus in Africa. Amina is special to me as is her daughter Noraya. I met them abruptly in the middle of the road of my life. They endured the worst circumstance in the worst slum of Korogocho surrounded by four generations of an HIV family,, and

Noraya was week with pin legs, purple, bruised, and was nearing her death. We prayed and then I offered a micro loan. Hope takes a second as does belief. Later Amina built her business, educated her children and wore pretty clothes and was a proud woman. Noraya got to grow into a fine young woman. Today they are immense women amongst millions of women today who are at the forefront of re-creating our world. Are you with them? Now it is your time to Re-Create with confidence.

Then there is the sideswipe that comes at anyone of us at any time that rocks our safe existence. A job that is lost with no warning. A partner who suddenly cheats.

One friend of mine, Brad Cummings, stands out for being sideswiped and demonstrates the cause and effect of what may then come as part of a true destiny. He was the young associate pastor of the church that I went to every Sunday during the year before 9/11. The Vineyard church in Malibu was packed every Sunday, with overflow areas outside and great speakers, cool community and young Christian rock music inside. In fact the lead singer of LifeHouse, which was the single of the year in the mainstream Billboard charts in the USA, was the youth worship singer. The senior pastor was one of the most engaging speakers you could ever wish to hear, and the services were full of Hollywood actors, Malibu surfers and home owners, anyone who wanted a great experience of God and community on a Sunday morning. Services were added to accommodate the need. The call from the altar often said God had descended on Malibu's coast line and we all sensed this. Brad was honest and he was direct about church outside the institution of church and I would go to the Sunday evening services as well which Brad led himself with again incredible music.

Then out of the blue of the Pacific Ocean that the church overlooked, suddenly cracks appeared. Without going into the story and drama of the goings on, the church fell apart in an instant. Brad did what he felt was honorable and integral and exposed things within the church. It struck to the core of the board and the senior pastor, which was very sad for us all to hear. Chaos ensued, as the old habits tried to hold on yet within weeks the church and all that we all saw as a safe central community was no longer. We were all side swept and bewildered, but nothing like Brad who had a very young family of four children.

Having been at the center of this incredibly thriving community impacting so greatly upon the area of Malibu and Los Angeles, Brad found himself out. Everyone close to Brad and his family said, "Just start another church" and everyone who was not close to him blamed him for the church falling apart. Brad did not look to fix the issue. The way church has often reacted to issue with churches is to just say, "let's start another one." Yet Brad knew this was not for him. His thoughts and ideas were in relation to mainstream media. For years we would sit and talk about this and Brad would continue to be tested. To pay his bills Brad spent years doing laboring as a landscape gardener and became recognized by the Malibu set for his hard work.

Then after a few years one of his friends gave him a copy of a manuscript that he had written. The man had never had anything published and he wrote the novel for his children. Yet I remember the day Brad come to me with it. He knew its importance. It was a novel about forgiveness. Brad gave it to me and I did not read it. He sent the manuscript to twenty four Christian publishers and they all turned it down as it was not Christian enough. They said give it to the secular publishers. They turned it down as too Christian. It fell through the cracks of all their right and wrong checklists. What did the experts hear when they read "The Shack" that made them all reject it? Brad charged up twelve credit cards to the maximum and set up a publishing company out of his home with his fellow out of church blogger, Wayne. The two of them went out and promoted the book themselves.

To date they have sold over fifteen million copies of the manuscript. "The Shack." It has become the biggest self-published book in the history of the New York Times Best Seller list. They set up an international joint venture company with the established publishing house, Hodder Hachette. Brad didn't know that he was being fashioned by "this or something better" for his highest good, and that there was supreme confidence in him. Yet seasons continue and the confidence in one moment can be tested in the next. Clarity, or what we know as clarity, can turn to confusion and conflict as with the contract relationships that then surfaced amongst the principals. Massive financial success can often introduce us to personalities of others that we also did not know that we knew. It is critical to remain in an open compassion-filled re-creating energy.

This is a story like so many that perhaps you know of people that had apparent disasters hit them, and yet years later they point to that very chaotic time in their life as the very turning point of their life. A choice point that may not have been able to avoid, or a direction they may not have had either the courage or the foresight to take. Yet in their seemingly helpless vulnerability, the choice been choreographed for them from on high, and then time allowed for something better to emerge.

What is critical, at all times, whether it be during acute crisis for yourself, your family or even your country, is to not lose your own confidence. It can be so hard when unemployment rises, when you see graduates with law degrees lining up with everyone else to find a job in every city, when you do not have money.

What is vital is not to lose.....................Your Mojo.

CONFIDENCE

When anger rages, despair spiraling.
When hurt vices the heart,
causing floundering in the abyss of despair.
When all that you see and hear tells how you are
different, alone, persecuted,
and every circumstance around you seeps fear, distrust and
darkness.
When now as you judge that God has deserted you
And believe why would he leave you at this time of need
Breathe a moment and reflect inside this solitary thought,

Could it be that this supreme moment
is God's confidence within you,
Knowing that your next step towards light can be without need,
Content that He waits in the wings of your shaping

As you are all that it takes to make this choice of freedom.
You are all that it takes. Your freedom.
And in our reflection of your own connected self,
May this simple prayer grant insight
That our differences give liberty
For you to look out upon how great our world's beauty is.

Chapter 27:   GLOBAL SHIFT HERE AND NOW

A constant question that we ask on behalf of the world is "Can we have a Global Shift?

We are faced with either living out our individual lives determined by our histories - legacies of our past, or we can save the human race from itself by serving our world and uniting our technologies and capabilities to be the co-creators of our human destiny."

I believe the answer is a resounding, triumphant "Yes" to the new emerging alternative!

You are IT. A light is alive inside of you and you are connecting with millions of others at this time.

It is so obviously the only path we should be choosing yet how many of us still exist apathetically in the trance of "someone else can take care of that." Through awareness rather than ignorance and through awakened action, we can no longer consciously give ourselves permission to be asleep to the converging crisis and chaos that is seen, experienced and felt by you, this generation. It propels us to urgent action and choice for change. Now.

Importantly we also have birthed a generation, like no other, that is collectively capable: able to respond to this world situation. We are a generation that in our chaos, can give ourselves the choice to confess, to be compassionate towards ourselves, connect together and have a conscious response-ability to support an earth worth living on,

You are IT. The IT man. The IT woman. The IT girl. Go get It. Most importantly Go Be It.

How do I do this? How do we do that? This is all the discussion needs to be about.

Throughout HEAR I trust and hope that you have become more aware of what is possible, where the journey has taken you and how you can make your choices to help you continue to move towards a more meaningful life. The How is critical now for you and for all of humanity. How can you be stimulated into these choices?

Nutrition

We eat forty nine billion dollars worth of ice cream a year, yet choosing to spend only nineteen billion dollars per year would mean we could end malnutrition on the planet.......yet we have malnutrition that both kills in areas of famine - and kills in the streets of your city from obesity.

If we grow high yield crops such as Moringa Trees - in Africa and other areas of our world, we would create super nutritional meals to deal with malnutrition for those that starve and also create an active ingredient that can combat obesity. This would create a dual purpose product providing local and international trade.

What other innovative ideas can we employ to end malnutrition? We can listen and follow the direction of people like Jamie Oliver who at twenty-four simply said, "I want to change the world through food." Who has a clearer statement of purpose than that? What ever Jamie says...do (at time of writing anyway, I am a huge fan!)

A world that is a garden of Eden, but still without food?

There are between seventy and one hundred million land mines in the world. No one is quite sure how many. Someone has an incident with a land mine every twenty minutes and as governments put them there, governments don't often take responsibility to clear them. The consequence is that immense fertile lands lie idle like giant kitchens without any food. These mines cost on average over one thousand dollars each to remove, until now, until technology changes humanity. Innovation transforms. Sir Richard Branson and Mike Kendrick birthed Mineseeker with the support of Nelson Mandela and the help of their friends: an organization with a radar that maps the world at one hundred square meters a second. Every land mine can now be identified, and since currently landmines cover only fifteen per cent of the designated land mine areas of our world (previously it was extremely difficult to know where they are and where they are not). Identifying where they are will result immediately in eighty five percent of fertile, food producing land being returned to its people even before the first land mine is taken out of the ground. Then the cost of de-mining drops to three dollars per mine. A seemingly endless problem has a solution. Yet .... have we seen this innovation funded by governments? Not yet!

Technology must play a vital role in the fields of compassion of our world. How can we support innovation for humanity better in private enterprise?

Education

We know that we spend one trillion dollars on protecting ourselves from ourselves yet ten billion dollars would have every child in primary education..... yet out of the four fifths of our global school children, only one out of five go on to a basic secondary education. It is pathetic that we can't pool our resources, collaborate and circulate our brilliance to have every child educated. Sixty percent of children in Africa are not in school, which adds up to more than all the kids who are in school in the USA. One mobile or tablet company could change this tomorrow. Let us hope, trust and believe.

There is no more powerful weapon than education.

What can you learn today and how can you help teach this to another tomorrow? How can we train up teachers and get children connected all over the world? How can we set up vocational training and empowerment colleges everywhere? How can you build one school and empower many?

Health

We give health care insurance of thirty five cents per family per month to micro loan recipients within the poorest slum in Nairobi. In addition nearly ninety eight percent of those on the programs pay back the loans - and have the benefit of health care for their families. Yet in 2014 in the USA fifty million nonelderly people are uninsured and a mother who has no health care gives birth every minute, while the rest of America had to give away sixteen percent of their entire domestic spend to health care. Which is the first world?

Health care for all - How do we achieve this in countries where it is not available like this, such as in the USA. Even the simple health care issues of our world need fixing: It's not easy to find a cure for cancer or AIDS, yet it is easy to find a cure for the disease bearer that kills more people than AIDS, Malaria and TB put together.......Dirty Water! Can you help us fix this today?

How can you save or catch water today? Can you not run the tap whilst you are brushing your teeth? Can you put a rain harvesting drum on your house and add a purifier to it? How else can you help reduce the cost of your water or recreate a situation where you don't have to pay for it again? Who can invent inexpensive applications to give pure water to all? A great example of this is the water straw that purifies the water as you drink through the straw.

We are using up our last supplies of fossil fuel too quickly.

What ground breaking solutions can you make possible - and who is going to create a shared resources web site for our world? You?

Who is going to invent and facilitate community owned and run energy supply, with pricing not controlled to gauge you?

How can we continue to find innovative re-cycling opportunities for waste management?

Seven billion poops a day. Every body poops and one billion of us don't have lavatories. Now microbe bacteria are being attached to waste tanks and can eat through the solids and the paper to leave clear water as they pass through three tanks.

I sense if we can shed light on poop consciousness, each of our own poop consciousness not to labor the point, we should be able to be conscious of everything else in our day.

There is so much for you to innovate today. So many of us are waiting for your brilliance to innovate, so we can join together around your inspired ideas, and to assist in their implementation into the fabric of your world.

You have a choice right now as to the culture you are going to demonstrably embrace through your own actions and promote to others. I champion the choice of this "the WE generation" now as we circulate "abundance" away from a few to "we the people" it is for us to combine food +water + health + energy + education + micro-loans + social enterprise promoting fair wage and move from immediate and immense scarcity to creating "an enough world" so we secure a thriving planet.

Today directly because of the economic and environmental crisis, the West is learning faster than it ever has to now face its issues and be authentic. It is re creating itself in the face of ultimate need. The West had better take a closer look at Africa and even countries like Vietnam. Bangladesh, Sri Lanka and Liberia as they are teaching themselves fast to benefit and serve each other.

Over one hundred and twenty million micro social entrepreneurs linking together through micro investment, micro production, micro distribution.

Our world is moving itself into good hands.

Chapter 28:   THE HEAR TOOL BOX

Taking a leap of faith on to your learning line.

Its time in HEAR for you to bring it forward. Whatever "it" is.

The learning life of life is where you have arrived at, so whatever goal line you have been comfortable defending, now is the time to take the defense down. Let everything come at you.

What is the destiny of you, your world, our planet? You are to recognize your purpose by buffing your own mirror, releasing yourself from your own road blocks, and instead creating your Ideal Scene and Priority Projects in the exercises that follow; then you will be innovating by shining in your brilliance into your fellow human-beings and as a result of what is possible within you, your world will be destined to hear better and all will become good.

However Awareness is nothing without Action.

Destiny requires Action and a sustaining demonstration of cultural change. A new demonstration of a We-Culture. You and I must choose to take action. Faith, belief and hope must be coupled with good works, or they will die.

When we do and we are united in action then "We the People" is destined to re-introduce the Insignificant to being Significant. To the very least the most is given and the Kingdom of Heaven resides right now in the hearts of all men and women. The ability to interpret and action dreams lies with every father and mother, each child, all people, all races, all colors and every creed.

Now that you have reached this point in HEAR, you are more able to hear inside and know a little better in your next second. So these tools are here to help you implement and find what you are looking for and then support you to achieve these goals and integrate their results over the next period of your life.

Ah-ha Moments are to be captured by you, nurtured and blossomed into the brilliance from whence they originated. The brilliant you, the light that chooses now to come out from behind the bushel that you yourself set up as you judged yourself.

In the past you may have had the most fabulous of ah-ha moments, when passion for an idea that will change your life or your business's direction for ever, was so clear. Yet a week later it was forgotten in the garbage bins of judgment or forgetfulness. "I am not rich." "I don't have time." "Who am I to do that? I am not Oprah so I can't do that." "I can't convince my team mates and management." "It's clear in a confusing way to me that I can't connect with anyone to hear me. "

So what happened?

Brilliance, Passion, God-ing within you through Enthusiasm. All Ah-has are alive and well as you put your head on the pillow, excitement keeping you awake, but then paralysis.

The tragedy is the cause and effect of this.

There may be no great ailment than the expectation that, "I can't."

In the dawn of the next day you lift your head off the pillow, yet the Ah-ha lies there paralyzed on the pillow, and the din of doubt is deafening you to your own silence.

Until now. No longer is this necessary if you choose to HEAR and intuitively act in the next second of your life. I use these tools as my own tool box for life. I measure my life performances with them, just as I recognize where an idea, relationship, business idea or issue is during the journey of the 13Cs.

It's time to realize that you are brilliant enough to own and implement any and all of your "Ahas," to demonstrate to yourself that you can shift your own demo-culture.

7 Tools to add to 13Cs

Since so much of HEAR is about: "How do we do this now for ourselves and our world?" I wish to serve you with additional support to help you activate yourself and then sustain you along your journey. I hold a belief that the 13Cs have given you a wonderful canvas and road map to live your life thoroughly. If you are able to retain an awareness of the C signposts as you come up to them, you will be propelled through the flow of them. Now is the time to help with the birthing of your ideas, then how to expand them and then how to keep you on course.

I therefore offer you seven sequential tools, so simple to use, that can help you find your way today, and which will facilitate you to hear yourself and know better what to do in any and all situations. This applies to all of you, wherever you are in your life, what ever your belief and faith, whatever challenge you may face and whatever brilliant ideas may be coming from you.

I know this for myself as I use them. I trust them for anyone.

I work them with Liberian child soldiers and with Mayan villagers and the poorest of the poor around the world. The tools work easily with them as their thirst for education is evident, as is "to the least the most is given."

I work with them with business leaders and billionaires and the tools work easily with them as they constantly look to "tune themselves up" and thirst most understandings about the world they live in and to help them with the direction of their legacy and destiny.

It doesn't matter who you are, they meet you wherever you are at in your life. They are simple and they are all founded within the good books. Everybody can use them fully. They need no PhD education, no vast user manual. Some of these have been aired in similar form derived from what was central, others I have re-designed for myself and now gift them to you. None of them are new.

There are no follow up to them, no course that you have to do to be successful. They are simple ways and tools that I enjoy and have seen immeasurable benefit uttering. They are as proven as the tool kit in my garage, as a hammer is at thumping nails or a saw is at cutting wood. I have learnt not to question their form, or their methodology and I therefore have every confidence in them when I do pick them up, and when something doesn't work I don't blame my tools!

What I hope here is, that by carrying this tool box with you for the rest of your life in association with the Holy Spirit consciousness that you possess through the 13Cs of HEAR, that you are saying, "Yes" to this vital opportunity of being an ambassador to your own possibilities. If you are the best you can be, you will become better at serving others and ultimately your world. To start with you can simply accept the tools to better support Ah-ha moments and a more conscious insight and outlook as to how to manage more effectively with all that will come towards you to deal with in your daily life.

Please note you will be required to choose to Vision, and then you will require to take Action as:

Vision + Action = Mission

It is while you take action, any action and experience the resistance or flow of implementing action steps, that you will be gifted the opportunity of how to integrate HEAR through a few out of the box tools into any situation or encounter you are to have.

The more action steps you take, the more you stretch into your unknown, the greater the opportunity for you to confront "the issue is not the issue, it is how I am responding to the issue which is the issue."

The more you consciously meet an issue, the greater the opportunity you have of finally releasing a block or barrier.

HEAR OUT-OF-YOUR-BOX

Taking Inventory

Tool 1   Silence. What do you hear?
Tool 2   Where are you in your life?
            Current NOW Scene with 13C signposts
Tool 3   What is limiting you?
            Unblocking your hearing and reclaiming your
            brilliance

Emerging into living

Tool 4   Identifying your quality and
            Positive projection purpose statement

Implementing your life

Tool 5   Creating your Ideal Scene and
            Priority Project
Tool 6   Putting your Priority Project into Action

Integrating your life

Tool 7   How Am I?

PREPARE TO HEAR

The journey you may have been experiencing through this book and now are embarking on for yourself is designed to bring forward your gifts, talents, skills, and resources so you can become a most impressive force for the positive transformation of your own life, your business activities and the lives of everyone on the planet. This journey opens your heart and connects your mind both to yourself and all of humanity for the highest good. You are stepping into your brilliance or up through the gears in the necessary work with your fellows, partners and business colleagues.

For this to be accomplished I believe that you have to be conscious in your innovation methodology for yourself and your world. This commences with clear insight and is carried out with a converging plan made up of your Ideal Scene and inner and outer action steps to accomplish your goals.

In HEAR, through the journey of the Cs, you have been asked many questions and given the opportunity to pause, ponder and journal some insights and outlooks around your life. I suggest before you move on to the HEAR tools that you go back and review your thoughts. Then I suggest that you do the exercises in sequential order.

As you go through the exercises, especially as you have just experienced the 13Cs, you will notice new or familiar thoughts and feelings coming to your consciousness. It is also very possible that you also may experience resistance at times. Please be compassionately accepting of yourself, as the old does not like to disappear and will keep trying to hang on and this includes your historic habits, character and energies. This is natural and just needs a little consciousness to move through. You also need to be prepared to add the ingredients of trust, hope and belief if they are missing. Armed with the awareness and consciousness of the 13Cs use this process as a way to compassionately discover and become more and more the re-creation of who you were clearly created to be. You were created with irrevocable skill sets and HEAR, combined with these tools, can now help you bring these forth in a way that empowers and fulfills you at the deepest level.

Tool 1:   Silence – Space for Healing and Wellness

For any meaningful exercise that you look to apply to yourself the most universal tool to apply initially is - Silence.

So be quiet. Infact hear this. Please be quiet....for a while.

Silence is the first tool of any counselor when working with a client. In psychology we are taught that the first two skills of counseling are heart centered listening and silence. Silence allows the client to actually hear themselves more easily and also, as no response is given to their story or detail of blame towards another, the client then speaks again and usually hears themselves better, going deeper and deeper to a place of authenticity and then reflection of their own involvement in the story.

Silence is golden.

Like HEAR's 13Cs peeling you first back to creation, silence gives you the best place to start. You are about to talk to yourself and create in your life. You should be able to hear yourself. Look to have silence around you and through your own body and mind. Do nor look to bring things and thoughts into your mind, although you can pray initially that God speaks through you and to you.

Try to have your mind clear itself. Be in as quiet and nurturing place as you can find. I am rushing around a lot and seem to find a shower, or a run brings me to a place where the chatter stops and I find myself in my own silence. Planes, trains and automobiles too, although be careful too. The policeman did not forgive me when I ran a red light in Los Angeles one day whist meditating!

If you can meditate in bed for only one hundred and twenty seconds in your early morning, your life with change.

Imagine yourself as a great conductor and you are now listening to the assembled orchestra in front of you. An orchestra made up of instruments crafted through your life by your own hand. You are the player of each instrument. In your own silence you are about to hear your greatest symphony. The space between the notes brings forward wellness.

Chapter 29: TAKING INVENTORY

Now lets look at you. Right away let's examine where you are and what's holding you back. There are HEAR Cs that you must bring to these tools and the exercises around them. These include:

Choice - that you are prepared to take ownership of who and where you are today.

Confession - that you identify everything you can.

Compassion - that you are not punishing yourself. Knowing that all your circumstances have been played out with you doing the best you knew how, even if in hindsight you do not admire or like what you see or feel about yourself.

Navigation - It is very unlikely that you will be able to end up where you want to go if you don't know where you are starting from. It is essential that the initial tools help you, compassionately and consciously, to be clear as to the circumstance and map of your life. Right now where is your life and how are you doing in it? This has no energy or focus on what you hope for but what is really happening to you.

Tool 2: NOW Scene Creation - and identifying where you are within the 13Cs.

NOW Scene Creation is a first step exercise designed to take inventory and stock. It's an exercise many of us collectively have been taking for the world. Yet for us to be effective in dealing with our global issues, we must be prepared to also take stock within ourselves.

Not easy when it comes to yourself? Not easy to truly understand your own world. Many of us don't. Yet it helps you clearly view all the ways in which you are spending your time today, so that you can make conscious decisions about your focus as you create your future. This is hugely beneficial whether you view it as the creative flow of where you are at today or as a gut retching confession about the deepest of isolated past secrets that have you seized in mire actions.

The power of this exercise comes directly from revealing and choosing to acknowledge with yourself how you choose to spend your time today. This enables you to hear accurately about yourself. Also I would like to stress that the deeper the cut you take with yourself, the greater the risk of exposing yourself and really looking to be truthful in the situations of your life, the more likely it is that you will be freeing up these spaces filling them with positive energy and actions. Let it all out!

Start writing as freely as you can everything that is happening in your life at the moment. Be sure to write down everything you are currently doing, working on, and thinking about. Note any judgment reaction in your mind as well as any feeling shifts in your emotions or in your body. Do not write about anything tomorrow or in your future.

Areas to contemplate: business, spirituality, relationships and or sex, family members health and wellness, personal finance, travel, humanitarian, service, philanthropy, or any other important area in your life. As you contemplate each of these areas, take the time to focus your energy on those elements of each that cause the most intense emotional reaction.

Observe your own reactions. Where are the 13Cs showing up?

Be conscious and take note of which Cs are showing up in each area of your life at any time. In every incident of my life, business building, relationship with myself or other, whether physical, mental or emotional response, I know today that anyone of the Cs can be in action, often shuffling themselves around based on how different aspects of my life are in their own evolution. If it is early in an idea it is likely to be creation or childhood. If it's in 'the should we do this or that' I might sense confusion. I look at compromise that an action may be bringing up in my beliefs and the judgment that is in my mind because of its emergence as a life scene topic. Occasionally I sense conflict within and it can then show itself outwardly as a crisis with a clear choice of how I want to react to it. How great it is to know that the issue is not the issue, but how I choose to hear and react to the issue which is the issue.

I may have a project or relationship or personal exercise that has gone from creation to confusion and now I have broken through with greater clarity and clear conscious action and it is with ease and grace that I move forward. There may be areas of my authentic self that I am now showing clearly and am easily able to share with others in connection and co-creation. I may even have the freedom now to circulate my abundant resources.

Know then it is OK to have ALL the 13Cs showing up in aspects of your life scene today.

It is natural and it is progressive circulation that continues to help you shift from old to new emerging brilliance. Therefore with the NOW Scene Exercise look to mark off the Cs that are showing up for you. Is your current core relationship with another in chaos or compromise or indeed have you just felt the flutter of Cupid's gentle arrow across your heart as you enter into the creation of possibilities with another?

Apply the 13Cs to money and finance, relationships, business, travel, your own well being, your relationship with your children and others. Know always that this is an ever-emerging process since however wonderful and committed you are to this process, you are still ultimately limited to what you know you know. You will know more once you have completed the 7 Tools for the first time and been involved in your own actions. The learning line of life never ceases to introduce new self discoveries!

Pause to be conscious and reflect. Have you confessed to all that is present?

I recommend that before you do the next exercise, you take some time to go within and reflect on the areas in your NOW Scene Creation. There are those that for you are most passionate, rewarding and fulfilling. There may be others that intuitively you know you should be dealing with yet you have been ignoring, such as taxes, divorce or separation issues, company restructuring or solvency, bill payments or debt repayments.

This will help you recognize the activities, environments and experiences that strengthen you and bring you the most personal satisfaction and joy. It will also serve as a guide to direct you toward areas to focus on as you create your Ideal Scene (Tool 5).

Put your experience into words.

As you have identified your reality you actually have begun the process of journaling. Try to be as free form as you can be, as quickly as your ideas come into your mind you write it.

Initially it may center around what you predictably do every day like getting in the car and driving to work or driving the kids to and from school. It may relate to the fact you have found yourself traveling a lot and are now settling into a new city. You may have just fallen in or out of love or lost all your money and are struggling today to pay this month's utility bills. Also please, be honest with yourself and that means let yourself go deeper and don't ignore the patterns you want to liberate.

If you want to take an extra step on this second exercise as you lay out your life that is LIVE today, you may also feel you want to check in with someone that knows and loves you. You can let them know that you are doing this exercise for yourself and ask for their reality check in support. You do not have to take on what they say, however in this context you may find, with your heart exposed, that you hear something that can have a profound affect on your next steps. If you feel like it, you can share what you have written and have your supporter give you feedback.

Equally you may wish to quietly and intimately take your own thoughts and journal and move on.

Unblocking your hearing so you can re-create.

Navigation: It's time to pull up the anchors that have kept you from moving you into a full flow of life. Beyond the circumstance of your NOW scene you have had heavy unseen weights below the surface, weighing you down: old weed in your propellers. It is time for a new season clean! Let's identify the limiting beliefs that we can see have showed up in areas of your NOW Scene, and reframe them so you can step into action immediately.

What holds you back is only judgment and a lack of self-trust and a distortion of belief - Irrational Limiting Beliefs.

Many of the 13Cs will be showing up in this exercise. Adding to your understanding and clear energy around confusion, compromise, conflict and crisis will be a conscious re-shifting applying choice, confession, compassion and clarity. The use of this tool is essential as you witness your own chaotic emergence to authentic expression.

Tool 3:   What is Holding you back? – Until now!
Identifying And Reframing Limiting Beliefs

What beliefs about yourself are standing in your way of your being yourself?

Now that you carry the 13Cs in your conscious backpack, this tool is a positive way to work through any challenge and see the opportunity that is presented for growth and transformation, helping you work through the process of releasing limiting beliefs. When you use this tool, you will be constantly excited to know how easy it can be to release any thought that holds you back from expressing your talents and brilliance and moving forward to live an exceptionally fulfilling life.

So often we think something is a certain way, when in fact it is not the way we think it is at all. Realizing that everything in life is an opportunity can bring you closer to manifesting anything you set your heart and mind on. Letting go and surrendering to "what is" will allow you to walk in the freedom and power of who you really are. Remember *"Don't judge lest ye be judged."* Please, please don't keep judging yourself. This is really an exercise about turning your beliefs from being negativity defined and an "I can't do" attitude to a more positive approach, one of "I CAN do this."

For example, if you had the belief that you didn't know how to do a certain thing and therefore you would give up on yourself; you might now look at all the things you do know how to do relative to that goal. This awareness will help you see you "can do" certain things right now. You are always fully capable of anything you set your mind on. Once you have woken to hearing your unique message and voice, you will be open to every challenge ahead. Did Mandela or Gandhi possess or convey limiting belief? Do we today have any doubt that we can end poverty or come out of our own chaos?

There is always support available to help you as we connect, collaborate and co-create. In this exercise, you will work through any limiting beliefs that you may have about yourself and reframe them so that they become positive possibilities for you. This is how.

1.   Identify something in your life that has a negative emotional charge or feeling to it, such as a belief that you are "not enough" or that you "can't do" / "can't have" something that you are passionate about.

2.   Once you have identified the limiting belief, ask yourself the following questions:

o   〈   What is the judgment that I say to myself about myself?

o   〈   Does my intuition sense that this is a true reality or is it a false judgment?

o   〈   What am I not seeing or hearing about myself in this situation?

o   〈   What can I do differently?

o   〈   What have I being doing until now to self sabotage and hold myself back?

o   〈   What can I do differently to break through?

3.   When you have finished with these questions, ask yourself the following:

o   〈   What is the opportunity being presented to me that I can learn and grow from in this situation? What am I hearing now and what is this teaching me? What is the gift of this experience I may take with me on my journey from here?

o   〈   How can I use this situation to empower myself?

4.   Now do the following with each belief...

o   〈   Summaries how this limiting belief has limited you.

o   〈   Decide how you would rather be, act or feel.

o   〈   Create a statement that affirms the new way you hear yourself.

Here's an example of what this may look like:

Limiting Judgment:

"I don't have the money to start a resource sharing web site for young mums in my town, so why even try."

Reframed Belief:

"I will set up a Facebook or LinkedIn community group right now within my own post code and start sharing my ideas. I know I can make this happen as I have a Facebook or LinkedIn account."

Limiting Feeling:

"I feel small in God's eyes and not worthy to have success in my life as I worry about what so-and-so will think and say when I ask him/her for something"

Reframed Belief:

"I AM worthy and I have amazing God given gifts and talents that I will share with others. Nothing can stop me from being who I am and sharing my own resources with others. Nothing can stop me from asking others to share their resources with me, and I am not attached to how they will respond. I will not shrink so that others are more secure around me and it is clear I am powerful beyond measure."

As you can see, this exercise is about letting go of the old story you have been telling yourself, and getting out of your own way as you wake up to all the possibility that is within you.

For me one of the vital keys to freedom for myself and for living an authentic life is accurate self-forgiveness around irrational judgments I may have been carrying up until now. Until a set of unique circumstances and incidents have played themselves out exactly in a fashion that culminates at an insightful moment - a moment when I know that I did know what it is that I now know but until now I just didn't know I knew it! This is a great position to start self forgiveness. The data I possess or what I say to myself about the judgment is often not true and so the key for me is to apply self forgiveness around the judgment itself. So if my limiting belief was "I am not worthy to write my own book about a HEAR philosophy." I can now put my hand on my heart and quietly say to myself "I forgive myself for judging myself as not good enough to express this philosophy to others when the reality is I am worthy to express myself authentically and give the gift of HEAR to others."

I write in HEAR a repeated verse. "Don't judge lest ye be judged." Because I find I have been graced with knowing others are doing the best they know how, I mostly apply this verse inwardly towards myself about myself. The key to life is accurate self-forgiveness for the judgment that I may have held. If there is no judgment of what ailed me in the past, it is likely that my talents can flow most easily in support of myself and my world.

Chapter 30: EMERGING

Living Into Your Purpose

Navigation: Now that you have a clearer open horizon ahead of you, free of limiting beliefs and you know where you are starting from, it is time to prepare to start your innovative journey and to tap into living your authentic expression.

To aid this we are going to build the architecture and foundation of your success and create consistent tools that will help you gain momentum and keep you motivated regardless of what is happening around you. The Cs that you are actioning include: Choice, Consciousness and Connectedness.

Also do not forget to be led by Compassion with every breath, as sandbanks still linger below the surface in yet unchartered territories.

Tool 4:   Your Truth Emerges
Identify Your Most Collaborative Quality and Integrate your Purpose Statement.

This exercise is first about identifying the quality that most empowers you and that you want to exemplify in your interaction with others. This is an ideal way for you to become centered in a feeling of self-awareness. Collaborative Qualities opens your heart space allowing you to really feel present to a confident vibration of possibility within you. Living from this empowering possibility centers you in bringing forth the manifestation that you choose to hold in your consciousness. When you are connected with and live from qualities that passionately speak to you, you embrace and become those qualities and live them out in every situation and circumstance as you connect, collaborate and circulate yourself and your God given resources.

Who do you think the world of? First simply take a moment to think of the person that you most admire. I encourage it be someone in the world ideally living, although ascended or passed on is OK as well. (Living usually carries more of vibrant now energy and is recommended.)

Now that you have selected the person, think about the quality that you most admire in that person. Is it their positive outlook on life? Their creativity? Their integrity? Their freedom? Their strength?

Identify a quality you sense in them: Enthusiasm; Creativity; Unconditional Love; Exuberance; Light; Grace; Faithfulness; Beauty; Joy; Humility; Acceptance; Knowledge; Peace; Caring; Integrity; Compassion; Generosity. What is it?

Once you have identified the person you most admire, and the quality you most admire in them, you will have a clear vision of the characteristic that is most important and meaningful to you. Now please spend some time consciously connecting with this quality. It is this quality that also exists clearly in you and through your connection with the person you selected you can now start to feel the quality residing in you. Also you can start to comprehend when it has kept you safe or moved you forward as you look at pivotal instances in your life. Can you see the quality showing up that was pivotal in life changing moments that you can recount?

Second, write down all the ways in which you already embody and express this quality when you interact with others. Once you have done this, if you wish to add to this, choose a second quality that you possess and do the same. Go ahead, take time to write them down...Hold these qualities in your awareness every day. By focusing your attention and intention on that characteristic in yourself, you will experience a new level of personal fulfillment and joy. You will also notice that the characteristic will strengthen and become more prominent in your life. They will be the integral keystones from which you will encourage yourself to innovate and implement in your life.

Third, let's look outward and express these qualities into the world you want to create. Assume the world is ideal to you right now, what does this world look like to you and how is everyone connecting and collaborating with each other? What is the conscious feeling in this fun and exciting community? For example, 'everyone is expressing themselves authentically and sharing their resources and talents, working in harmony for the upliftment of all.'

Finally combine all the three sub-categories above, quality, expression and the vision of community and combine them into a single personal purpose statement that is you.

My own quality that I identify about myself is LIGHT. I recognize that I have always been graced with shining light energy towards people I have encountered along my journey and that they have seen that quality in me, even if there were times I did not see it in myself.

When I first did the exercise the person I identified was Nelson Mandela. This was years before I travelled down to Mozambique and entered his Maputo home! The light of hope and belief that he carried in himself and for his people together with the fact that he traveled light, discarding judgment of others as much as he could humanely do, meant Mandela to me was Light.

For me as I look at engaging with others all aspects of my life defines Light to me as "Traveling Light" rather than heavy, as well as automatically bestowing a light into people so they can see, hear and feel more effectively.

Speak your Purpose daily.

Begin your day by saying it so that you "program" both your conscious and subconscious mind with the knowingness that you now radiate this quality in every situation and circumstance you find yourself in.

The purpose statement should start with "I AM," and be stated in the present tense with positive and action-oriented language. You should also state that it will be shared with others.

Here's an example using LIGHT as the empowering quality...

"I AM Light Being, and through my Spirit filled heart, I am a Love Crusader, being of service to my Self and sharing my gifts with you."

This statement happens to be my own quality and my own affirmation that I have carried with me sixteen years now. It reminds me not to hide my light under a bushel; that I choose to recognize the Holy Spirit within myself as a child of God; the choice of actioning this by crusading in the simple unconfined realm of love; and the knowing that for me to be of unconditional support to others, I must choose first to be of service to myself and receive what it is that I am to know.

After you've written an affirmation that inspires you, I recommend you say your affirmation aloud regularly.

You and the World - Purpose Statement

Another interesting exercise would be what happens when you select the planet as your positive projection:

1. What are the qualities you sense that are empowering about the world?

_____

_____

_____

_____

_____

2.   How do you like to express those qualities when you interact with the nature of our world?

_____

_____

_____

_____

_____

3.   Assume the world is ideal and thriving, how are you and everyone else in it innovating and interacting in it?

_____

_____

_____

_____

_____

4.   Combine these three exercises into a single statement of how you are being and living and interacting for the betterment of the world.

_____

_____

_____

_____

_____

Chapter 31:   IMPLEMENTING YOUR LIFE

Tool 5:   Your Ideal Life
Visioning, Creating and Actioning Your Ideal Scene and then Identifying your Priority Project.

This is personally the most simple yet powerful implementation and manifestation exercise I can do to help me create what truly can show up in any area of my life, often beyond anything I think I can wish for.   I believe this to be true for you.

Your Ideal Scene is the very blue print that allows the two key role-players in your life to come together in their ideal harmony for the highest good of you in your life and for your world.   The role-players of your mind and your heart, connected together through the energy of your Creator. The Trinity at work. It brings forward hope, then trust and belief. It is your truth.

This is how you wish for your life to be and now that your limiting beliefs are history it is your time to offer yourself your life, and let destiny show up. All this is to occur in the Cs of Creativity, Choice, Clarity, Consciousness, Collaborative Co-operation, and Circulation. Know that everything you are about to put forward will produce a result of "this or something better for your highest good!" Let God get to work in you. Miracles can happen, especially when permission is given for the Holy Spirit.

Since being introduced to an Ideal Scene exercise during a Masters course in Spiritual Psychology in 1998 at the University of Santa Monica in California, I have helped thousands of people both in groups and as individual clients, business colleagues, or friends experience this exercise. Whether they arrive at my door or office in total despair from the most tragic of personal experiences and they are beaten up physically, mentally and emotionally, I set them the immediate task of a make-over or personal re-creation through this particular personal exercise of the HEAR Tool Box.

Sometimes the situation is so dire, like being beaten up and left on the side of the road by someone on their honeymoon (and thank you Miss S for your brilliance shining ever since), or waking up to be bankrupt (and thank you to all the thousands of you). We then will sometimes have to go into emergency mode and bypass Tools 2 and 3, which may be too much to take on in the midst of the upheaval of a fear focused distortion of mind and body, and we go straight from comprehending and connecting to the issue in Tool 1, with silence and the ability to breathe during your crisis, and move straight to a YOUR LIFE Ideal Scene.

However what I always see and feel is that in whatever state a client or friend arrives in front of me, I sense a knot that they have tied for themselves and they are tangled in it. Everything may be too much for them and their own vision is clouded. Just starting the Ideal Scene loosens everything in and around them and gives them eyes to see and ears to hear.

If only all the threads of their life could be unknotted and allowed to flow freely, un-touched, free to feel and grow in their own spirit driven quest for brilliance. This is the finest and most simplest exercise to allow anything you desire to show up. However always remember what you desire may or may not be for your highest good.

Remember earlier in the book the ancient Jewish translation of "I am that I am" is also "I shall be that I shall be"

What can you be? What are you to accomplish? This moment is your time to create what you want to show up in your life. If you are incredulous and don't believe me. Just start and do the exercise once and then look at what you wrote in nine weeks and then nine months from today.

How to create a first Your Life Ideal Scene?

Vision all aspects of the life you desire today and project it into your life nine months from today. Where do you want your life to be in nine months time?

If you have particular reaction to one area (i.e. relationship with another or the subject of money and financial freedom) you can later choose to develop and create one separate Ideal Scene for each of those, going to into greater detail. For now it is a complete life plan that you are publishing.

Use or copy the Ideal Scene template on page 374 to do this exercise. As you are filling out the template, remember to use powerful, positive and action-oriented language. Speak in the present tense and see yourself in the experience. That way, when you read YOUR IDEAL SCENE after it's complete, you will feel like you are already inside the experience. This technique is a powerful tool to help you manifest what is on the page.

Also this exercise is an enhancement to the very small manifestation prayer from the Bible. "Jabez called on the God of Israel, saying, Oh that you would bless me indeed, and enlarge my border, and that your hand might be with me, and that you would keep me from evil, that it not be to my sorrow! God granted him that which he requested."

First, Jabez asks God to bless him. Second, he asks God to

enlarge his territory or increase his responsibility. Third, he prays that God will be with him and stay close. Lastly, Jabez asks that God keep him from harm so that he will be free from pain.

This exercise can unite you with your divine destiny and change your life. Go for it!

Creating your Ideal Scene – simple guidelines

1. I repeat always write in the present tense: "I Am ..." Make sure you can see (and feel) yourself in the scene that you are the role player in. Please speak about your experience as if you are having it now in the present tense. This is vital as you are allowing spiritual energy and your prayer work and meditation time to manifest all over your clear consciousness.

2. Make sure everything you write is at least 50% believable by you. You must believe you can create this in your life in order for it to manifest, however even if you are reaching for your own personal stars, it is possible you are still shrinking in your limited belief about what you are capable of ... SO STRETCCHHHHH.

3. Use language that excites you, such as descriptive adjectives and adverbs. "I am enthusiastically ... I am wonderfully experiencing .... I am graciously ... I am passionately ... I am gracefully ...

4. Remember to use positive language, no double negatives, such as "I am not unhappy." Instead, use "I am joyfully ..."

Ideal Scenes are not goals - they are experiences.

Be sure not to get into the mindset of how things will happen or "what you need to do" to achieve something. Instead, keep focused as if you are already living in it. If you focus on the "what," the "how" will start to show up.

Why nine months?

I suggest for you that you lay out Your Life Scene to be accomplished over the next nine month period for trusted reasons: Very often, elements of your visions manifest before nine months because of your powerful declaration and implementation, but nine months is a birthing process in life and for you. (It is possible that in absolute crisis I would recommend speeding up to ninety days.)

The nine month period allows you time to work on all that you have written, and most importantly allows for what you don't know you know to show up and have its way within your Scene. The words "this or something better for your highest good" are vital and often some of your Ideal Scene details need to be re-ordered and help is needed from above. Nine months allows for this help to be given, to be received by you and then acted upon!

Putting your experience into words

After you have identified those areas that you are most passionate about, you will begin the process of recording them using powerful, positive and action-oriented language. You should always create from the present using the words "I AM."

For example you might detail scene lines like...

"I AM creating a fabulous and loving relationship with my partner as we do the things we love that bring us closer together."

"I AM working, innovating and utilizing all my talents as I effortlessly am able to embrace greater opportunities."

"I AM freely supplying my skill sets into my world, serving the collective collaborative consciousness with unconditional actions, delivering authentic expression."

"I AM creating a healthy practice of eating nutritionally and exercising and I am maintaining my optimum health."

"I AM effortlessly developing multiple streams of income for myself as I live a life that is financially free."

"I AM loving God to my fullest and feel his love for me"

"I AM writing my book, feeling good about the process and having fun doing it."

"I AM writing lyrics and letting my voice be heard as I

majestically sing my songs"

"I am connecting with my children, enjoying being their father/mother in ways that compliment all aspects of my life.

I hope you understand. Show up into your life scene and then let your life scene show up in you! There is no time limit on this. Thirty Minutes to three days could be good to complete Your Life Ideal Scene. I have done them for the last four years lying in bed on a January 1 morning. I have done them in a crowded train or sitting in a slum gutter in Africa.

If things are clearly in transition for you, wait until you are settled a while into your new surroundings.

This year my partner and I did one together in March after moving to the Yucatan Peninsular in Mexico in January. We therefore waited a few months into the New Year to allow ourselves to integrate a little with our new surroundings.

Once you complete this, I also suggest sharing the creative page with a friend or your partner and speaking it in your present tense as if you are living it now. Be proud of it and don't hide it! My partner's and mine is usually framed in our bathroom, and it's a great navigational aid and early warning system if I have taken myself off on a distracted side track, which happens!

Also be prepared to add or alter something tomorrow. The person who first introduced me to the Ideal Scene, Mary Hulnick the co founder of the University of Santa Monica, constantly revises her Ideal Scene as new ideas of living as a healthy being are heard by her.

In fact there is something about Mary (and her partner) Ron that allowed me to take my deepest cut when I graduated from USM in 2000. When I was invited back to the graduation of the class of 2013 I was able to reflect on how deep a cut I have taken since, directly due to having the freedom to project into the action of many Ideal Scenes!

Remember there is no right or wrong, only this or something better for your highest good. I have found that what I know that I know in this exercise is not what God knows for me and my highest good may be about to be revealed. It is irresistibly exciting when I know God has ideas for me that I do not know I know.

MY IDEAL SCENE TEMPLATE
This or something better for my highest good

Chapter 32: EVOLVING WITH YOUR CHOICES

Implementing your Priority Project

It's time to put ideas and thoughts and visions to the test of action in your real world. It's time to test yourself in "the issue is not the issue, it is how I respond to the issue which is the issue." It's time to check in on your own responsibility and consciousness around the 13Cs. We shall journey together on two tandem paths.

The first path is set over the next nine months as we watch your ideal scene unfold and show up.

The second path is to be forged as we work on your Project together. Yes, the project that you are pregnant to create and bring forward. Know right away that every C will show up as you implement your Passion Project to a successful outcome.

I added these 7 tools as part of HEAR because they each facilitate clearly my ability to hear. I know this especially in the action of a Priority Project - a project of the moment that may or may not be a world or career changer, but something I want to do or bring forward as a priority action in life. For me a priority project may be daily flow writing to my children, either in letter, or email or silently in a journal by my bed. When I do not see them it is a priority to me that they know my love for them. As I navigate this project there are times when I sense compromise when I say to myself I don't have time or worse still I forget to complete the days communication. There are other days where it flows effortlessly and over time the writings give clear indication that my intent became integrated action.

Selecting your Priority Project

Within a period of one week from completing your Life Ideal Scene (and it may take you one second as you already know what "I AM ...." is) please select one area of your life identified in the initial Life Ideal Scene and it is to become your immediate Priority Project. It may be the innovation idea, or around your career or relationship. It is certainly is pressing, and because it is you may be trepidation or nervous when you think about it.

Choose one that your mind is chattering about right now! The one that says, "Gosh I said that" ... Yes you did and now stretch through the limiting beliefs and see it happen.

What is the Priority Project and What outcome do you want to see in 12 months from when you start?

_____

_____

_____

_____

_____

_____

_____

_____

_____

_____

_____

_____

_____

_____

Tool 6:   Actioning A Priority Project

To step into your Priority Project immediately and efficiently it is important now to clearly and consciously define every month your "next steps" and monitor accountable results around how well you are accomplishing what you have set up for yourself. Please create initial output actions for month one, and then layer more outer criteria action steps and inner criteria you believe you need to have accomplished by the end of each additional month so that you stay on pace to accomplish your goals at the end of month nine. We will then have three additional months to course correct or monitor results, which because they are financial, business, relationship or health related require this additional three months for us to gauge a correct assessment of the project.

I have always noticed in life, as I look to live and work through or accomplish anything involving myself, that choice points are consistently being presented to me. Hopefully I hear them and recognize them when they arrive. Often every day there are hundreds if not thousands arriving for me to allocate a direction! Since I seem to stretccccch myself in a variety of diverse yet inter connected ways I have thousands of choices to field every day. So do you.

How we respond to the choice points usually determines the direction and the ultimate outcome of what is happening or about to happen. For example since the age of thirty-four I have responded very differently and sought different outcomes. I have also continued to make interesting choices, many of which were logical at the time and were affirmed by clear outcomes. Other choices were made from nothing more than "gut" feeling or deep intuition that I could not choose to ignore. Mystery in many ways surrounded them and the outcomes that were played out became the interesting learning. Could these choices be justified? No. Could these choices be deemed to be the right ones or the wrong ones? Who knows that they know the answers to that question?

How many times have you said, "If only I had chosen to do it that way." Choice determines outcome.

To aid you accomplishing your Priority Project, I am now requesting you identify and work with your own CHOICE Points. This is to serve two brilliant functions. The first is of course to move you forward in a more organized yet expanded way to help you best achieve the results you desire. The second is that now armed with the 13Cs you are aware that you are to face whatever comes up as you move forward.........and you are ready to HEAR it and flow through it. Ultimately the choices will always be yours.

Exercise: CHOICE Points

Using CHOICE is an important way to both navigate chaos and to create success in every area of your life. Each letter of the word CHOICE has meaning and stands for a component in the effective monitoring process of your journey to accomplishing the endeavor you have set yourself. Utilize CHOICE to accomplish what you set out in your Life Ideal Scene & Priority Project.

C	Clarity
H	Help
O	Outer Criteria
I	Inner Criteria
C	Confidence
E	Engage

Clarity - Clear vision allows your conscious mind to be in action towards what you are looking to accomplish with your Priority Project and like voicing a prayer, also allows Mystery to do its wonder.

Help - Asking for and receiving help is usually the best way any new project can get kick-started. You can even be encouraged by the effectiveness of "please help" sites Kickstarter and Indiegogo.

When to ask, how you ask and how you react to the way someone responds to your request is usually going to determine how successful you are to be.

Also we often forget to ask ourselves for help? How can you best help yourself is frequently determined by how clear and conscious you are to what you are looking to accomplish?

Outer Criteria - What do you believe needs to be done in what time schedule for you to accomplish your project? – i.e. If you are learning the guitar, this would include the following: buying a guitar, stringing it, hiring a teacher, turning up to a series of lessons, practicing, and perhaps the project is completed with you performing to an audience by a specific date. As you review your choice points you will quickly see whether you have passed each of your outer criteria signposts and if not what choices can you make to help yourself and even course correct if necessary.

Inner Criteria - What can you do to support yourself inwardly to accomplish your outer ideas? We know that outer experiences are often a reflection of inner reality. What criteria can you design yourself to best prepare and give you the confident attitude to accomplish what you have set for yourself?

Confidence - What have you confidently completed? Now what's next? Set yourself a series of tasks along the way that you know are attainable and achievable. By accomplishing many small steps the big huge project is reached. Acknowledge yourself and have gratitude for what you have completed. Recognize what is not being completed with ease and grace and with a confident attitude apply clarity as you look at the criteria you have set up.

Engage - In my experience nothing is accomplished unless you are engaging yourself and others in your process. Collaborating with others provides help, solicits feedback and allows you be experiential which is really good to move a project forward. You cannot accomplish much from the sidelines. Whatever your project is, it is likely that practice will make it better if not really good!

I do not seek "perfect" in project-setting as I do not believe in the word perfect when it comes to intentional goal setting. For me it is an attachment to the result of a set of criteria that the mind has set. What seems perfect for one person's reality is nearly always different for another. Also having reached this position of the mind, perfect often then gets us to feel a tinge of disappointment as to "is this it?" and confused as to what is next and there is always more to be next!

Stay engaged.

Here is an example of what to do and what not to do when setting CHOICE Points round a common theme of weight loss.

Be Clear - Include Who, What, Where, When, Why, and How.
 ⟨ YES: Shed two inches off my waist line in the next sixty days to feel healthy.
 ⟨ NO: Lose weight

Grounding your project and criteria in time sets a target and creates a sense of urgency.
 ⟨ ASK – What is a realistic start date?
 ⟨ ASK – What is a realistic end date?
 ⟨ ASK FOR HELP – Who do I know that will support me and / or keep me accountable to these dates?

Ask for Help - Create a system to track and measure your progress.
 ⟨ YES: Can you be my exercise trainer and set up a class schedule with me?
 ⟨ NO: I will lose a lot of weight soon.
 ⟨ ASK: Who should track my progress? Is it best for me to do it or should I have an accountability partner to help?
Set up support networks when you can.

Outer Criteria - Ensure your criteria points are stretching, yet attainable for you in the period of time you've defined. Stretched criteria projects motivate you. Easy goals create boredom and stagnation.
 ⟨ YES: I will shed a quarter of an inch off my waist each week for the next eight weeks, and rate my feeling of "healthiness" on a scale of 1-10 (10 Is feellng super healthy) each week. The 3 ways I will do this are X, Y and Z.
 ⟨ ASK: Have I broken up my large goal into manageable chunks?
 ⟨ ASK: Do I believe I can achieve the criteria within the time-frame defined? - make sure your project is more than fifty percent believable.

Inner Criteria - There is a ninety per cent probability that it will be your own inner attitude that will result in the level of success you have, including this project. What can you do differently to set yourself up consciously for success?

Around weight loss, there is the tangible physical results and you and every one around you will feel wonderful if you achieve your physical goals. However if you do not also have a mental and emotional exercise program, it is 90% plus probable that the weight will come back on. Always work the three levels at the same time, Mental, Emotional and Physical.

Engage - Have fun and enthusiastically share your priority project. Every successful entrepreneur shares their ideas and products and takes on feedback so they can course correct when necessary. Engaging and sharing with others increases the energy flow around your project and often can give you vital course correction if required sooner rather than later. The choice is yours.

In my own world as I bring ideas forward both as individual business ventures or life scenes, it is essential for me to carry out both Ideal Scenes and Positive Project Plans on a regular basis. I love being conscious to *Vision + Action = Mission,* and then equally seeing how Spirit shows up "with this or something better for my highest good." I am usually amazed by the result!

Chapter 33: INTEGRATING WHO YOU ARE

Tool 7:   How Am I?
Recognize Your Brilliance – The Mirror Exercise

Speak to yourself so that your heart can hear yourself and then heal. For the next few days at least, take a few seconds before you go to bed each night to stand in front of a mirror and acknowledge yourself for all that you have accomplished during the day. Make eye contact and look at yourself in the most unconditionally loving way, thinking only of the positive experiences that you have created, attracted and manifested. See yourself looking back at you as you do this. Connect with all that you know in your being.

Focus on the positive

I believe we have now entered an age where it is vital we shine the light on all things positive in our world.

To do this we have to do this with our Selves and the Faith we have in our Self. Take the time to truly recognize yourself for all the positive things that you have and are achieving (business, spiritual, financial, humanitarian, etc.), any personal disciplines you kept (exercise, meditation, diet, etc.) and any temptations you did not give in to (sabotaging behavior, negative future fantasy, etc.). Recognize with compassion the Cs that you have faced through your day and even how you moved through them from one minute or hour to the next.

At the end of the exercise, say, "I love you and I APPRECIATE YOU" and take a few moments to have a deep heart connection.

This exercise might feel a bit strange at first, but if you push past the discomfort, you will develop a deeper connection with yourself that will remain for ever.

My own life changed its course with one glimpse in a dirty mirror in a Hollywood bar. I did not expect it to happen, but it did. I do not believe that Dante expected his life to change when he wrote "In the middle of the road of my life, I awoke within a dark wood where the true way was wholly lost.'"

Did Jesus expect his death to have its eternal resurrection when he turned at the very end to his Father and said *"Why have you forsaken me."*

Jesus showed up inside of my life in that bar and has been present, allowing me to live LIVE ever since.

I personally therefore also add "I Love you Jesus" as this integrates my whole Being and Self beyond the physical form I know. I seem to find myself smiling. I also recognize with contentment the reflective lightness that exists with the mystery of the Holy Spirit that is clearly alive and well.

The mirror exercise reinforces what HEAR brings to the surface to be heard. I know most of you are like me and there is way more that connects us that separates us, however fundamental differences can be quantified by the extent of our willingness to give and receive love, as well as our own individual battle between the love of power as it wrestles with the power of love, which of course can be quiet in its own defense. For much of my life I found it easy to give love outwardly. To look to love another person, the people I was drawn to care for and those that were suffering. Yet until I recognized how to love and care for myself, I did not know what love was as there was a block in the giving and the receiving of love.

There are many ways of identifying any blockage on how to receive love. Here are a few:

1. Have people applaud you all at the same time with their full energy and attention on only you, or have a friend praise you around your kitchen table over a cup of tea

2. Be thanked for a caring action by women or children in the slums of the world or by a homeless person on your street, for a caring action by you for them.

3. Receive and give a hug, or warm embrace.

4. Recite the Prayer of Jabez from 1 Chronicles 4:10. Then spend a minute connecting with your sense of worthiness in God's eyes to receive the blessing of this wish. (if there is another positive spiritual message that you resonate with which supports you to ask for help and expand your territories/resources then recite this quote from your own favorite messenger.)

5. Stand in front of a mirror and tell your Self how much you appreciate and love yourself. How are you?

Hopefully after 345 pages of HEAR you won't find a request of you talking to yourself as weird. When you can truly receive love from yourself, and acknowledge the positive nature of this virtue, then you can truly know that you know what love is and you can then truly hear. Perhaps you can even try singing into your mirror!

I'm starting with the man in the mirror
I'm asking him to change his ways
And no message could have been any clearer
If you wanna make the world a better place
Take a look at yourself, and then make a change
Take a look at yourself, and then make a change

Man in the Mirror
© Siedah Garrett and Glen Ballard
R.I.P Michael Jackson

HEAR

EPILOGUE

Recreating life itself

This was the furthest thing from my mind. At no time in my past did my mind think this would happen in my future.

I sat across the table from this person. We had been sitting for a long time. There was space between us and yet we were connected. Intense conscious meditation with a connectedness of energy that I had not experienced in this lifetime. Our trust of absolute recognition within ourselves was evident, beyond the data of our lives, which were of no consequence to the circumstance of this time. We sat like this for what seemed an age.

Then a very strange and unique event played itself out for me. Lights entwined and expressions ruptured and it was if all had become One. Suddenly her face melted away. The very face I was in front of changed. In a few seconds the face had recreated itself, remolding itself like a wax-work to reveal another image. Then it happened again and another, each re-creation seemed even more pure, then another, and another. Perpetual transformations revealing what appeared as lives of differing ages yet connected as one to the last. Young infants, the most vibrant of youth, older women, a young man. It was as if I was dreaming at night, but I was awake and it was the middle of a bright day.

I was witnessing the re=creation of one being through many physical forms, all encapsulated in a unifying of timeless radiating energy. I would see the face change, yet in its complete form the same set of compassion filled eyes settled gently on me. Eyes piercing my soul, the mercy, the grace, the faith and the trust; and the innocence of belief, of love. Each gaze of each form penetrated deeper into my soul. My heart was stretching in its ability to hear.

The hair was amazing too, as golden long locks changed to mid length dark and even braided grey. The style of hair would hide a forehead and ears and then expose them. Every image was fleeting yet fully formed for seconds, one came and morphed one after the other. I was awake, I was in Her presence. I felt my heart was being poured into. For weeks after I felt and cared at unbearable levels for my mere self. I found myself expressing emotions of incredible joy and of caring tears.

A heart that hears the old as it merges with the new.

Over the years I have found myself in many caring circumstances where I saw the beauty in another. There were moments like on Heaven's Hill that I felt I was home. There were other times when apparent chaos or crisis surrounded me, that a serene peace descended. All these moments of past hearing became support to sensing what I knew on this occasion, that the Kingdom of Heaven is within. Home for me is within my Self!

I sense I have been blessed to be witness to the truth of the divine passing through life, beyond any intrusion of human experience. Kept safe by a caring source unable to be challenged through time. It is this Being who carries the truth of life itself. The Tree of Life. Blood Royal. The Grail was before me. She is simply the spiritual Being having this human experience. She is also Him and also You and she is also Me!

I traveled on.

Four years later, in a far off place known as Maya, beyond the mind fields of my mind, an encounter with an Angel took place. It was the first day of 2013, when huge wings were to be healed and the nails, which had been put into so many female hearts and killed so many physical human lives, were being pulled out.

The Divine Being was free again, unencumbered by human experiences brought on by man's history of time.

Free, the Angel flew again.

There are many times I do not expect to hear what I do hear. When I hear, I am blessed to acknowledge the Angel of Grace leading the way - An Angel that leads me, through the light of Jesus, to me fulfilling my own capacity to love.

Love has been recreated a lot in my life, and the sum of it all is: as I discover how to care ever more deeply, and also to be cared for, the comprehension of love becomes ever clearer.

I thought I knew what love was. Today I think I know what love is.

Yet tomorrow, as I apply greater care, it is likely that another dimension of love will reveal itself. As my sub conscious becomes conscious I will know what love is. It is our caring that releases our suffering, bringing us wellness, which releases us to even more love.

MY LOVE FOR YOU

My Love for You,
The awakening of my unconditional love.
Awakening, a moment spirit's eyes meet and fall
In to this deep velvet abyss of shared souls.
Clandestine hearts passionately entwining,
surrounded by human sleep, yet with each secret breath
our instant alliance driven by cupid's gift of love's angelic armor.

My love for you, the early morning dew of God's blessings.
A dew, nurturing a bed of Holy flowers, friendship forged in our
earthly destiny,
illuminating each others light through eternal times,
surely guiding us along His path,
dancing now so lightly, His reflection a trampoline catapulting us to
Heaven.
Heaven, a vista where our awaken souls are Being triumphant in
Graduation.
God's angel, a gift from the Lord, a Divine being.
My love, You are all these to me.
Thank you Being, Thank you Light, I Thank God. Amen.

Future Destiny

Who Knows?

It's easy to say we are at a cross roads, a choice point and that the future of human civilization rests on the answers we make and decisions we take today.

Yet I remain sensitive. I sense much quickening and urgency as "we the people" strengthen a collective voice and share what we know once we have confidence that we can be heard.

Color has in most geographical areas became far less of a choice point issue resulting in a black man entered the White House and African and Latino women becoming leaders of their nations.

Money? Who Knows what a dollar is worth. Will the very few, that have so much, continue to wake and be meaningful in their purposeful work for the planet. I see some, like the patrons around our work, influenced by the magnetic legacy of Nelson Mandela, doing amazing ceaseless work. Their earnings have increased since the days we were all in Mozambique, yet billionaires Richard Branson and John Paul deJoria, as well as the actor Brad Pitt, use their resources and talents to greater effect every year of their lives. They have learned how to be great people, channeling their creativity and passions with purpose. There are now many joining the ranks of wealthy purpose driven "we the people" citizens.

However there remains massive chaos today around money, and its future remains totally uncertain as the old institutional paradigms hold on painfully, hurting many. Fear and greed around "enough" still dominates as these paradigms struggle in their death.

Creed and religion may also be the last bastions of the karmic placenta fortress, holding on to their past doctrines and fearing their lessening vice on their people, who innately remain God loving, gifted the fruits of their spirit at birth.

I believe the future is in the final set of Cs. If we see people choosing forgiveness and self forgives of all that is able to be confessed to, and this is received with compassion; If we then witness consciousness within, co-operation with others and a thirst to collaborate and circulate our resources; Then our world is to be transformed. What price on recycling?

I ask what can amaze you as you journey on through your future? How can you marvel at the brilliance all around you? When can you move out of the box that you live in and be astonished by the pure genius of yourself, your world and the magnificence of your lands?

When will our love for our planet cause us to carry unbearable compassion? A compassion so utterly connected in our hearts and bodies that we cannot ignore a single whispered cry of poverty suffering, and disease until we hear it no more.

What does the future hold? Is there going to be undeniable global change and who knows the date? Millennium bugs and the media moment around December 21 2012 suggest that doomsday dates come and go, and we are still here.

Will weapons of mass destruction be destructed before they destruct us, and can the guns killing innocents all over our world be no longer in the hands of those that are twisted in judgment?

Who knows when Christ will return, and if he does who knows whether it will be the form chronicled by your ancestors, or will He and God show up in the Trinity of a Holy Spirit, uniting us all for ever in goodness and compassion? Has Jesus ever really left us?

And in the open unity of our compassion field – where are you with your God? Or where is your compassion if you have no God?

Will the business of charity become the world's biggest buyer of advertising media in its attempt to convince you to give more, or will the two billion people that have lived on less that two dollars a day, become our greatest force for good as wonderful standard bearers for the power of love? Will they be the examples we finally follow?

How will you recycle and who ultimately will profit from it?

Will you keep paying more for your water, with it more expensive a commodity than oil, and will water continue to be the biggest killer in our world or can we clean it? How much will you have to pay for energy from the sun, wind and waves, and will you have enough time and resources for a halcyon upbringing of your children?

Will you be able to hear and let the power of all our love conquer the love of power, and since I sense strongly it will, when will it happen? In the introduction to this book I detailed a story that highlighted the ignorance of one conscientious man, Captain Smith, of the Titanic. Do you need to be in the middle of the crisis of all crises, with your unsinkable ship submerging with no hope from human intervention, to awaken and act? Does a Revelation need to reveal itself to you, as the Power of Love, re-awakened within all of you, makes its second coming as the collective You?

How will this appear around the value of your money and the nurturing of your world, your community, your family and yourself? How many of us will demonstrate Joseph's spirit, with our hearts turned to each other - mothers, fathers, sons and daughters - showing humility, compassion for weakness, yet being bold and courageous, holding graceful wonder for each other strengths?

Will our ultimate fertility nurtured through our chaotic emergence bring us all to a place where peace on earth is guaranteed?

Who knows the answers to these questions and every other question? Perhaps anything we say we know can only be a projection of our minds, and HEAR has already shown us how little the collective answers of the past can mean as we judge that our systems fail. God asks us not to judge lest we be judged.

However what I do clearly sense is that the future of our world depends on you possessing faith and taking action, as the generation that is gifted the challenge of choosing its destiny.

There is so much that is good and holy, so many hundreds of millions that are not to be convinced anymore through prejudice and dogma, but are freely connecting with each other to birth in their world a future we all would love to behold. They now need you also to choose your future. A future where in your choices you hold loving compassion for all that has passed and all that is to be, where the clarity of our situation leads you to conscious connections and collaborations and where your resources are circulated to the maximum benefit of human kind.

My hope for you is that you possess a compassionate yet courageous heart and a convicted willingness to move forward through your life; that you now know no boundaries and that you are prepared to travel lightly, beyond what has been governed in the past by other people. Now my hope is that you desire so greatly to hear accurately and, possessed with trust, hope and belief, you know yourself better and you act with the best intentions imaginable.

It is my own intention that my future insight, outlooks and actions will be balanced through the questions I ask in harmony with the choices I am given day by day. In this life time I will continue to travel, like you, through the Cs of life and return to them over and over again, often in the same day and week. Some will give me the opportunity to climb vast mountain ranges and gaze across inspiring vistas exuding life, light and love. Yet others will emerge as unpredictably as a storm that catches a row boat on an endless ocean, and I will find myself again within the valleys of my world, to walk once again through trees in a dark wood. I am bound to experience this circulation, taking me from hero to villain as unknowns come forward to be heard.

My hope for myself is that on this journey through the forest of life, and through the shadows of past judgment, I may not ever again be wholly lost and indeed will continue to emerge lighter.

My vision for the future of my children is unclear. The Cs of life rock their little boats, and despite the attentions of their caregivers, they will ultimately be left, like I was and you were, to be buffeted by the winds of their own futures. This book has been written to the best of my ability, for them to know their daddy. I still cry for my children.

My trust for myself is that by the end of my life I will have thoroughly been spent as a force of good for those I love and for humanity.

My belief is in us. We are all divine children of God. We collectively can believe and recognize the opportunity of our generation, as we choose the destiny of our world. In our humanity this will be enough. We are enough.

PURPOSE

The purpose for me now in life is love,
Love unconditional is enough,...... is enough.
The gift of receiving by hearing,
And sharing with you now is gift enough..is gift enough.

Walking Christ's chartered course,
His never ending sustenance provided by accurate hearing,
An instinctive freedom
Resoundingly voiced by prayer filled intuition.

Hearing the voice inside provides reflective integrity,
Giving clear eyes to God's confidence.
Signed by my soul's breath so deep with faithful fullness
One choice of faithful fullness

This moment a boundless, open cargo of Spirit
So sure along that ragged coastline called past judgments,
And the safe harbor of this utter open vulnerability
Provides the greatest gift to me.
It is God's will that I do today.

Hearing gives me my chance to receive
And then to know in the next second of my life.
And in the dawn of this re-awakening
My reactions to my Self are all that concern me,

An instant that disintegrates the block of blame,
Always resulting in God's simple provision of forgiveness.
And through these portals of forgiveness
Shapes a heart of compassion.

Compassion is the act of giving gracefully
And giving gracefully is being of service
And service is being as Christ being.
And Christ being is my inner Light.

My Light that can shine more bright with every breath of my soul.
And in this light I rediscover what it is to receive love,
Which is enough, ...this is enough.
Today I am more able to choose to be.
And I Am.

If not YOU, Who?

If not NOW, When?

Now go and live your Future.

A future that has no time but now.

Hear yourself Now

And

Live LIVE

GOD BE IN YOU, WITH YOU AND THROUGH YOU

Who helped me to HEAR?

This book would simply not be without Daniella Hunter and her depth of caring for me. I love you. Complimenting Daniella's attention to HEAR is Sarah Hall with art design, Julie Gunn with her editing heart and also all our continual typo detectors!

I acknowledge the love of Gina Deeming and Adrienn Laki towards my children Arabella, Jamie and Sahana; and of Alex and Maia, who Daniella and I share Luca and Kai with; My own family - Mummy, and my immensely stretching sisters, Vivien and Louise. They stretched me as the kid brother as they now do others with their expressive living; All my teachers, friends and colleagues who have had a hand in blowing wind into my sails as I ran into them, traveling the Cs of life, including Andrew McPherson and Charlie Gordon Watson, my first friends; The boys of Spyway and Eton College, which did much to shape the ugly, bad and then good; Paul Eden, Robert Bair, Paul Dainty, Roy Hay, Townsend Coleman, Billy Sammeth, CHER, Frank Yablans, Mark Victor Hansen, Helena Huang, Larry Ross, Ron and Mary Hulnick, Ron Booth, Peter Willis, Spryte Loriano, Elizabeth Jarosz, Patricia Blum, Danny Seay, Richard "Sonny" Lee, and Trina Hart; and to all the people we are now with.

Also Joanna Owen, my enduring first love: and then others, Anna, Marilyn, Suzy and Lisa with her Isabelle. I also give very special thanks for the overwhelming love and support of David Woolfson, and Harold Davis.

I give thanks all the time to my father who was my God; and God who is my Dad. Within the Trinity I thank Jesus and also the Mystery of my Holy Spirit. Finally all of you who seek an authentic path for your own Selves - I thank you for being fan enough to read HEAR.

About the Author

Charlie Stuart Gay lives in the Yucatan with his family amongst the smiling faces of the Mayans. They own and operate Sanará. He is active in businesses around the world, as well as supporting humanitarian enterprise solutions. Charlie is a fan of our world.

HEAR

29804732R00203